THE ULTIMATE HOW-TO BOOK FOR NEWLYWEDS

In a guide that takes you from wedding daze to forever after, Arlene Modica Matthews charts a course for newlyweds of all ages. You'll discover how to negotiate:

- *The Unwritten Contracts*—about housework, love-making, children (his, hers, theirs), and more
- *Careers*—how to keep your work in perspective, deal with competitive feelings, and encourage each other
- *Sex*—what to expect once someone's sleeping in your bed . . . forever; and how to rekindle the embers if they're burning low
- *Leisure*—how to make your time together better than ever

"WHY DID I MARRY YOU, ANYWAY? is a lively, literate, and extremely perceptive guide to successful living for newlyweds. Partners should read it not only before they say 'I do' but after, and use it as a biennial refresher course in marital behavior."

> —Jean Baer, author of
> *How to be an Assertive—Not Aggressive—Woman*
> and co-author of
> *Don't Say Yes When You Want to Say No*

"A witty and wise, kindhearted and thoughtful introduction to marriage. . . . Should be required reading."

> —Dorcas Fick Mellecker, Ed.D.,
> President-Elect, New York Association
> for Marriage & Family Therapy

WHY DID I MARRY YOU, ANYWAY

A Practical Guide to the First Years of Marriage

Arlene Modica Matthews

POCKET BOOKS

New York   London   Toronto   Sydney   Tokyo   Singapore

POCKET BOOKS, a division of Simon & Schuster Inc.
1230 Avenue of the Americas, New York, NY 10020

For Bill, with love
Special thanks to Deborah Bershatsky

In love, every man starts from the beginning.
SØREN KIERKEGAARD

It's too bad that one must begin with the beginning.
We know so little of beginnings.
ERIK H. ERIKSON

Acknowledgments

This book would not have been possible without the contributions of the recently married couples who so graciously allowed me to pry into their private affairs that others might learn from their thoughts, feelings, and experiences. To all of these generous and forthcoming women and men, my heartfelt thanks.

My thanks also to the experts who contributed their ideas to this book, including psychologist Dr. Robert Sternberg, psychoanalysts James Morrell, Dr. Joan Ormont, Dr. Benito Perri, and Dr. Hyman Spotnitz, attorneys Raoul Lionel Felder and David Larsen, and financial planners Jim Polos and Eric Riedman.

I am especially indebted to a great many friends both for their suggestions and encouragement. Thank you, Kathy Walton Banks, Russell Banks, Michael Barson, Jeanne Behren, Jeanne Wilmot Carter, Paul Dinas, Kate Duffy, Pat Eisemann, Pat Follert, Joyce Fredo, Lynn Goldberg, Dan Halpern, Chip Logan, Gary Margolis, Susan Horton Polos, Bill Stulbarg, Margaret Norcott Stulbarg, and Barbara Uva. Thanks to computer wizards Claudia Goodman and Greg Peters for helping me master

Acknowledgments

my Macintosh, to director/choreographer Barry Ivan for helping me select the lyrics quoted in the text, and to Joan Goody, Bill Morelli, and Chase Twichell, for providing some of the lovely far-from-the-city spaces where this book was written.

I am grateful also to Ryoko Toyama and the staff of Columbia University's Butler Library; to my agent, Robin Rue, who believed in this book when it was no more than a gleam in my eye; and, of course, to Peter Davison, with whom working is not only a pleasure but a privilege.

Last, but certainly not least, I would like to thank my parents, Frances and Vincent Modica, who are celebrating their forty-fourth wedding anniversary as this book goes to press.

September 1987

Contents

From "I Do" to "I Did?":
An Introduction

"Why did I marry you, anyway?" is a question most newlyweds are tempted to ask their sometimes exasperating, sometimes inscrutable, oftentimes imperfect husbands or wives at some point—or *many* points—during their first married year. Few of them, of course, actually pose such a query aloud. A good thing, too, since doing so could well reduce anyone's chances of winning the World's Most Sensitive Spouse award.

But, despite outward restraint, within a few months of marriage, women and men who happily and eagerly said "I do" usually find themselves waking up one morning thinking, *"I did?"*

I did. And just about everyone I knew did. And that is how this book came to be.

When I married, several years ago, my wedding was one among so many weddings of friends, relatives, and colleagues that it proved nearly impossible to find a free date on which to schedule the happy event. For months, it seemed as though the only topics of conversation were wedding ceremonies, wedding receptions, wedding wardrobes, and honeymoon plans. Proper wording of invitations was debated, menus were selected, seating charts were drawn up, torn up, and drawn up again. The only thing that wasn't talked about much was marriage itself.

Were we happy about getting married? Sure. Were we nervous? You bet. But if anyone had asked us during that frenetic season if we were ready to make all the adjustments that marriage involved—yes, even for those of us who had lived with our mates before marriage or who were veterans of marriages gone by—we probably would have ignored the question and blithely asked our well-meaning interlocutor to go rain on someone else's parade.

Of course we knew all the old adages: The course of true love never runs smooth, and so on. And we knew the statistic that one out of two marriages ends in divorce. We even knew, though we may not have liked knowing that we knew, that our soon-to-be-sanctioned relationships would have their highs and lows. Whose didn't? But potential problems were, we believed, a long way off. And by the time that distant future presented itself, we vaguely assumed we'd be prepared for it. After all, we were bright, kindly, civilized people who deeply loved and, just as important, liked our spouses-to-be. So, while *other people's* marriages might split at the seams, our nuptial bonds, we were certain, would make even Ozzie and Harriet's pale by comparison.

A few months after we took our respective vows, however, we brides and grooms were humming different tunes. Of course we were still in love with our partners. It was just being married to them that seemed to be the problem. Sometimes we felt wonderful about the decision we'd made, but sometimes we wondered if we'd made that decision in some sort of fugue state, wholly in the grips of inexplicable temporary lunacy. Sometimes we experienced a sense of déjà vu, noticing that difficulties we had in our present relationships were eerie echoes of those we'd had in previous ones. Sometimes we felt a sense of *jamais vu,* and our partners, with whom we'd thought we were so familiar, seemed alien.

How did something that seemed so simple become so difficult? we wondered. And why had it become so difficult so soon? Was there something wrong with us that we were such evident marital misfits? Or was there something wrong with our spouses, who, having cleverly presented themselves as princes or princesses, had now revealed that under their royal veneers lurked some rather froggy qualities?

In an attempt to try to figure out what, exactly, was going on, in my own life and in the lives of those I cared about, I started doing some serious talking to the women and men in my informal "newlywed network" and to colleagues at the psychoanalytic institute where I had, perhaps presciently, begun studying around the time of my engagement. I also read extensively about marriage past and present. As my formal and informal research, as well as my own soul-searching, progressed, I began to suspect that a big part of what was "wrong" was that, although most of us want to marry, and most of us do, many of us embark upon our marriages with little to guide us except romantic myth, folklore, and fantasy.

Popular literature and mass media are both culprits in perpetrating misconceptions of the married state. Literary works from fairy tales to Jane Austen novels have presented marriage not as a beginning but as a "happy ending." Television and magazines bombard us with rapturous commentaries on royal weddings. Marriage, their cooing correspondents assure us, allows us all to enter a magical kingdom of heaven-on-earth.

Let's face it: marriage is a less-than-ideal institution (though it's the best we've got) entered into by less-than-perfect beings, who had better be prepared to exercise a good deal of effort, patience, and understanding if they want their relationships to stand the test of time. Unfortunately, however, many new couples who don't feel as "happy" as they thought they would, or as quickly as they hoped they might, imagine that the joy which eludes them can be found only in the arms of more "compatible" mates. No doubt more marriages would prove durable if people abandoned the misbegotten notion that marital myth and marital reality are one and the same. But where and how can they learn this?

We spend countless years preparing to succeed in business or work in a chosen profession. We may spend countless hours and dollars mastering skills from tap dancing to scuba diving to kung fu. But when it comes to living harmoniously with the person we wed, we assume we can play it by ear.

A certain amount of trial and error is a natural part of all ultimately successful endeavors. But try telling the manager of a new major league baseball franchise that if he just leaves well enough alone his team will win the pennant sooner or later. He'll tell *you* that your elevator doesn't go all the way to the top. Try such a theory out on a scientist and he'll tell you about entropy, the tendency of systems to fall apart unless new energy is introduced into them. If we want to create something that really works, *we* have to work—hard.

The goal of *Why Did I Marry You, Anyway?* is, therefore, to help you tolerate the inevitable early frustrations of your marriage while working to improve it, and to help you keep loving your spouse while you learn to live with him or her in the married state. It is a book for the recently married, the about-to-be-wed, and for those who are simply at the stage of contemplating this giant step and who want to know what to anticipate once the ink on the marriage license has dried.

The book argues that while the first year of marriage can provide newlyweds with many pleasures and exciting discoveries—not to mention some hilarious moments, which, with hindsight, evolve into terrific anecdotes—it also invariably provides moments of stress, disillusionment, anger, and doubt. It can be a year in which couples lay firm and unshakable foundations for their relationships, but it can also be a year in which bad habits and attitudes get set in psychic stone.

The dynamics of the first year of marriage are as crucial to its future as the period of infancy is to the development of the human personality. Indeed, not since the first years of life itself are we required to process so much new information and make so many adaptations while defining our own sense of ourselves and our sense of what others mean to us.

And as difficult as marriage has always been, it is even tougher now. Today, men and women are, on the average, marrying later than ever before, and many come to their marriages equipped with long histories of freedom and independence, not to mention their own careers, credit cards, and circles of long-time friends. They are faced with the dilemma of building a life for two in a world that glorifies the individual. What's more, the subtle, unspoken rules that, in past generations, kept most people from marrying outside their own social or economic class have grown increasingly relaxed, so that many new couples need to find ways of bridging differences that, in another time and place, would have probably kept them from dancing together, let alone pledging to live side by side until their dying day.

While some people are reluctant to discuss the many kinds of difficulties they encountered in the transition from single to married life, I was fortunate in finding some fifty recently married women and men who realized that the confusing and conflicting thoughts and feelings they experienced early in their married lives meant only that they were human. These people—whose stories and comments I have conveyed through fictional composite characters in order to protect their privacy—ranged in age from early twenties to mid-fifties. They had varied family backgrounds, geographic backgrounds, income levels, professions, and, of course, temperaments. Some were in their first marriage and some on later go-rounds. And some who were remarried already had children. But for all their differences, they had in common a certain sensitivity, candor, and articulateness, which made this book all the more enjoyable to write and, I hope, will make it all the more useful and enjoyable to read.

Why Did I Marry You, Anyway? also draws on the expert opinions of couples therapists, psychologists, and psychoanalysts who shared with me their perspectives on the psychological quandaries of marriage's first year, as well as attorneys and financial planners who discussed pragmatic concerns, such as prenuptial agreements and merging funds. And because the first year of marriage, one hopes, will be the first of many years, the final chapter of the book includes comments from husbands and wives whose marriages have endured for fifteen years or more.

Why Did I Marry You, Anyway? does not purport to be a sweeping survey or a scientific study. No one who contributed to this book was asked to fill out a questionnaire or rate his or her spouse on a scale of 1 to 10. All they were asked to do was talk, and all readers must do to benefit from that talk is to listen with an open mind. You'll find no graphs, grids, charts, or statistical tables here; what you will find instead are ways of becoming more aware of how marriage will, very early on, begin to challenge and reward you, as well as ways of meeting those challenges with good humor and good sense.

Granted, each marriage is *sui generis,* a thing unto itself, but that should not prevent newlyweds, or those who are soon to be newlyweds, from learning certain emotional and practical fundamentals that can help them get things off on the right foot and, with a little luck and a lot of love, keep them that way.

As children learning the alphabet, we begin with A, B, and C, but as grown-ups learning about marriage, let's begin instead with E. E is for expectations . . .

WHY
DID
I
MARRY
YOU,
ANYWAY
?

1

Heading Down the Aisle

IN THE MOVIE *Diner,* Eddie is about to marry his high school sweetheart, Elise—provided she can pass his one-hundred-and-forty-question football quiz. While Elise struggles mightily with true-and-false, short-answer, and multiple-choice questions, Eddie explains to his half-admiring, half-incredulous buddies that unless she scores a minimum grade of sixty-five the marriage is off. "It's out of my hands," he says. She scores sixty-three, but he magnanimously marries her anyway.

In the musical *Guys and Dolls,* a nightclub performer named Adelaide hopes that marriage will cause her fiancé of fourteen years, notorious gangster and gambler Nathan Detroit, to trade in his floating crap game for an honest job and a baby buggy. To underscore her point she sings:

> Marry the man today,
> Trouble tho' he may be,
> Much as he likes to play,
> Crazy and wild and free.
>
> Marry the man today,
> Rather than sigh and sorrow,

WHY DID I MARRY YOU, ANYWAY?

Marry the man today
And change his ways tomorrow.

Though Adelaide says of her beau, "I've always thought how wonderful he would be, if he was different," she does marry him in the end.

Obviously, both Eddie and Adelaide have expectations about what their married life will be like and what kind of spouse their loved ones will be. But while Eddie lets Elise know in no uncertain terms that he expects his wife to share his passion for the gridiron—and she complies—Adelaide takes care to sing her ditty well out of Nathan's earshot.

Everyone who is about to marry has certain ideas, beliefs, hopes, and fantasies about what lies ahead. It's only natural that, in order to compensate for giving up our past way of life, we want to exert some sort of control, be it real or imagined, on what the mysterious future holds. While we may share some of our expectations with our partners, many more of them tend to go unspoken. We may be embarrassed to talk about our expectations aloud, and we may fear that rejection will result if we do (after all, not everyone is as understanding as Elise). Sometimes we simply don't bother talking about them because we assume, usually falsely, that our partner has expectations identical to our own.

Mark and Claudia Howard had been married for two and a half years at the time I interviewed them. Each of them remembered certain expectations they had when they married—he for the second time at forty, she for the first time at twenty-seven—as well as the surprise and annoyance they felt when they discovered they were operating under two entirely different sets of assumptions.

"Mark has always loved to ski," said Claudia. "While we were dating he would spend at least two weekends of every winter month at his Vermont country house, skiing

2

with his two teenage sons. Since I was in law school I would either stay at home in New York and study or bring my books with me and curl up with them while Mark and the boys were on the slopes. Sometimes I would get teased about not being a skier, but basically I thought Mark knew how frightened I was to take up the sport and how much a North Carolina–born girl like me dreaded being outside in the cold. Somehow I figured that once we were married Mark wouldn't ski as much. I assumed he wouldn't want to leave me alone on weekends, and that the kids could just as well visit us in the city as in the country. Boy, did I have the wrong idea!''

As it turned out, Mark assumed that as soon as Claudia finished law school, she would develop an interest in his favorite activity. ''I guess I never really took her objections seriously. I figured as soon as she wasn't so caught up in studying that she would be a good sport about the whole thing and give skiing a try. I was floored when she refused.''

Like many couples, Mark and Claudia found that their first year of marriage was a time to come to terms with their differing expectations. During January and February, Mark skied and Claudia stewed. But by March, this brave bride decided to take a beginner's skiing course. ''I thought I'd try, break my leg, get a lot of sympathy, and put an end to the whole thing,'' said Claudia. 'But to my everlasting surprise I found I loved it! Now we ski together whenever we can. It's been great for us and it's been a wonderful way for me to get closer to Mark's children.''

I talked with Dave and Megan Brown, both thirty-four, just before their second anniversary. They told me they shared some mutual moments of shock and dismay early in their marriage when they found that their somewhat stereotypical assumptions about the day-to-day responsibilities of husbands and wives didn't apply to their own situation. Though they had lived together for nearly a year before formalizing their relationship, that experience seemed not at all to prevent them from bringing false assumptions to their marriage.

When the Browns married, Megan automatically assumed that Dave would tend to all the items in their apartment that needed repair. "Megan grew up in the kind of family where, it seemed, every Saturday her father and brothers would rewire the house just for fun," Dave explained. "As soon as I became an official family member, she expected me to be the same way. I'm an absolute klutz when it comes to that kind of thing. I don't know a nut from a bolt—never did and never will."

For his part, Dave assumed that Megan's culinary skills, not much in evidence during their cohabitation, would suddenly spring to life. "As soon as we got married, Dave expected me to cook up a three-course meal every night," said Megan, "even though before we got married he seemed to accept the fact that the most complicated thing I could do in the kitchen was to heat up a frozen pizza. Somewhere in the back of his mind he thought, Wife equals meal."

Clearly, the Browns were faced with the need to redefine their marital expectations, and they did. They continued to eat lots of take-out food until Dave decided to take up cooking himself, and they continued to endure their leaky faucets until Megan finally accepted the fact that Dave was "all thumbs" and charmed the building superintendent into taking pity on them.

When two people get married, they make formal contracts with each other. They sign a marriage license, which assures that their bond will be viewed as legitimate in the eyes of the state. They stand up in front of witnesses, usually relatives and friends, and make a public statement to the effect that they will love, comfort, honor, and cherish each other for the rest of their days. In many cases, they have their union blessed by a priest, pastor, or rabbi. But, as the Howards and the Browns and virtually everyone else I spoke with rapidly discovered, these formal contracts and vows and sacraments, as important and meaningful as they are, do not have nearly as much day-to-day impact on a marriage as the informal contracts between two people.

Informal contracts are what govern such nitty-gritty issues as who will do the laundry, who will do the driving, and who will send out the thank-you notes for the eight coffee-makers and seventeen serving platters received as wedding gifts. They also govern more weighty matters, such as what a couple's spending priorities are, how each spouse will treat the other's parents and/or children, and even how, and how often, they will make love.

Informal contracts, as we've seen, are based more on unspoken expectations than on spoken ones, but, as marital therapist Clifford Sager, the first to write extensively about the different levels of marital contracts, points out in his book *Marriage Contracts and Couples Therapy,* they can also be based on *unconscious* expectations. On a level outside our awareness, we may look to marriage to cure us of our personal emotional problems, to provide us with an ideal mother- or father-figure, or to right the wrongs life has dealt us in the past. We can't help keeping such expectations secret from our spouse, because they are also secrets we've kept from ourselves.

When Sandy Farrell married her husband, Jack, she had an unconscious expectation that did not creep into her awareness till about six months into her marriage. "I think I believed on some level that by marrying Jack, I would marry into a perfect family," Sandy said. "I was the only child of a mother and father who divorced when I was young. I had a lonely childhood, going back and forth between the two of them. Jack came from a big family that always seemed to have so much fun together. I thought they would make me forget about my own unhappy family life and that finally, at twenty-four years old, I would have what I'd always dreamed of.

"When I got to know his family better, I saw that they weren't perfect after all. I don't mean they were bad people, I just mean they were normal people who sometimes argued or complained about each other and had their little rivalries. But whenever they did any of this perfectly routine stuff I got depressed. I didn't want to have anything to do with them and of course that upset Jack. It was only after we talked it out that I finally figured out what was going on. After that, I came to appreciate Jack's family much more, even though they weren't some made-up TV family like the one I'd always fantasized about."

After Sandy's unconscious expectation was brought to light, she was able to make a necessary change in her informal contract with her husband. She allowed herself to enjoy a relationship with Jack's less-than-perfect relatives, and she relieved him of guilt for not providing her with something that no one could have provided.

Informal marriage contracts, whether conscious or unconscious, are fluid, dynamic agreements. Any married couple will revise and refine these contracts throughout their marriage, but I think it is safe to say that never will there be so many contract negotiations on so many levels as there are in marriage's first year, a time when husbands and wives face every day the task of exchanging fantasy for reality.

In theory it might be nice if all of those who were about to marry were able to discover and articulate all of their own expectations before the wedding. This would at least serve to cut down the sheer number of surprises in store, though in practice it is really asking too much. In the weeks and months leading up to a walk down the aisle, brides- and grooms-to-be are often simply too overloaded with conflicting emotions to plumb their innermost thoughts, let alone find a way to communicate them. On the one hand, they're busy being happy and anticipating the best; on the other, they're busy being anxious and fearing the worst.

"A" Is for Anxiety

Fran, about to become a bride at twenty-five, had the following dream:

"It's my wedding day and I wake up wearing the clothes I'm supposed to be married in. But instead of a white dress, I find I'm wearing a red dress. My hat is white, but of all things it's a white, fur-covered toilet seat and it's held on my head by an elastic band that ties under my nose. I feel completely ridiculous. Someone tells me to go to the church and take a number, which I do. It turns out there are lots of other brides at the church, all wearing white, and all of us are clutching slips of paper with numbers on them. The brides are finding their husbands by matching up *their* numbers to the numbers of the men who are standing around the church, but my number is forty-nine and I can't find a man who has the same one. Finally, a boy I dated briefly in high school turns up with number forty-nine, but he tells me that although he's not my husband-to-be, he's going to marry me by proxy. It seems my real husband is too busy to get married today."

Kevin, about to remarry at thirty-six, dreamed that he simply could not get out of bed on the morning of his wedding. "In the dream I'm so tired, and my arms and legs feel so heavy, that I can't move. My parents are in my bedroom and so are some of my friends and even my ex-wife's parents! They're all shouting at me to get up. My mother keeps yelling that the photographer will leave if I don't hurry—he has other weddings to photograph. I just keep lying there, wanting to get up but utterly incapable. I keep saying I need just five more minutes of sleep, just five more minutes."

One doesn't have to be a psychiatrist to sense that these were anxiety dreams. In the clever shorthand way that dreams have, they express many of the fears and apprehensions that Fran and Kevin were feeling with relation to their impending nuptials. To marry is to take leave of the past, which might explain the cameo appearances of Fran's high school beau and Kevin's ex-in-laws. To marry is to face an unknown future, which might account for Fran's lottery-style dream wedding. To participate in a wedding ceremony is to put ourselves on public display to be ogled, inspected, and oohed and aahed over by Aunt Gertie, Uncle Mortie, Cousin Guido, and the like. It's no wonder Fran's dream found her so embarrassed by her foolish costume, or that Kevin preferred sleeping to being photographed.

All of us fall prey to anxiety when under stress and strain, but there's nothing like the approach of our wedding day for producing a whole grab-bag of anxieties at once. First, there's separation anxiety, a factor in any situation in which we bid adieu to the comfortable and the familiar. Freud believed that all separation anxiety stems from the early anxious feelings we had when separating from our mothers, even back to the birth experience itself, when we were all forced to say "Good-by, cozy womb, hello, bright lights, big city!" A wedding can't help but call up feelings of separation on many levels, for there is much we leave behind us as we head down the aisle.

In getting married we are symbolically exchanging our

8

own babyhood and childhood for the cares and responsibilities that accompany adulthood. At ancient Japanese
weddings, in fact, this symbolic tradeoff was acted out
rather literally by pitching all of the bride's girlhood play-
things onto a roaring bonfire. We are also leaving behind
the comparatively carefree existence we enjoyed as single
people. In many cultures, including our own, friends and
relations of the groom may acknowledge this by treating
him to a rowdy prewedding party, a kind of "last fling
with the boys." As for brides, their transition to the responsibilities of wifehood has, through the ages, been
noted by "showering" them with practical adult items
from crockery to Cuisinarts, but now that women, like
men, are generally understood to have "pasts" before
marriage, these pragmatic events are sometimes supple-
mented or replaced by nights-on-the-town with "the
girls." As Tolstoy wrote of such festive prewedding rites
of passage, "There is a good reason for taking leave of
one's bachelor life. However happy you may be, you can't
help regretting your freedom."

Of course, in marrying we are also, quite literally, separating from our families of origin. In times gone by, the
departures of brides and grooms from their parents' homes
were often accompanied by elaborate pageantry. In the
United States today, most of us have already lived apart
from our parents and siblings by the time we marry, so
our separation from them is not so much physical as psychic—and it is often accompanied by a lot of angst on
everyone's part.

Many people I interviewed, and especially those who
had recently married for the first time, recalled family-
related conflicts in the weeks or months leading up to their
weddings. Many mothers and fathers, even those who had
never shown much interest in matters of etiquette before,
suddenly evinced an encyclopedic knowledge of wedding

minutiae, from invitation typefaces to table centerpieces, and demanded that their wisdom be put to use. Brothers and sisters, too, were determined to contribute their two cents on wedding-related matters great and small, *including* handy suggestions for coping with overenthusiastic moms and dads (e.g., "Surrender and surrender now," or, "Stand up for yourself for once").

The interesting thing about most prewedding family feuds is how they re-create each family's time-worn power struggles and how everyone involved, fired up by new enthusiasm, plays his or her role to the hilt. One bride's mother (described to me as being in the habit of getting her own way and then claiming it was what her children really wanted all along) insisted her twenty-six-year-old daughter be married in a particularly opulent catering hall instead of the smaller, less pretentious setting her daughter preferred. When the hall rental contract was signed and her daughter burst into tears, the woman turned to her future son-in-law, exclaiming, "Look how happy she is!" One father, legendary in his family for his lifelong determination—and inability—to master even the simplest photographic equipment, insisted on recording his son's wedding with a portable video camera and an eight-track tape recorder, resulting in three hours of footage of wedding guests' feet, orchestrated by an eerie high-pitched sound.

Brides and grooms and their families, on the eve of weddings, unconsciously reenact old family dramas because they fear they may never have another chance to do so. No matter how happy our parents and siblings may be when we marry, there is certainly some level on which they regret how fast we've grown up—and therefore away—and resent the fact that we're now in a position to choose a new family member for ourselves: a spouse. They are feeling as much separation anxiety as the bride and groom themselves. One way to alleviate it is to deny the impending future by repeating what has gone before.

Just as separation anxiety is bound up with the past, anticipatory anxiety attaches itself to thoughts of the future. In certain situations, anticipatory anxiety is extremely useful. It can serve as a warning signal from our brains to our bodies, alerting us to real danger and readying us for the "flight response"—as in, "Whoops, here comes a tiger, I'm outta here!" But when anticipatory anxiety focuses on imagined rather than actual danger, it leads to worry, worry, worry.

Not many of us consciously equate marriage with danger, but to the unconscious mind, the unknown *is* danger. Anytime it is faced with a journey into *terra incognita*, anxiety results. As the wedding day approaches, it's only natural that those about to wed worry about the kinds of questions that can really only be answered with the passage of time: Will marriage bring me happiness? Will I be a good spouse? Have I given this whole thing enough thought?

Charlie and Robin Turner, married for a year and a half at the time of their interview, described to me the anticipatory fears they each felt on the threshold of marriage. Robin put it this way: "I had to pick a major in college when I was eighteen. I picked art history, but then I changed to psychology and then to sociology. Then I dropped out of college altogether. I had lived with and broken up with two boyfriends before I met and fell in love with Charlie. Right before the wedding I began to wonder if I could ever really trust my own decisions. Maybe at twenty-nine I was still too immature to know what I wanted. Maybe I was just indecisive and flighty by nature. I knew I loved Charlie with all my heart, but was I going to change my mind about him, too?"

Unbeknownst to his fiancée, Charlie had some doubts

of his own. "I was madly sexually attracted to Robin from the day I met her, but before that I guess you could say I was something of a Don Juan. Right before the wedding—even though I was really satisfied with our sex life—I got scared. Suddenly thirty-three seemed awfully young to be committing myself to having one lover forever. Would I be able to stay faithful for the next forty years or so, or would I have affairs like so many married men I knew, including my own father? I really worked myself into a state."

Their fears and doubts caused Charlie and Robin many a sleepless prenuptial night. In fact, after their wedding, both laughingly admitted to having briefly entertained fantasies of heading for the hills or taking a slow boat to China, rather than going through with things as planned. Talk about the flight response!

As if all these nervous-making forces were not enough to contend with, most couples involved in a marriage countdown are also faced with an overwhelming degree of performance anxiety regarding the wedding itself. "Performance anxiety" is just what is sounds like: anxiety focused on the outcome of a crucial event. It is what actors may feel before they go onstage opening night, or what a baseball player may feel as he steps up to the plate in that all-important seventh World Series game. A wedding is a complex set of events all happening at once. It is a private and romantic event, a legal event, often a religious event, and, with very few exceptions, it's a public and social event—a kind of performance.

As soon as a couple decides to have their wedding witnessed by friends and relations (as opposed to sneaking off to City Hall and getting married during lunch hour), endless anxiety-provoking decisions ensue, sometimes causing those who take the former path to lament not choosing the latter. How many guests will attend? What happens when the guests want to bring guests? What music will be chosen? Can we keep Cousin Guido from playing his accordion without appearing rude?

With so many interfaith marriages occurring nowadays, these choices are often harder than ever. What do you serve at a wedding when the bride's family keeps kosher and the groom's family refuses to eat anything that's not doused in tomato sauce? Who performs the ceremony when Mary-Margaret McBride marries Sun Yat Woo? Moreover, with fewer etiquette imperatives to follow these days (assuming Mom and Dad have been soothed), the number of choices that those planning weddings must make has increased tenfold. Take fashion as one small example. If no one insists that the bride wear a white floor-length gown complete with veil and train, what *should* she wear? A blue suit? A pale beige cocktail dress? Jane Fonda Workout gear? What about the groom—a tux? An unconstructed Italian blazer? Golf pants?

Our contemporary world being what it is, wedding plans are often complicated by some very touchy situations. Sandy and Jack Farrell, for example, had to contend with the fact that Sandy's divorced parents hadn't seen or spoken to each other in years (a temporary truce was ultimately declared so Sandy could be escorted down the aisle by her father). Robin and Charlie Turner, married in San Jose, California, on a Sunday, had to introduce their immediate families, respectively from New Jersey and Ohio, to each other at their Friday night rehearsal dinner. And Mark and Claudia Howard had to coax Mark's ex-wife into letting his two sons attend their wedding, which Mark had unwittingly scheduled during a family vacation she had planned.

With so many internal and external stresses to contend with, it's no wonder that people who are about to wed sometimes feel the need to blow off a little steam. Many a tearful bride has threatened to sue the contentious caterer who insists on garnishing every dish with kiwi, and many an irate groom has threatened to punch out the procrastinating printer who is two weeks late with the invitations, but for most wedding professionals, dealing with prewedding wrath is all in a day's work. Unfortunately, some of the steam that a couple blows off gets blown off in the direction of each other.

Premarital spats are so common that Miss Manners, in her *Guide to Excruciatingly Correct Behavior,* provides a checklist of fights that engaged couples are expected to have "so as to be ready and tired enough for a peaceful marriage." Though the thorough Miss Manners provides, in the very same chapter, advice on how to announce that the wedding is off, engagements aren't broken at the last minute as often as one might fear.

Many engaged couples find that their positive, loving feelings toward each other give them enough strength to withstand a few spats. Indeed, lots of prewedding "lover's quarrels" are resolved easily enough by quid pro quo negotiations (e.g., "You get your mother to forget about singing 'I Love You Truly' and I'll get my aunt Eustasia to leave her three cocker spaniels *outside* the church"), after which the couples involved have a great time making up. But all couples' situations differ, and some couples, because of the temperaments of the people involved and/ or of an overwhelming number of circumstances outside their control, find that though their ardor is still strong, it becomes eclipsed by anxiety and the arguments that spring from anxiety. Such couples may be helped by consulting a neutral third party.

Premarital Counseling

Premarital counseling comes in three basic varieties: instructive, predictive, and therapeutic. Instructive premarital counseling is usually what you get when you seek counseling through your church or synagogue. Ministers, priests, and rabbis will generally discuss with an engaged couple what marriage means in a broad spiritual and social context. Most will also give general advice, informed by psychology as well as their religious beliefs, as to how to appreciate the "better" parts and tolerate the "worse" parts of your "for better or worse" married life. Depending on how well the religious counselor knows the couple, of course, this general advice may veer toward the specific.

Some couples seek instructive premarital counseling on their own; others undertake it because their religion requires them to do so before they can be married under its auspices. Usually those who take the initiative themselves have a more open attitude and find the experience more rewarding. On the other hand, some couples who enter into instructive counseling with the idea that it is just another prewedding chore to cross off their lists are pleasantly surprised by the experience. One woman I spoke with told me, "It was a real relief just to have a few hours where I was encouraged to think about what marriage really meant instead of what kind of chicken we should serve at the reception. I actually felt much calmer after it was over. I thought, Hey, who *cares* about the chicken, I'm getting *married!*"

Predictive premarital counseling is favored by psychologists who put their faith in collecting data and making statistical prognostications. If you seek premarital coun-seling from a clinician with such a bent, you may be asked to respond to questionnaires designed to measure how alike or different you and your betrothed are in everything from hygienic habits to moral values. The psychologist inter-prets the answers and tells you how good—or poor—your chances are for marital success, assuming you want to know.

Some predictive counselors even use the similarities and differences of a couples' parents as a yardstick. In one such method, engaged couples are asked to imagine the marriage of the woman's mother to the man's father and her father to his mother. Where such hypothetical match-ups are deemed unthinkable, slim chances for marital bliss are predicted.

Couples who go in for this sort of thing would do well to take such predictions with a large grain of salt. Ques-tionnaires may do a fine job of measuring surface similar-ities and differences, but the more important, unconscious ways in which partners are alike and unalike are hard to pin down. What's more, to predict marital success based on the personalities of people's parents is to assume that people can never rise above their parents' patterns. They often can if they are willing to try.

Therapeutic premarital counseling can be enormously useful to couples who are motivated to explore their indi-vidual expectations for marriage and to share them with each other. It can also help couples who are struggling under an excessive or unmanageable prewedding anxiety load to *rediscover* some of the happiness and affection that may lie buried underneath their fears, distractions, and doubts. Therapists who work with couples therapeutically may be social workers, marriage and family counselors, psychoanalysts, clinical psychologists, or psychiatrists, but whatever their credentials are and whatever theoretical framework guides them, you can tell good ones from not-so-good ones by their willingness to listen instead of lecture, their disinclination to show favoritism or take sides in disputes, and their ability to help both members of a couple talk to each other constructively.

Can everyone benefit from premarital counseling? To some degree, yes. For many people in our society, premarital counseling is the only opportunity they will have, in the frenzied period before the wedding, to reflect on what they're doing and why they're doing it. Though certain counseling techniques and styles will obviously be better suited to some couples than to others, the sheer number of options out there practically guarantees that any couple can find an approach that will benefit *them*. By the way, premarital counseling is just as useful to couples who have lived together before marriage as it is to those who haven't. It's amazing how marriage changes the dynamics of any relationship, and counseling can often help cohabiting couples become aware of this.

On the other hand, premarital counseling is no panacea. As useful as it is, it won't in any way alleviate all of the difficult adjustments that arise after signing on the dotted line. As psychoanalyst James Morrell told me, "Marriage is like a flower that unfolds. You can't force a flower to open up before it's ready to, and you can't resolve problems that haven't come up yet." Perhaps it's best to think of premarital counseling as you would think of tuning up your car before a cross-country journey. Changing the shock absorbers and the oil may give you a smoother ride, but there's not much you or your mechanic can do to guarantee that you will never get a flat tire en route.

Prenuptial Agreements

Premarital counseling is a tool available to couples who would like to see their marriages work out. Prenuptial agreements are tools available to couples who would like to see their marriage work out but would like to protect their individual interests just in case they don't. Prenuptial agreements are quite an anxiety-provoking subject in and of themselves. Lots of engaged people get squeamish at the very thought, but no discussion of heading down the aisle would be complete without making mention of them.

Though they're usually thought of as something new, prenuptial agreements have actually been around since biblical times, and apparently people haggled over them even then. In his book on marriage contracts, Clifford Sager notes that infrared photography used by scientists to inspect a prenuptial agreement from 449 B.C. revealed many cross-outs and erasures on the document (all changes, interestingly enough, being to the advantage of the bride). Through the centuries, prenuptial agreements continued to be common, since families of brides and grooms in many cultures would not even entertain the notion of marrying off their children before financial arrangements were duly spelled out.

Today, of course, it's the partners rather than their parents who negotiate these agreements. What's more, while they used to deal primarily with financial arrangements for the course of the marriage and/or provisions for inheritance, they now deal largely with what will happen in the event of a divorce. Most of today's prenuptial agreements should actually be called *postnuptial* agreements.

The number of prenuptial agreements being drawn up

in this country is on the rise for many reasons. First, there are the unignorable statistics on divorce, combined with the fact that many people who are marrying come from broken homes themselves. Second, the predominance of two-career couples means that both parties usually bring assets to the marriage, and the older people are when they marry, the more considerable those assets are likely to be. Third, many people execute prenuptial agreements to protect children of prior marriages from being left out in the financial cold.

Yet for all the people who do have prenuptial agreements drawn up and signed, many more talk to their attorneys about them, then change their minds. There are many good reasons for this as well. Prenuptial agreements force people to think about the worst-case scenario when they are staking their entire emotional lives on the best-case scenario. Moreover, prenuptial agreements are hardly what one would call romantic. It's one thing to send your fiancé a tender love sonnet, but another thing entirely to hand over something that reads, on the first of its zillions of pages:

> The parties hereto, in anticipation of their marriage, desire to define and limit the rights which each will have in the estate and property of the other by reason of their marriage and the rights and liabilities that each may have in the event of permanent physical separation, annulment, dissolution, legal separation, or divorce.

Even if both parties agree to try to hammer out a prenuptial agreement, that may be the last thing they agree on. Though marital attorney Raoul Lionel Felder, who has one of the largest premarital agreement practices in the country, recommends drawing up such agreements as protection against today's incredibly complex divorce laws, he also cautions: "These agreements can turn into a divorce before you even get married. They can catch people at the most vulnerable time of their lives and make them instant adversaries."

Those couples who can bring themselves to execute prenuptial agreements should also be aware that if these agreements are ever utilized, one party or the other is likely to cry "no fair." "When you have a life preserver on board ship for an emergency," says Felder, "everyone is hoping it will work if the emergency really happens. This is different. This is one case where an instrument is prepared for an emergency and one party hopes it won't work."

In order for prenuptial agreements to stand up in court, they can't be prepared on the eve of the marriage, because one spouse may later claim he or she gave in to emotional blackmail—"Put your John Hancock on this or I'll leave you standing at the altar." What's more, each party signing the agreement must be represented by his or her own lawyer, and each must disclose all assets at the time of the marriage. Many people, by the way, consider this last stipulation a good reason *not* to draw up a prenuptial agreement.

While prenuptial agreements deal primarily with financial matters, some couples like to add expectational clauses about everything from what religious faith their children will be raised in to who will take out the garbage. There's no law against putting such things in writing, and doing so may make both partners feel honor-bound to stick to their promises. From a legal standpoint, though, Felder says such clauses are completely unconstitutional and would be laughed out of court. Fortunately, we live in a country that guarantees us all freedom of religion and that furthermore upholds everyone's inviolable right to refuse to take out the trash.

Wedding Days, Wedding Daze

Whether or not lawyers have been consulted, whether or not couples have been counseled or caterers duly cajoled, sooner or later it's time for the wedding preparations to end and the curtain to go up on the big event itself. One might think that after enduring months of psychic acrobatics and arduous planning, brides and grooms would vividly remember those precious minutes during which they said their vows and those precious hours of celebration that followed.

But, alas, most people are so overwhelmed by emotional and sensory overload during their own weddings that they remember them only in the vaguest way. Many newlyweds I interviewed said they succumbed to what I've come to think of as "wedding amnesia." Charlie Turner said that "a kind of glaze" came over him as soon as the ceremony began. Sandy Farrell said that, in spite of her efforts to force herself to pay attention, she "felt as if everything was a blur." After Mark Howard's wedding, his mind was a blank. "All I knew was that I must have smiled a lot," he said, "because my face actually hurt."

What did all these people miss? What actually happened while they were in their nuptial daze? Well, first, as we know, they pledged, in the presence of witnesses, to honor their formal marital contracts. Second, they and their wedding guests took part in various rituals, most of which grew out of ancient customs designed to cement the symbolic husband-wife bond, to ward off evil spirits that might cause marital disharmony, and to ensure all-round good fortune for the happy twosome.

The giving of rings, for example, as much a part of

wedding custom today as it has been for many thousands of years, is a dual-purpose ritual. The exchange of a valuable token between bride and groom has long represented the solidification of the marital union. But rings also became an important part of marriage rites early on because of their circular shape. Many ancient cultures held the circle in veneration as a symbol of perfection, and its use in ritual was thought to ensure good luck. At one time it was taboo to decorate wedding rings with stones, engraving, or anything else that diminished their perfect, unbroken roundness.

Wedding cakes, too, symbolize good wishes. Way back when these "cakes" were actually dry, unleavened biscuits, it was considered efficacious to break them over the head of the bride before eating them. This rather messy tradition held up even after ingredients like eggs and almond paste were added to the original recipes. It was only when sugary icing became part of the standard formula that wedding guests began to content themselves with having the cake cut up and distributed without first demolishing the brides' coiffe.

Even today, the tradition of showering newlyweds with foodstuffs continues, but contemporary brides and grooms who complain of having to pick grains of Uncle Ben's Converted Rice out of their hair ought to thank their lucky stars that they did not live in days of yore. In those "good old days," guests sought to ensure the nuptial couple's abundance and fertility by pelting them with everything from dates, figs, nuts, and seeds to wheat, raisins, and barley—in short, all the makings of a hearty granola.

Wedding rites often also include customs that symbolically ward off any future antipathy between the husband and wife. When a bride and groom drink from the same cup or glass, or feed each other from the same plate, fork, or spoon, they are following age-old practices designed both to illustrate the couple's capacity for harmony and sharing, and to prevent evil spirits from pestering newlyweds by planting seeds of discontent in their minds. Slightly more graphic methods of assuring the absence of evil spirits, such as animal sacrifices at the wedding altar, have, thankfully, been laid aside, and I'll wager that no small number of chickens, oxen, goats, and sheep are delighted with this turn of events (*especially* sheep whose gall bladders the ancient Romans removed after their sacrifice to symbolize the removal of bitterness from the marriage).

Though many wedding rituals today have been toned down from earlier ones, they are nonetheless thick with meaning. And like most rituals and superstitions, those connected with weddings are really about control—or, more correctly, the attempt at control. Deep in the collective unconscious, the knowledge that marriage is no simple business seems to be accompanied by the wish that it *were* a simple business. The creation and preservation of wedding rituals reflect humankind's desire that the married state be divine rather than human, trouble-free rather than occasionally troublesome, easy rather than complicated. Rings and rice and cakes, however, can only express that desire; they can't make it reality. Would that they could!

When newlyweds leave their wedding festivities behind and go off into the world as a married couple, they take many things with them (I mean *besides* the gifts). They take the good wishes of their guests, their own foggy but happy memories of the day, and their expectations for what is to come. But, as George Eliot wisely wrote in her novel *Middlemarch,* "The door-sill of marriage once crossed, expectation is concentrated on the present." Let's see what happens when the long-awaited future finally arrives.

2

The Infancy of Marriage

The moon, the moon, so silver and cold,
Her fickle temper has oft been told,
Now shady—now bright and sunny—
But of all the lunar things that change,
The one that shows most fickle and strange,
And takes the most eccentric range,
Is the moon—so-called—of honey!

—Thomas Hood

When a couple are newly married, the first
month is honeymoon or smick-smack;
The second is hither and thither; the third
is thwick thwack;
The fourth, the Devil take them that brought
thee and I together.

—*John Ray*, English Proverbs

JUST HEARING THE WORD *honeymoon* can be enough to make us smile. We may well envision a man and woman alone together, strolling hand in hand on a beach at sunset, gazing rapturously at each other and thinking thoughts perfectly suited to the interior of a Hallmark card. In pondering the origin of this romantic-sounding word, some linguists, too, seem to have been influenced by sentiment.

Some etymologists think the *honey* in *honeymoon* stems from a Scandinavian tradition that called for newlyweds to toast each other with mead, a wine made from honey. Some think the *moon* in *honeymoon* stands literally for the first month of marriage, when, to quote *Samuel Johnson's Dictionary*, "There is nothing but tenderness and pleasure." So far, so romantic.

But what's this? The much-respected, no-nonsense *Oxford English Dictionary* makes no mention of honey wine in its history of this word and contends that in its earliest usage, *honeymoon* did not refer to the period of a month but rather compared "the mutual affection of newly married persons to the changing moon which is no sooner full than it begins to wane." What a depressing genesis for such a pleasant word! Can there be some mistake?

As the two verses quoted at the start of this chapter illustrate, there seems to be some belief that newlywed affection is bound to change its nature shortly after the threshold of married life is crossed. But how does it change? Does it really "wane"? I think not. It actually does something far more complex and interesting: it gradually transforms itself from something illusory and fragile into something realistic and durable. The painfully circuitous route it sometimes takes, though, may make newlyweds *feel* as though it's on the wane.

The Urge to Merge

Many marriages start off with a honeymoon trip, a well-deserved vacation the purpose of which, to quote *Middlemarch* once more, "is to isolate two people on the ground that they are all the world to each other." But even couples who have neither the time nor money to spend a weekend at Niagara Falls, a week in Miami, or a month on Maui begin their life together in a mutual psychic paradise.

The "honeymoon phase" of marriage is a period of time—perhaps a month, perhaps two, three, or more—when newlyweds feel a deep, almost magical emotional connection with each other. The stress of the wedding is behind them, the nitty-gritty details of married life have not yet begun to be addressed, and all seems just as it should be.

The honeymoon phase of a marriage resembles nothing so much as the first phase of infancy, when babies experience a sensation of complete oneness with their mothers. This feeling is something we long to recapture our whole lives through, and who can blame us? When we enter the world as babies, we and our mothers form a kind of symbiotic team, meeting each other's needs instinctively, communicating with each other intuitively. Indeed, mother and child are so merged in the first few months of a baby's life that the infant is virtually unable to distinguish the boundaries between them.

Newlyweds, bonded together in what feels like an inviolable bubble of bliss, are in much the same situation. They tend to view each other not as separate beings but as extensions of themselves. They believe firmly that they are empowered to read each other's minds, and indeed their mutual telepathic powers at this state of marriage can be impressive. They are in touch and in tune.

The British psychoanalyst and pediatrician D. W. Winnicott has written that "there is no such thing as a baby." By that he means that a baby cannot exist by itself nor survive without its mother's attention, protection, and love. During the honeymoon phase of a marriage, it *feels* to the two people involved that there is really no such thing as a separate "husband" or "wife"—only a self-supporting system of two interlocked beings, each of whom assumes he or she is capable of providing the other with all that is necessary to survive and each of whom feels confident that he or she will receive the same in turn.

Not many newly married people recognize and express their unconscious feelings about this union (a fortunate circumstance, all things considered), but if they did, they might say the same sorts of things a newborn would say to its mother if endowed with the power of speech: "Make me the center of your world as you are the center of mine. Hold me, comfort me, take care of me always. Don't ever hurt me, don't let anyone else hurt me, and don't let me hurt myself."

This, to put it mildly, is a tall order, but at the beginning of a marriage, both partners feel equipped to meet tall orders. They are walking on air. Sooner or later, though, the time comes for them to vacate Cloud Nine and get back to terra firma. Just as babies gradually begin to discover that their mothers are separate and independent beings with their own agendas, so this realization dawns on the newly married.

Good Spouse/Bad Spouse

In the weeks before and after a wedding, aspects of everyday life get put on hold. Somehow work gets done, bills get paid, and socks get washed, but such menial details are floated through. They are hardly the focus of couples getting ready to wed or tasting the sweet early fruits of marriage itself.

Then one day funny things begin to happen. A wife may tell her husband of two months that she isn't going to "turn in early" with him because she wants to tackle the work she brought home from the office. A husband may tell his bride that he doesn't think a dinner at *Chez Très Expensive* to celebrate their three-month anniversary is appropriate, considering the size of their last American Express bill. A couple married four months may have a difference of opinion about who last did the laundry and whose fault it is that the only socks that seem to match have holes in them.

What's going on here? For one thing, the pesky problems and banalities of everyday life are reasserting themselves, as is their wont. For another, the personal preferences, habits, styles, and idiosyncrasies of the two distinct individuals that make up a marriage are reasserting *themselves,* as is *their* wont. Husband and wife no longer seem to be wishing each other's wishes and thinking each other's thoughts. On the contrary, they are making it quite clear to each other that they have wishes and thoughts of their *own* and that they plan to resume coping with life's little predicaments in their own ways. Poof!— the spell of the honeymoon phase is broken.

Now newlyweds begin to realize that marriage did not miraculously turn their spouses into flawless beings who only aim to please. Their mates' imperfections and peculiarities have not only not *dis*appeared, but have *re*appeared with what seems like a vengeance. Quirks that may have seemed minor during courtship or even during cohabitation have a way of looming larger under the magnifying glass of marriage.

Ben and Barbara Simon, a widowed man and divorced woman who remarried in their early fifties, recalled feeling put off and put out by each other's habits once the permanent nature of their commitment to each other began to sink in. After their first few months of marriage, Ben became agitated by the length of time it took his wife to bathe, dress, and "put on her face" each morning. About the same time, Barbara, a stickler for neatness, grew frustrated at Ben's lackadaisical approach to housekeeping details. As Ben said, "I knew Barbara's morning routines before we married. I think the reason they upset me so much afterward was that I felt as if I were stuck with them forever, that there was no escape." As Barbara put it, "I knew Ben liked a more casual, cluttered environment than I did. When we first got married I felt so happy I didn't let that bother me. But pretty soon I had visions of spending the rest of my life following him around with a dustpan and broom."

Newlyweds in the post-honeymoon phase may also find themselves annoyed by traits in their mates that before marriage they considered admirable or charming. One woman who encouraged her fiancé in his literary ambitions during courtship was aghast when, after marriage, he spent most weekend hours at his typewriter attempting to write a novel. Another woman who appreciated the way her fiancé doted on his eight-year-old daughter found herself resenting her husband's painstaking attempts to build his child an elaborate handcrafted wooden doll house for her ninth birthday. And one man who found his girlfriend's love of animals endearing was less than thrilled to find his bride "feeding all the stray cats and dogs in the neighborhood."

When the honeymoon phase passes, husbands and wives begin to realize that many of their unspoken expectations are not shared by their spouses ("Good grief, he *isn't* going to give up skiing!" "Good grief, she *isn't* going to take up cooking!"). It's also at this time that newlyweds realize that some of their spouses' vague premarital promises were, well, vague.

About four months into their marriage, Robin and Charlie Turner had a spirited difference of opinion over a casual promise Charlie had made to quit smoking after marriage. "I quit during our engagement and asked Charlie to do the same. He said he was too tense right then but that he would quit sometime after we got married. One day I decided it was time for him to keep his promise, so I got up early and hid all the ashtrays. Pretty helpful, huh? It turned out that Charlie and I had different definitions of *sometime*. He didn't see his continued smoking as breaking a promise to me. In fact, he's still planning to quit—sometime."

Ron and Carol Clarke were married four years when I spoke with them. Carol at twenty-eight gave up her job as an account executive for a Boston advertising agency and moved to Los Angeles to marry Ron, a thirty-six-year-old film editor. The two had met on a vacation and carried on a bicoastal courtship for two years before marrying.

"Carol promised me she would give life in L.A. a fair shake and not get into a complaining syndrome, the way a lot of Easterners do when they move out here. But about a month after our wedding, she started complaining all the time. She didn't like my friends, she didn't like the freeways, she didn't like the smog, she didn't like the fact that the ocean was on the 'wrong' side. She was on the phone to Boston every night, complaining *and* running up huge bills. When I reminded her of her promise to try to be a good sport, she said she wasn't complaining, she was just commenting."

The Clarkes, the Turners, the Simons, and a number of other couples summed up their post-honeymoon-phase feelings toward each other and toward marriage in general in one word: disappointment. Though many seemed embarrassed to admit this—as if they believed they were the only ones who had ever had such an experience—statistical surveys and clinical observations by couples therapists show that within a few months after marriage nearly *ev-*

eryone suffers disappointment and feels that marriage is different from what he or she anticipated. And long before therapists and statisticians had their say, George Eliot, in describing the first year of marriage, observed that "some discouragement, some faintness of heart at the new real future which replaces the imaginary is not unusual."

If all this disappointment is so common, we may well wonder why so many newlyweds have such a hard time coping with it. After all, everyone has foibles and no one can stay on his or her best behavior forever. Right? It's no big surprise that new husbands and wives exhibit the perfectly natural human tendency to stop running once they catch the bus. Right? So the simplest thing for newlyweds to do is to deal with their disappointment rationally and stop making mountains out of molehills. Right?

Well, sure, that *would* be the simplest thing *if* newlyweds in the post-honeymoon phase were able to think about and behave toward their spouses in completely rational ways. The hitch—if you'll pardon the pun—is that they're not. There are some situations that, as a matter of course, stir up some of our earliest infantile insecurities and defenses, and marriage happens to be one of them. Early frustrations in an intimate circumstance such as marriage can cause us to regress emotionally back to the point in our life when we were first frustrated by our original love object—yes, Mom again!—and to have some of the same kinds of impulsive, irrational feelings toward our spouse that we once had toward our mother.

In the second phase of infancy, the baby's feelings of ecstatic unity with its mother give way to an awareness of separateness. The baby, less than delighted by this new awareness, reacts to it by a skewed perception called "splitting." Splitting is a psychic defense that causes the infant to perceive its mother as two distinct objects: a "good" mother who gratifies wishes, and a "bad" mother who frustrates them. In the post-honeymoon phase of marriage, splitting is also common.

How is it, newlyweds wonder, that the person who so recently seemed to be the embodiment of all things good and kind is suddenly capable of actions that disappoint, offend, and thwart? They suspect that their spouses, too, are comprised of a "good" and "bad" self, though the latter had been cunningly concealed until now. Newlyweds may begin to fear that they married wolves in sheep's clothing and to believe nineteenth-century pundit Samuel Rogers was right when he said, "It doesn't much signify whom one marries, for one is sure to find out next morning it was someone else."

When we perceive something a certain way, we start acting upon that perception. Like infants, newlyweds act on their split perspectives by directing their aggressive impulses toward the "bad" object and their loving impulses toward the "good" object. When they think of their spouse as "bad," they may feel they have nothing at all in common and wonder why they married this person, anyway. They may even fantasize about how wonderful life would be if only they could get rid of this incorrigible ogre. They're hardly disposed to do anything to please the bad spouse. And since they feel the bad spouse is unwilling to give them the all-accepting, unconditional love they crave, they may reject the spouses's attempts to give them anything more down-to-earth.

On the other hand, when they think of their spouse as "good," they feel content, perhaps even irrationally euphoric. Since the good spouse gives them pleasure and seems willing to meet their needs, they bestow in return all the tenderness and concern they can muster, perhaps even to the point of overdoing it. They no longer want to break with their partner; in fact, they want to hold on tight. They long to stay fused with the good spouse, to reestablish oneness with this benevolent being, even if it means giving up their own sense of self. But just when it seems their fantasies are on the verge of being fulfilled, here comes the bad spouse again.

Albert Camus wrote, "We always deceive ourselves twice about the people we love—first to their advantage, then to their disadvantage." But the nature of splitting is that we deceive ourselves over and over again. What inner turmoil this stage of marriage can bring! How perplexing it is when a spouse seems to be the ideal partner one minute and the next minute seems to do nothing right. And how confusing it is to be on the *receiving* end of a split perception, sensing a spouse's total approval one moment and disapproval the next.

It can seem to newlyweds as if they're doomed to spend the rest of their married days plucking a kind of double-sided daisy, chanting "I love you/I love you not. You love me/you love me not." And it can seem to anyone spending a lot of time around a newlywed couple—especially children of one spouse or the other—that things are in a perennial state of confusion and upheaval. Instead of marriage bringing stability, it seems to have had the opposite effect.

It's at this stage that newlyweds may begin to wonder if they are crazy, if their spouses are crazy, if marriage itself is crazy. It's at this stage that they may nod their sadder but wiser heads in understanding of Montaigne's ironic observation: "The land of marriage has this peculiarity, that strangers are desirous of inhabiting it, whilst its natural inhabitants would willingly be banished from it."

But wait! Things may not be so bad after all. Just as newlyweds repeat infantile patterns of love in their honeymoon and post-honeymoon phases, they are apt to move on to yet another stage of marriage that mimics the infant's changing relationship to its mother. When the baby first perceives its mother's separateness, the months that follow constitute a natural psychological crisis, but this crisis begins to resolve itself in a phase known as "rapprochement."

In the rapprochement phase of infancy, the baby begins to view its mother as a whole, multifaceted being, embracing both good and bad qualities. If a new marriage is to proceed in a healthy way, newlyweds must also engage in a rapprochement process. They must come to terms with their ambivalence, with tolerating the conflicting feelings that result from interacting with less-than-perfect others.

A Mixed Bag

In the Stephen Sondheim musical *Company*, Robert, a curious bachelor, asks his friend Harry if he is ever sorry he married. Harry responds by singing philosophically:

> You're always sorry,
> You're always grateful,
> You hold her, thinking,
> "I'm not alone."
> You're still alone.
> You don't live for her,
> You do live with her,
> You're scared she's starting
> to drift away,
> And scared she'll stay.

What Harry is really describing is marital ambivalence. Ambivalence is a part of the human condition we all must learn to live with. We are all born with the capacity for love and the capacity for hostility and aggression. Both these basic drives will at times be directed toward people with whom we are intimate. Logically enough, our loving feelings tend to predominate when we are pleased, and our nonloving feelings tend to predominate when we are displeased.

In the honeymoon phase of marriage, pleasure prevails mightily over displeasure, and loving feelings usually drown out nonloving ones. When newlyweds first experience displeasure at the hands of their spouses, their negative feelings may come as an unwelcome surprise, but in fact they are only experiencing what Freud would have called "the return of the repressed," the reemergence of feelings that were hanging around in the unconscious all along, waiting for an opportunity to break through.

When occasional antagonistic feelings toward the spouse surface, newlyweds may feel ashamed and guilty, as if they themselves were "bad." They may also fear they are experiencing the death of love. But such utterly normal emotions mean nothing of the kind. As philosophers have long expounded, the opposite of love is not hate but apathy and indifference. If you are experiencing strong feelings of any kind toward your spouse, consider yourself ahead of the game. The next step is to understand, accept, and modify those feelings instead of swinging back and forth on an emotional pendulum.

It's hard to see the forest for the trees, and it's hard to view a spouse as a whole and integrated being unless some distance from him or her can be obtained. Distancing in marriage is a natural phenomenon. When married people first realize they do not necessarily want to spend every spare moment in each other's company, they may wonder if this is the beginning of the end, but a parable told by the philosopher Arthur Schopenhauer illustrates why distancing is so useful:

WHY DID I MARRY YOU, ANYWAY?

One cold winter's day, a number of porcupines huddled together quite closely in order through their mutual warmth to prevent themselves from being frozen. But soon they felt the effect of their quills on one another, which made them again move apart. Now, when the need for warmth once more brought them together, the drawback of the quills was repeated, so that they were tossed between two evils, until they discovered the proper distance from which they could tolerate one another.

Schopenhauer used this allegory to make a point about living amidst one's neighbors, but its applicability to marriage seems clear: too much closeness can cause just as much trouble as being too far apart.

As babies we instinctively knew when it was time to distance ourselves from our mothers. One day we began to turn our eyes away to see what else the big, wide world had to offer, and slowly but surely we began to obtain some of our satisfaction from reaching out to that larger world. When we turned back to Mother, it was with an enlarged, more realistic perspective and a better sense of who we were in relation to her and who she was in relation to us.

The time comes when a newlywed couple too must end their total absorption with each other, focus some of their attention outside the relationship, and gain some portion of their happiness from sources other than their mate. In doing so, they will find their "optimum distance" from their partner, a space in which they can be themselves while still caring deeply for someone else.

The eighteenth-century author Mary Wollstonecraft wrote to her husband, philosopher William Godwin, "I wish you, from my soul, to be riveted in my heart; but, I do not desire to have you always at my elbow." Wollstonecraft and Godwin had very definite ideas about how to establish distance between them. They worked in separate quarters and saw each other by appointment. Not many people find it necessary to go to such extremes, but many newlyweds I spoke with recalled that they appreciated their partners more once they allowed themselves to enjoy time alone, time with friends, time devoted to a creative project all their own. When they stopped putting all their eggs in one basket, it was easier for them to accept their mates for all that they were—good, bad, and in between.

Distancing is one way to help resolve ambivalence in marriage. Another is to deliberately recall good times at times when things don't seem so good. Infants in the rapprochement phase already have memory traces stored in their developing minds. Their recollections of happy exchanges with their mothers help them to tolerate frustration. So, whenever your partner's behavior strikes you as less than ideal, it's not a bad idea to smile to yourself and remember the times when he or she planned an especially romantic evening, surprised you with flowers or a silly gift, or came through for you emotionally when you needed cheering up or calming down. Now might be the perfect opportunity to ask yourself why you married this person, anyway—and compile a mental list of *positive* answers to it. Dwelling on your partner's positive qualities and giving him or her credit for a good overall track record will make it easier to overlook an occasional misstep.

No matter what we do, we can never completely work through ambivalence in marriage. As the noted psychoanalyst Otto Kernberg writes, "Mature love relations are not 'postambivalent,' but remain ambivalent with the predominance of love over hatred." In healthy marriages, couples come to learn that just because they have *mixed* feelings doesn't mean they can't emphasize some over others. Psychoanalyst Hyman Spotnitz employs a wonderful analogy when he compares human feelings to an orchestra and the people having those feelings to musical conductors. When we are functioning well, we have the power to choose which instruments are played *fortissimo* and which are played *pianissimo*. We have the power to stress positive over negative emotions.

The Constant Husband/
The Constant Wife

Once newlyweds come to terms with their ambivalence, they have successfully negotiated the rapprochement phase of marriage and are well on their way to achieving "constancy." Constancy implies the intactness of the self and, therefore, the integrity of any relationships in which the self is involved.

When we have constancy in our relationships, we have trust and confidence: trust that another person loves us and is there for us despite his or her flaws and foibles; confidence that we can accommodate our commingling feelings of love and hate without destroying that other person or being destroyed ourselves. What's more, when we have constancy we have objectivity and empathy—we can see the world through another's eyes, and in marriage that's no small achievement.

When an infant achieves what is known as "object constancy," it stops viewing the mother only in terms of what she can provide and what she can take away. When married people achieve constancy, they stop viewing their spouses primarily in terms of their own desires and fears. They are less likely to blame their personal problems on their mates and more likely to take responsibility for their own actions.

The process of developing constancy in a child is strange and wondrous. It reconciles the longing for unity with the equally strong longing for separateness and personal identity. In marriage the process is much the same: in finding out who we really are, we learn many things about our spouses; in finding out who our spouses really are, we learn much about ourselves. Constancy is the way out of illusory oneness with our partners and into what Erik H. Erikson has called "true twoness."

In some marriages, though I suspect they are rare, ambivalence is resolved and constancy is achieved almost without the couple's being aware of the process. For other couples, passing through the first year's stages can be more taxing. The consensus seems to be that people who are raised in families where mixed emotions are tolerated, where conflicts are negotiated, and where the parents' marriage is happy have a somewhat easier time adjusting to the married state than others do.

But no one's childhood is perfect and, with the possible exception of Wally and Beaver Cleaver, no one's parents are perfect either. Even those with relatively idyllic pasts still have a few things to learn about intimate relationships. Our families of origin may provide the setting for our emotional elementary school, but lessons that are not learned there can certainly be learned later, provided we are willing to do the work involved.

Some of the people I spoke with described the learning process of the first year of marriage quite eloquently. Sandy Farrell had this to say: "I used to go into a panic whenever Jack did something that made me realize we weren't going to be joined at the hip, doing everything together and thinking about everything in the same way. At first I had the fantasy that we would become so symbiotic that we would start to look like each other—you know, the way pets and their owners seem to. But by the time our first year was up, I knew we could live with our differences. I realized how wonderful it is to be with someone who wasn't like me in every way. Jack and I can now often see each other more clearly than we see ourselves, and I can't tell you how much we both have come to appreciate that.''

Robin Turner said this about her first year: "I remember having days when I was absolutely euphoric about Charlie, and I treated him like a king. Then, one little thing would go wrong and I would feel differently about my connection to him, as if he was fading away somehow. I think I felt he would abandon me if things weren't perfect. But after a time, those feelings occurred less and less often. I became more secure about myself and about the relationship. I knew that bad times would always pass and when they did Charlie would still be there. My love for him can still change from day to day, but that doesn't bother me. I'm sure his love for me is not 'the same' every day either. But if we loved each other 'the same' every day, it wouldn't have any meaning.''

Ron Clarke recalled, "Talking about this now it's kind of hard to admit, but there were points in my first year of marriage to Carol when I remember actually asking myself whether I had made a bad deal. I used to look at her and wonder if she was the person I thought she was all those romantic years we spent commuting, or if *that* person was someone I had made up. Then I began to see she *was* who I thought she was before we got married, but she was other things, too. It seemed she was always full of surprises, some of them terrific, some of them, well, surprising. Yet the more things she seemed to be, the more I began to love her for them. I began to think, Hey, this is a person who is much deeper and more complicated than I originally thought. Good—our live will never be boring!''

Getting Stuck in
"Together-Together Land"

Couples who are still enjoying their honeymoon phase may be a bit confounded by all this talk about learning and working and passing through stages. It's only natural for very recent newlyweds to wish that their initial sense of ultra-togetherness would go on and on, but they should actually rejoice when they find that it does not. Marriages that linger in this phase are highly vulnerable.

In 1958 psychologist Harry F. Harlow did an experiment with rhesus monkeys, which, because of their instinctive clinging behavior, he called the "together-together" animals. He raised a pair of these baby monkeys in isolation, allowing no one and nothing to interfere with their gratifying holding of each other. The result: the monkeys never developed signs of adult behavior and could tolerate no interference from the outside world. Had anything come along to upset their fragile existence, they would never have been able to adapt.

Little monkeys need to experience and tolerate frustration in order to mature. The same goes for little humans and for big humans who have recently joined their lives to those of other big humans.

Some couples waste a lot of emotional energy trying to prolong their honeymoon phase past its time. Such "together-together" marriages may look so good on the surface that friends and neighbors envy the "lucky" couples who have them. Paradoxically, though, such couples are actually working harder at keeping reality at bay than are couples who are facing up to it. It may not be the easiest thing in the world to learn to tolerate and cope with frustration in marriage, but it's easier to do this than it is to try to forestall change, stifle creativity in the relationship, and persist in behavior that is ungenuine and rote. Together-together couples find it all too easy to engage in mutual distortions and get into psychological ruts, never giving each other the opportunity to become acquainted with their own true selves.

On some level, each of us searches for what Theodor Reik called "our better self and the best of ourself" in a marital partner. By pursuing what psychoanalysts call our "ego ideal" in a mate, we look for a spouse who will confirm our own self-worth and elevate our self-esteem. As Reik said, "Tell me who you love and I will tell you who you are and, more especially, who you want to be."

While it's certainly nice to admire one's mate, together-together couples don't know when to quit. They unreasonably expect each other to be able to live up to impossible standards of perfection and to fill in the "missing pieces" of their own personalities. This is a problem, not only because no one can meet such standards for any real length of time, but because the human mind is capable of embracing many contradictory wishes at once. Thus, someone may long for a partner who is impulsive and daring and seek such a person out, only to discover later that he or she also longs for a partner who is stable and predictable. Pity the poor confused spouse who is ultimately expected to live up to both ideals simultaneously!

To further complicate matters, some people unconsciously look for a mate who embodies some of their own not-so-good qualities. This phenomenon goes by the rather fancy name of "projective identification."

Each of us has aspects of ourselves that we don't like and are not proud of. Some of these may be constitutional traits we are born with and some may be character traits and attitudes picked up from the people who raised us, through a kind of psychic osmosis. According to psychiatrist Harry Stack Sullivan, we try to deny that these aspects of ourselves exist and so think of them as "not me." One of the handiest ways to rid ourselves of these "not me" parts is to displace them onto others, and it's especially handy to find spouses whose own personalities predispose them to accept our displacements.

Say you are a person who is hot-tempered by nature but likes to appear to the world as calm, cool, and collected. Your anger, then, remains in a passive state. If you choose a spouse who is prone to having temper tantrums, you can remain calm while your spouse does all the active ranting and raving. If someone is inwardly depressed but outwardly cheerful, he or she may find a mate whose idea of a good time is to have a good long cry now and again.

Passive-active alliances between husbands and wives are extremely common because projective identification is such a deeply rooted psychic mechanism. Just about everyone engages in it from time to time. You can actually see the process at work in children who conjure up imaginary friends whom they blame for their own misbehavior (as in, "I didn't spill the milk, Casper the Ghost spilled it!").

As newlyweds regain a sense of their own boundaries, they should, for the most part, stop expecting each other to act out their own hidden impulses. Together-together couples, however, unable to distinguish where one of them stops and the other begins, persist in excessive projecting and set themselves up for marital Catch-22's. Eventually, they may tire of being defined by the other's projections and grow weary of being exposed to traits they have tried so hard to deny in themselves.

It's really no fun to be stuck in together-together land. For that matter, it's no fun to be stuck anywhere. Ideally, of course, all couples would pass Honeymoon 101, Post-honeymoon 101, and Rapprochement 101 with straight A's, and continue to do graduate work in Constancy for the rest of their married days. But development neither in the first year of life nor in the first year of marriage follows a smooth, even curve. All newlyweds are bound to have moments when they start slipping backward just when their spouses may least expect it—or appreciate it. This is just part of the process and not at all a cause for alarm. All newlyweds need to grow up on each other's time a little bit, and sometimes growing up requires taking two steps forward and one step back.

3

Newlywed Games

IN *Anna Karenina*, Leo Tolstoy describes the feelings of one of the book's principal characters, Konstantin Levin, after three months of marriage:

> Having embarked upon married life, he saw at every step it was not at all what he'd imagined. At every step he experienced what a man experiences when, after admiring the smooth, happy motion of a boat on a lake, he finds himself sitting in it himself. He found that it was not enough to sit quietly without rocking the boat, that he had constantly to consider what to do next, that not for a moment must he forget what course to steer or that there was water under his feet, that he had to row, much as it hurt his unaccustomed hands, that it was pleasant enough to look at it from the shore, but very hard, though very delightful to sail it.

Poor Levin! Like any other newlywed he is discovering that navigating the waters of wedlock can be very rewarding, but that keeping the marital ship from capsizing requires practice, patience, and effort. He is learning that launching a marriage means making countless adjustments and accommodations, tending to endless practical details, and making decisions that affect the fate of not just oneself but someone else too.

Had twentieth-century psychologists been able to observe our nineteenth-century hero, they would doubtless have noted that his post-honeymoon revelations were causing him a great deal of stress. Recent research makes it clear why stress goes hand in hand with marital adjustment. People typically experience stress when they feel they have lost autonomous control over certain aspects of their lives and when the intrusion of the unexpected prevents them from making things happen according to their preconceived notions.

Getting married *means* giving up some degree of autonomous control over one's life and confronting the unknown on a daily basis. It means taking someone else into consideration. It means tradeoffs and compromises, and, on the way to those, it can mean contention.

The marriage-stress connection is so strong that marriage has been afforded a whopping 50 points on the Holmes-Rahe scale, an index that measures the stressfulness of various life experiences. (As one's score approaches 300, chances of stress-related illness increase.) According to this widely used stress barometer, getting married is more stressful than getting fired, going bankrupt, or losing one's home to foreclosure. The only things more stressful than marriage are the death of a loved one, a major disease or injury, a jail term, and—here's something that speaks in favor of working through first-year stress and *staying* married—separation and divorce.

During the symbiotic honeymoon phase, the marital ship sails smoothly along and it is easy to keep stress under control. It is the very nature of a symbiotic relationship that a state of equilibrium exists. But when married people begin to see their partners as separate and different from themselves, things can get out of balance and stress levels can begin to climb.

In the post-honeymoon phase, not only are both parties trying to figure out if they really married Jekyll or Hyde, they are also trying to make sense of marriage itself: trying to define their rights and obligations to each other, trying to determine what they can expect from their spouse and what their spouse has a right to expect from them, trying to figure out how "joint" decisions get made and who really makes them. And just as regression causes newlyweds to go to extremes in the way they view their spouses, its influence can cause them to go to extremes in many of these other matters as well.

Dependence and Independence

In long and strong marriages where constancy has firmly taken hold, partners achieve *interdependence*. They help each other, draw on each other's strengths, and feel a sense of mutual obligation—yet they leave each other enough room to do and pursue things on their own. Early in marriage, however, many newlyweds tend to go overboard in the direction of either dependence or independence. Either extreme can upset the equilibrium of the relationship and rock the marital boat.

The first year of marriage is so reminiscent of the parent-child relationship that the "take care of me" theme is common. Even those who were paragons of self-sufficiency before marriage may suddenly find themselves feeling needy in ways they can't understand or explain, and their neediness may confuse or even annoy their partners.

Ben Simon recalled his wife Barbara's sudden bouts of overdependency that began shortly after their marriage. "I thought of Barbara as a very independent woman. She was one of the most capable and self-directed people I ever saw. In fact, that's one of the things that appealed to me about her. Well, we weren't married long when it seemed like she couldn't do anything for herself. She wanted me to manage all the money because I was 'better' at it. So I had to do everything from balance the checkbook to stand on line at the cash machine. She wanted me to do all the driving because I was 'better' at it, too. Even on long trips, she didn't want to take a turn at the wheel. Maybe I should have been flattered, but I felt taken advantage of.''

Megan Brown said her husband, Dave, became more socially dependent on her soon after marriage than he was when they lived together. ''It used to be that I could say to Dave, 'I'm going to the movies to see such-and-such. Do you want to come?' If he didn't like what I was going to see—which was more than half the time since we have different tastes in films—he'd say, 'No thanks,' wish me a nice time, and that would be that. After we got married, he would sulk if I wanted to see something he wasn't interested in. He would ask me what he should do while I was at the movies. I'd ask, 'Well, what did you used to do when I was at the movies?' and he'd sigh and look so forlorn that I'd end up changing my plans. The same thing happened when I went out with friends from work. Suddenly, Dave always seemed to want to tag along, and he'd feel left out if the conversation didn't include him. I was pretty confused by his behavior. I'd thought I was getting a husband—not a shadow!''

Ben Simon and Megan Brown both felt that they had taken on more responsibility than they had bargained for. That rattled them. It's nice to be needed—to a degree—but having someone rely on us for darn near everything can be nerve-racking, even scary. On the other hand, it can be just as unsettling to have a spouse who is over-zealous in the assertion of independence as it is to have a partner who is a clinging vine.

Nowadays, lots of newlyweds enjoy a good deal of liberty before marriage. It takes some of them a while to come to terms with the fact that marriage won't afford them the same sort of personal latitude they had living alone, or even with roommates. They're so used to being "free agents" that they don't automatically think of themselves as being part of a team. So it's no surprise that many newlyweds occasionally neglect to call home when they're going to be late, make plans without informing their mates, buy a painting, or bring home a pet without feeling obliged to prepare their partners. Though they may not be aware of it, many new husbands and wives harbor a good deal of nostalgia for the days when they were accountable to no one but themselves and occasionally "forget" that they've now got another person's interests, tastes, and schedule to consider.

But some newlyweds have more than occasional lapses in this area, and chances are those who take an overly independent stance again and again are doing so as a defense against dependent feelings that make them uncomfortable. This sort of dynamic was at work in the first year of Ron and Carol Clarke's marriage.

"Before Carol moved out to L.A.," said Ron, "I had fun thinking of all the weekend trips we would take together. I wanted her to really get to know my part of the world. I wanted to take her to the Sierra mountains, out to the desert, down to Mexico. But Carol had some old girlfriends from college who were living in San Francisco, and she went through a phase where she seemed more interested in spending her weekends with them than with me.

"Sometimes she'd invite her friends down for the weekend without letting me know until after they'd accepted. Then they'd show up, and I'd be pretty much ignored for two days. Once Carol made plans to visit *them* for the weekend and didn't tell me until after she'd bought a plane ticket. She hadn't even asked me if I'd wanted to go along. I felt so slighted. I couldn't imagine what she was trying to prove—or why. Fortunately, she seemed to get whatever it was out of her system after a while."

Thinking back on her behavior at the time, Carol explained: "Of course I see now I was being thoughtless, but I was uneasy depending on Ron for so much. He had a regular job, and I was just freelancing. He knew L.A. like the back of his hand, and I kept getting lost on the freeways. He had pals all around, and my only West Coast friends were four hundred miles away. I kept thinking that if anything went wrong between the two of us, I would be stranded. I know it was irrational, but I thought of my San Francisco connections as some kind of back-up insurance, and I wanted to keep those relationships more or less to myself."

Newlyweds who behave the way Carol did are like defiant children who say to their mothers, "Leave me alone. I don't need you to take care of me," when what they really mean is, "I'm afraid of needing you too much." Unfortunately, their spouses may interpret their signals as meaning they don't care enough about them or their relationships. And who can blame them for feeling neglected and hurt?

Selfishness and Selflessness

Veterans of long and strong marriages almost unfailingly talk about their relationships in terms of give-and-take. But many novices find it hard to strike a balance between the two. Some go through a first-year phase of selfishness and territoriality. Like children dickering with siblings and playmates over who gets to play with what toy, who gets to claim what marbles as his or her exclusive property, and who gets to eat the last Eskimo Pie, newlyweds may initially have a hard time with sharing.

For many couples, distinguishing between "yours," "mine," and "ours" can be an especially high-stress endeavor. Couples I spoke with told me of the anxiety they felt when first getting used to the idea of sharing everything from favorite records, tapes, and books to grown-up toys like cameras, computers, and cars. Claudia Howard's anecdote was, for all intents and purposes, an adult version of the Eskimo Pie dilemma.

"Before I married Mark, I lived with three roommates," she said. "Each of us had a shelf of her own in the refrigerator and the rest of us kept our hands off whatever was there. So for years, my food was *my* food. If there was a box of chocolate chip cookies or a bottle of cranberry juice or whatever on *my* shelf before I went to work, I knew it would be there when I got home. When I first got married, I'd get really upset to come home from work and find that something I'd been looking forward to eating or drinking was gone because Mark—or one of his omnivorous children, if they were staying with us—had gotten to it first. I'd get angry at him and he'd sulk. I know he thought I was being petty and selfish, not to mention an ungenerous stepmother, but I thought he was being selfish, too, because he never thought to save me the last cookie or the last sip of juice, and he never thought to replace what he or the kids had finished.

"I feel silly admitting this now, but I started stashing a few goodies in a cupboard where I thought no one would find them. Naturally Mark found them, which turned out to be the best thing that could have happened. We were both so embarrassed that we quickly began to 'share and share alike.' Now Mark knows that he and the boys are welcome to sample my special 'goodies,' but he'll also fill the fridge up with treats from time to time."

Claudia went to one extreme with her proprietary tactics, but some newlyweds go to the other. In their desire to be loved and appreciated and to be perceived as "good," they bend over backward to accommodate a spouse's desires even when doing so means completely ignoring their own self-interests. Like Claudia, Jack Farrell was distressed by his spouse's appropriation of something of his, but he took an opposite tack.

"Sandy would use my razors to shave her legs. I'd get up at my customary five-thirty, grope around for a razor, wind up with a dull one, and go off to work with my face looking like a road map. But I felt awful about asking my wife not to use something of mine. I didn't want to seem selfish or small. It took quite a while for me to ask her to get her own razor, but I finally realized I had to save my own skin!"

Mark and Claudia discovered the pleasures of giving, but Jack discovered something equally important, something family therapist W. Robert Beavers calls "enlightened selfishness." Understanding enlightened selfishness means understanding that marriage and martyrdom don't mix well. Giving to a spouse is all fine and good, as long as it doesn't mean seriously undermining oneself.

Getting the Upper Hand

In parts of Germany in the nineteenth century, when a bride and groom's hands were joined by the clergyman officiating at their wedding, each partner would, literally, try to get the *upper* hand. If the clergyman tried to put an end to their symbolic power struggle by placing the hand of one or the other on top, the couple would usually begin the process anew—this time with their feet.

Though we don't acknowledge it as openly as nineteenth-century Germans did, most newlyweds seek early in their marriages to gain some measure of power over their partners. Faced with making decisions on everything from how to split up the Sunday paper, what time to eat dinner, and how to appropriate closet space, to how to manage finances and how to accommodate two sets of parents, or even two sets of children, most newlyweds, not surprisingly, sometimes think about how simple—and how very nice—life would be if they could have the upper hand in the decision-making process.

Some newlyweds make no bones about wanting to captain the marital ship. One woman I interviewed even presented her new husband with a hand-stitched sampler reading, "Let's compromise. We'll do it my way." But most people are embarrassed to admit to wanting to wield power over someone they love, and a lot of people marrying today consider themselves too enlightened or sophisticated to run around bellowing, à la Ralph Kramden, that they want to be "king of the castle." But newlyweds who don't claim power *overtly* sometimes, without admitting even to themselves what they are doing, try to get it *covertly* by manipulating their partners into doing things their way.

The intricate maneuvers involved in gathering marital power can be subtle and deceptive. In fact, it's often hard to tell from outside a relationship who is manipulating whom. Spouses who go to extremes of independence and self-interest are often able to gain the upper hand by implying, ever so subtly, that if they don't *get* their way, they are "strong" enough to go *on* their way alone. But spouses who are very dependent or who insist that they have no wish other than to surrender to their partners' whims may wield enormous power through their very "weakness." Such people can gain the upper hand by manipulating their partners' guilt feeling.

When children are part of a newlywed couple's life, they too may be used as weapons in the power-guilt game. Partners who are also parents may insist they want certain concessions not for their sake but "for the sake of the kids"; and partners who are stepparents may demand that their desires be indulged "just this once" as compensation for "always" putting their mates' offspring ahead of themselves or their own children. While the needs of youngsters faced with the daunting prospect of forming a relationship with a new stepparent should not be overlooked by either spouse, using one's kids as bargaining chips is no way to meet their needs or the needs of the marriage.

Needless to say, a spouse who feels manipulated is not going to feel any happier than a spouse who feels bullied outright. What's more, it's a sure bet that *mutual* resentment will occur if marital power doesn't end up pretty evenly divided. Partners with less than their share of power will ultimately experience a sense of loss of dignity from too much giving up and giving in. Partners with more than their share will eventually feel burdened with too much responsibility—especially if their slighted spouses blame them for every decision that turns out badly.

Research shows, and common sense knows, that the happiest marriages are those in which there is an equal distribution of power. Equity makes a relationship more exciting and stimulating. It helps keep boredom at bay, it keeps partners from taking each other for granted, and, as studies show, it helps keep a couple's sexual relationship interesting. It's hard to feel turned on by a tyrant, or passionate toward a pushover. Besides, when power is equal, it's easier for couples to achieve interdependence, a sense of reciprocal obligation, and a healthy balance between enlightened self-interest and concern for each other. Instead of expending too much energy trying to get the upper hand, newlyweds would be better off to stop playing games and get serious.

Serious About Marriage

In marriage, getting serious means giving up the idea that there are winners and losers in marital relationships, and understanding that when one person feels defeated, the relationship itself is defeated. Getting serious is probably one of the most important things newly married couples can do. But because it involves a fundamental change in the way they conceptualize their relationships, it can also be one of the most difficult.

In the early stages of a marriage, partners tend to view their relationship in terms of how well it meets their needs. Getting serious involves looking at the relationship in terms of how well *they* meet *its* needs. It means asking not what your spouse can do for you but what you can do for your marriage.

As soon as a man and woman become husband and wife, they begin to create a new entity, a kind of imaginary "third person" who is bigger than both of them. This third person evolves throughout the marriage as the result of give-and-take between two loving and committed people. It is a result of the many things they learn from each other, the things they do for each other, the empathy they have with each other, and the compromises they reach together.

Getting serious means keeping this developing third person in mind. It means being willing, on occasion, to put immediate personal desires on the back burner in order to ensure greater *inter*personal rewards down the line As psychoanalyst Benito Perri says, "The more each partner can do things for the sake of the long-term relationship, the greater the chances of the marriage growing and giving more pleasure to each partner."

There's no question that trading immediate gratification for more distant and, therefore, less tangible pleasures involves some amount of sacrifice. One 1950s marriage manual says, "Sacrifice is difficult and irksome only in the absence of love. Love makes it easy, and the more perfect the love, the more joy in sacrifice." I think it's safe to say that most contemporary newlyweds would respond to that statement in a word: baloney. Sacrifice is always difficult and irksome—that's why it's *called* sacrifice—but it is possible to better tolerate necessary sacrifices when we do so on behalf of the third person that we and the one we love are creating together.

Getting serious helps keep newlyweds from going to extremes. It helps them to recapture a sense of control over their destinies and keep marital stress in check. What's more, a broader, more long-term perspective will help newlyweds to stop viewing their first year as a series of contests and conflicts and start looking at it instead as a series of tasks they must master together.

The idea that whatever is seen as a conflict can also be

experienced as a task is a cornerstone of the theories of Erik H. Erikson, a leading figure in psychology and human development. Erikson says we must master different emotional tasks at different stages of life if we are to construct healthy personalities. Likewise, if we are to construct healthy marriages, we must master certain tasks at different stages of our relationships. The tasks we master, or at least begin to master, in the first year of marriage help us resolve ambivalence and work toward constancy. They strengthen us as individuals and they strengthen the character of our third person.

Task 1: Developing Trust

According to Erikson, the first emotional task that infants face is developing basic trust. This is also the first emotional task for newlyweds. If asked, most newlyweds would of course say they trust their partners, but they often don't act as if this were so.

When we really trust people, we don't feel the need to cling to them; we just know in our hearts they'll be around to rely on. We don't fear counting on them for some things and letting them count on us for others; we feel free to nurture and be nurtured. When we really trust people, we don't try to maneuver them into doing what *we* want all the time. We respect their judgment and assume that they, like us, are competent grown-ups who can share power wisely.

In the confusing post-honeymoon phase, a lack of basic, implicit trust of a spouse is par for the course. Until newlyweds know who's who and what's what in their relationships, they may sometimes wonder whether their partners have completely honorable intentions. When we think of someone as a wolf in sheep's clothing, it's only natural to fear that he or she may be trying to pull the wool over our eyes.

Developing implicit trust in marriage is to some extent a matter of time. A certain amount of trust automatically results when two people share positive experiences. But if implicit trust can't be created overnight, it *can* be helped to grow by taking *explicit* leaps of faith.

If you feel tempted to question your spouse's motives, try giving him or her the benefit of the doubt instead. *Choose* feelings of trust over feelings of mistrust. *Assume* your partner is acting out of decent motives. Assume that *your* instincts in choosing this person as a spouse were trustworthy to begin with and that, although your mate may not be a saint, he or she is worthy of your confidence.

Taking conscious leaps of faith will help you feel more secure about your partner and, perhaps even more important, doing this will help your partner feel more secure about himself or herself. When people feel more secure about themselves they actually *become* more reliable and more nurturing toward others.

When we think the best of people, they often go out of their way to prove us right. Unfortunately, when we think the worst of them, they may *also* go out of their way to prove us right. As one man I spoke with recalled about his first year of marriage, "When I had the sense that my wife mistrusted me, I felt guilty—even if I hadn't done anything wrong. The guiltier I felt, the more I was tempted to do something worth being guilty *about*. On the other hand, when she gave me the message that she had faith in me, the more I wanted to do my best not to let her down."

In a marriage, showing faith in each other's integrity contributes to the integrity of your "third person." And when you can put aside doubts, fears, and suspicions, you'll find sacrifices and compromises on behalf of that third person easier to bear. Mutual trust makes it easier to sacrifice without feeling sacrificed—and easier to compromise without feeling compromised.

Task 2: Flexibility and Role-Switching

"Why did I marry you, anyway?" is not the only question most newlyweds ponder now and again. Two other common queries are: "Why is my spouse behaving so oddly all of a sudden?" and "Why am *I* behaving so oddly all of a sudden?"

As we've already seen, some of this "odd" behavior isn't odd at all. It's just newlyweds reasserting their individual characters. But when newlyweds start acting in ways that are truly *out* of character, chances are there's something more involved.

People marry, on a conscious level, because they love each other. If one accepts the definition of love—by far the best around—offered by Yale University psychologist Robert Sternberg, this means they feel passion *for* each other, intimacy *with* each other, and a desire to be committed *to* each other.

Passion, says Sternberg, is love's "hot" component. Analogous to what psychologist Dorothy Tennov has dubbed "limerence," it is tied up with sexual energy and physical attraction. Intimacy, love's "warm" component, refers, in Sternberg's words, to "feelings of closeness, connectedness, and bondedness." Commitment, love's "cold" component, implies cool reasoning, an objective decision to enter and remain in a given relationship through bad times as well as good.

But that still leaves us with a question, one that takes us out of the realm of the rational. What makes us find person X, rather than person Y, so compelling and compatible that we want to make him or her a constant part of our life? What is that certain "something" that draws us to one specific and, in our eyes, very special partner, even in cases where all our friends are shaking their heads in consternation and muttering, "What's *he* doing with *her?*" or "What's *she* doing with *him?*"

Perhaps we can never know the full answer to such a complex question, but often at least part of that certain "something" is a phenomenon known as "transference." And transference is also a major cause of strange behavior early in marriage.

When we are attracted to someone based on a transference reaction, it means that person unconsciously reminds us of a significant person in our past, most often one of our parents. The notion that we marry our parents in disguise is so well worn as to seem a cliché. But think about it. The first learning we all have is unconscious, emotional learning, and the first people our unconscious learns *from* and *about* are our mothers and fathers. Since we all tend to gravitate toward the familiar anyhow, what could be more natural than searching for a mate who we imagine resembles the woman who nurtured us or the man who protected us when we were small?

Once someone we think of as a lover and friend—even a long-time, live-in lover and friend—becomes, through marriage, part of our actual family, the unconscious transference that played a part in forming our unions to begin with starts to take on a more assertive role. That's when newlyweds may actually begin to *relate* to their spouses in ways they related to members of their families of origin. If, for example, the way they tried to get affection from their mothers was by whining and complaining, they may "kvetch" and moan to their partners about every little thing that goes wrong. If they tried to earn their fathers' approval by never showing a fear or shedding a tear, they may well feel the need to be stoic in front of their spouses.

Some of a couple's transferences may be complementary. A son who enjoyed soothing a complaining mother may grow up to be a husband who enjoys soothing his complaining wife. A daughter who admired her "strong and silent" father may grow up to dote on a husband who is much the same. But even though some transferences are mutual and collusive, it's virtually impossible for any two unconscious minds to fit together like a lock and key. Some of the ways in which newlyweds treat their spouses like mother-clones or father-clones can create problems, misunderstandings, and friction.

Barbara Simon told me a story that shows just how this can work: "Quite a few of my early arguments with Ben came about because he wouldn't tell me about anything he considered bad news," she explained. "If a check bounced, if he lost money in the stock market, even if he broke a dish, he'd never mention it. I didn't mind that things went wrong. I think of myself as being pretty sanguine. But I really minded that he felt he had to hide things from me. It was only through talking to his sister and brother that I found out that when the three of them were growing up their mother would react to even the most minor pieces of bad news with total hysteria, as though the end of the world was coming. So the three of them had an emotional survival strategy: 'Mum's the word.' No wonder he didn't want to tell me about the down side of things. He was confusing me with her."

Though the confusion that transference can cause may seem like more than enough to deal with, yet another family-related unconscious mechanism often kicks in after marriage. While each of us is growing up, we absorb many of the habits, attitudes, and behavioral tendencies of our parents and make them our own. We *identify* with them.

Clinical observations show that in the first year of life infants are already imitating aspects of adult behavior, like hand gestures and inflections of voice. By the time we reach adulthood, our characters are influenced by hundreds or thousands of identifications, but the ones that are most deeply ingrained in our psyches are the earliest ones.

Our earliest identifications get stirred up early in marriage, partly because of emotional regression and partly because, on some level, many newlyweds miss their parents, even if they haven't lived with them for years. But early identifications also get reactivated by role confusion—confusion about what, exactly, it means to be a "husband" or a "wife."

Joan Ormont, a psychoanalyst and couples therapist, says, "People start behaving like their parents after marriage because they realize they're not children anymore, and because their existence seems more like that of their parents. They think, 'Here I am, a wife, and the first wife I ever knew was my mother.' Bing! Or, 'Here I am, a husband, and the first husband I ever knew was my Dad.' Bing!" When those little unconscious bells start to chime, many newlyweds may start re-creating the roles their mothers and fathers played in their own marriages.

Many newlyweds I spoke with told me of times, early in their marriage, when they behaved exactly like their parents or when they heard their parents' words coming out of their mouths. Robin Turner said, "I had never been particularly compulsive about cleaning or dusting until I got married. Then I started cleaning with a vengeance, even when the house was perfectly clean already—just like my mother. And I'd get furious if Charlie dirtied anything I'd just cleaned, which is just what my mother does to my father.'

Annie, thirty-four when she married for the second time, said, "I *became* my mother. I really did. She has a martyr complex. While everyone's out in the backyard having a good time at the barbecue, she'll be in the kitchen mixing coleslaw, getting angrier and angrier. Then the anger comes out in the weirdest ways. I did the same kind of thing when I married my first husband, but when I married my second husband I figured I had wised up. Yet suddenly there I was, getting up at six A.M. to make him a good breakfast and a hot cup of coffee even though I didn't have to be up until eight o'clock myself. Then I'd get mad if he didn't finish his eggs, or if he'd read the paper instead of talking to me.''

Steve, twenty-five when he married for the first time, picked up one of his father's all-too-familiar habits. ''My dad is a worrier, always anticipating worst-case scenarios. I remember that whenever my family went anywhere together he'd build in all this extra travel time because he was afraid we might get stuck in traffic or have a flat. We'd arrive everywhere much too early, which would leave lots of time for him and my mother to have an argument. I told myself I'd never be like that, and mostly I wasn't, until I got married. Then my wife and I would get into fights because I'd do things like insist we leave for home early Sunday afternoon after spending a weekend out of town because I didn't want to get caught in some mythical traffic jam.''

Obviously enough, marital behavior motivated by transference or identification can be bewildering—not only to the partners who are observing it but also to partners who are engaging in it. They may know their behavior is not quite compatible with their image of themselves, but they can't quite figure out what's compelling them to behave as they do. But what's particularly annoying about behavior that has motives buried deep in the unconscious is that it tends to be extremely rigid, and rigidity is often, as family therapist W. Robert Beavers writes, "the hallmark of marital difficulty."

The more stubborn a spouse is about not changing behavior that's clearly inappropriate to a current situation, the more certain it is that such behavior emanates from what Freud called the "compulsion to repeat." What this compulsion means is that in the present we try again and again to resolve, symbolically, conflicts rooted in the past.

Early in marriage, when we relive struggles between ourselves and our parents, or reenact conflicts our parents had with each other, we are really trying to achieve new mastery over old painful situations that still haunt us. That sounds like a noble cause, a kind of psychological "cleaning house," but in fact it's a trap. The past is past, and no matter how many times we unconsciously reenact history, we can't rewrite it.

Often—though not always—spouses can help each other steer clear of repetition traps by helping each other identify parentlike peccadilloes or transference behavior that just doesn't "fit" into the present. If we recognize our own repetitious behavior at all, we tend to do it from hindsight. *While* we're acting it out, we're pretty oblivious to it; we're functioning on automatic pilot. With the right kind of intervention, a spouse may be able to stop us in mid-flight and provide us with the emotional insight we need to override that automatic pilot.

As Charlie Turner discovered, gentle, loving, and light-hearted interventions are likely to work better than angry and defensive ones when a spouse is on a repetition roll. "When Robin first started going on her cleaning binges, I could hardly exhale for fear of dirtying something she'd just washed or waxed. It was so frustrating I started yelling at her to relax and cool out. Needless to say, that had the opposite effect. Then we visited her parents for a few days at Christmas, and I realized that her mom was the original Mrs. Clean. The next time Robin started brandishing her dust mop I didn't gripe, but I did sit her down and share my little insight with her, and she actually said, 'You know, you're *right!'*

"Robin didn't change overnight, but at least it was a start. From then on, we were even able to joke about her behavior. Robin would act like her mother and I'd say, 'Mrs. Clean, where has my wife gone? I might have to call in an exorcist to get your spirit out of her body.' After I went through that routine a few times, she became less compulsive about the housekeeping.''

With his good humor, Charlie helped Robin "exorcise" her mother. Sometimes strategies like the ones Charlie used are all that's required to help a spouse become more flexible, but sometimes, no matter how effective we are in reminding our spouses that *they* are not their parents or that *we* are not parents, nothing seems to change. The unconscious forces that resist change can be stubborn indeed, and sometimes people have a hard time giving up rigid behavior even *after* they've become conscious of its causes and even if, consciously, they *want* to give it up. Sometimes, the more we invoke rationality and reason to resolve someone's resistance to change, the harder their unconscious digs in its heels and says "no way." That's where role-switching can come into play.

Everyone's heard the phrase "If you can't beat 'em, join 'em.'' If your spouse persists in behavior that is irking you, and none of the helpful things you say seems to help at all, don't reproach your partner, try mirroring him or her instead. If your spouse is a procrastinator and you're a compulsive deadline-beater, try putting off until tomorrow what you can do today. If your husband or wife watches the household budget like a hawk, and your idea of a good time is buying out the local mall, try pinching a few pennies yourself. If your mate is the nervous type and you like to come off cool as a cucumber, try admitting to a little anxiety of your own (come on, admit it, you must be worried about *something!*).

Mirroring your partner's behavior should not be done out of a spirit of vengeance. The object is not to "get back" at your spouse; the object is to make your partner feel more understood by you, less threatened by your dissimilarities, and, given new behavior on your part, more amenable to change. The object is also to give you a new perspective on things and help you see that there *might* be some advantages to your partner's way of looking at the world after all.

Marital role-switching is a way to keep relationships in balance, to avoid getting into dangerous emotional ruts, and to increase the flexibility of both partners. Role-switching doesn't mean undergoing an entire personality overhaul—it just means rethinking, from time to time, the way you act within the context of your relationship.

Task 3: Tolerance

While flexibility on the part of both spouses is one of the most important elements in a healthy marriage, people are more apt to change their ways gradually than overnight. Besides, there are always going to be some areas in which your partner cannot, will not, perhaps even *should* not change. That's why one of the major tasks confronting newlyweds is developing tolerance.

In the first year of marriage, partners are often dismayed to find themselves immersed in "metabolism conflicts." Though they may have expected to live their lives in near-total synchronicity, they quickly find out that they have entirely different ideas about what time to go to bed at night, what time to get up in the morning, whether to sleep with the windows open or closed. Though they may have hoped to agree on most of the day-to-day basics, they may find they disagree about whether to buy caffeinated or decaffeinated coffee, or whether an invigorating breakfast consists of carrot juice and wheat germ or orange soda and a jelly doughnut. And though they may have anticipated taking life at the same pace, they may find that one of them is an unstoppably frenetic Type A personality and the other a relentlessly relaxed Type B.

Contrary to what some newlyweds may think, married couples are not akin to Siamese twins. In fact, they may have vastly divergent body clocks, body temperatures, and inborn temperamental differences. But it's perfectly possible, as many couples learn, for a night owl to be happily married to a lark, and for a tortoise to be happily married to a hare.

Jack Farrell discovered as a newlywed that he and his wife had different body clocks. "It bothered me at first that Sandy would sleep so much later than I would. I've always been an early riser, even on weekends. Sandy likes to sleep as late as she can, *especially* on weekends. At first I would get really impatient on Saturdays and Sundays, waiting for her to get up so we could do something together. I'd rattle around making as much noise as possible, hoping she'd wake up and get going. But I quickly found out that that getting my wife out of bed before she was good and ready usually meant she'd be grumpy all day. So, I learned to let her be. Now I think it's great to have the morning hours to myself. I can get a lot done and I've learned to enjoy the sense of solitude."

Mark Howard also found his pace was different from his wife's. "Claudia is always in a hurry, and I like to take things more slowly. We'll go to see a show at a museum, and she'll race through, while I like to linger and savor things. Trying to keep up with her made me dizzy, and trying to get her to slow down was useless. By now I've learned to do it my way and let her do it her way. We'll go to a museum together and agree to meet up somewhere afterward at a certain time, but whether each of us takes in five or fifty or a hundred paintings in the interim is up to us. We both get what we want out of the experience.''

It's even possible for a junk-food junkie to be contentedly wed to a fitness fanatic. Carol Clarke is a good example. ''Ron is kind of a health nut. At first he was always nagging me about giving up red meat, white flour, sugar— you know, all the really good stuff. I could see his point about some of it. I had lived alone for seven years before we got married, and I think my eating habits had become a little strange. I didn't mind him asking me not to eat potato chips for lunch, but the thought of renouncing hamburgers and french fries forever was just too much for me. He used to give me lectures or at least reproachful looks whenever I ate something that wasn't on his 'approved' list, but after a while we worked it out. He doesn't try to be my conscience anymore. He understands that there are times when I just can't be satisfied by tofu and bean sprouts.''

When all is said and done, it's unreasonable to expect your spouse to be able to be flexible about *everything*. That's why, as the Clarkes, the Howards, and the Farrells now know, a proverbial grain of salt can sweeten the marital relationship immeasurably.

Couples who have been happily married for many years often confound people who observe them. They cheerfully admit to having some widely divergent habits. They are able to laugh off each other's idiosyncrasies. ''Oh, that's just the way he is,' say the wives. ''Oh, that's just her nature,'' say the husbands. Such couples have learned that good-natured tolerance is one of the things it takes to make their "third person" strong.

Task 4: Pragmatism

Our first mode of learning in life is one of trial and error, and this is also our first mode of learning in marriage. Babies learn how to get along in the world through testing and experimenting. Though they are bound to topple over a few times before they learn to stand upright and successfully toddle across the room, they do inevitably learn from their own successful and *un*successful experiences. As infants grow, they discover, slowly but surely, how to distinguish between practical actions that propel them from one end of the room to the other and impractical actions that cause them to wobble and fumble and land on their bottoms. They also eventually learn to choose the former over the latter.

On their way to achieving a happy and fulfilling relationship, newlyweds too are bound to make some blunders. Their ultimate progress, like that of infants, depends upon their becoming pragmatic and gaining respect for behavior that works.

Being pragmatic means introducing a kind of Darwinian natural selection into your marriage. It means abandoning maladaptive actions, the ones that keep your relationship from evolving, in favor of actions that help move it forward. In the first year of marriage, there will be times when you honestly may not know what will help your relationship work and grow because you may not know the answers to some basic questions about your mate. But one thing is sure: as the marriage unfolds, you will learn the answers.

In your first year you'll learn whether your spouse wants to be cheered up when he or she is blue or would really rather be left alone for a while. You'll learn when your advice is welcome and when your mate would rather resolve a problem without it. You'll learn when it's all right to joke, when it's permissible to criticize, and when it's best to let sleeping dogs lie. In short, you'll learn what kind of behavior on your part leads to smooth marital sailing and what kind of behavior steers your relationship into the eye of a storm. Now all that's necessary is to learn to let your experience be your teacher and your guide.

Profiting from experience sounds simple, but it can be hard to observe the consequences of your own behavior and modify it. Doing so requires a little humility and a lot of objectivity. It also requires an understanding that your marriage is not a carbon copy of any other. Behavior that works for your best friends, your parents, your aunt Maude and uncle Abe, or the couple next door may be unworkable where you and your spouse are concerned. It's *your* experience you should learn to rely on—not someone else's.

Task 5: Optimism

The first year of marriage is bound to have its peaks and valleys. No matter how much progress you and your spouse make in getting serious, minimizing stress, and mastering marital tasks, peaceful times will inevitably be punctuated by more turbulent ones, and a sense of calm will occasionally give way to a sense of calamity. That's life. And more to the point, that's marriage.

Successful marriages are fueled by hopefulness and optimism rather than by hopelessness during difficult times or oversensitivity to minor failures. To suggest optimism as a task may seem a bit simplistic and Pollyanna-ish, but I'm not suggesting that you go around with a smile on your face and a song on your lips twenty-four hours a day. What I *am* suggesting is that you hew to the idea that all the hard emotional work you and your spouse are doing will pay off. To a certain degree, building healthy, viable relationships is a matter of fulfilling our own prophecies. If we believe we can do it, chances are we will. If we believe we can't, odds are we won't.

Everyone is prone to a little fretting and stewing about the future now and again, but each of us can choose to be an optimist rather than a pessimist, in the same way we can choose to stress positive emotions over negative ones. Just as adjusting to marriage entails living with negative emotions without dwelling on them, it entails learning to live with nagging little worries without dwelling on apocalyptic thoughts of a future in ruins.

Trust, tolerance, flexibility, pragmatism, and optimism are intrinsic to the healthy development of any marriage. In working on these tasks, you will expand your awareness of yourself, of your spouse, and of the dynamics that operate in your relationship. But when it comes to expanding awareness, there's another task that can't be overlooked. Task 6 is effective communication: the giving and receiving of all kinds of marital messages, from words and body language to giggles, grimaces, grins, and groans. Task 6 is so interesting that it deserves a chapter all its own.

4

All Kinds of Messages

It's not talk of God and the decade ahead that
Allows you to get through the worst.
It's "I do" and "You don't" and "Nobody said that"
And "Who brought the subject up first?"
It's the little things, the little things . . .

> —Stephen Sondheim
> "The Little Things You Do
> Together," from Company

COURTSHIP AND CONVERSATION go hand in hand. It's not unusual for a couple falling in love to spend hour upon hour, day after day, talking of their feelings for each other, telling each other about their pasts, sharing their hopes for the future, and even waxing philosophical on topics from the nature of the universe to the merits of modern art or the dilemmas of democracy. From all this talk, a sense of endearment and intimacy grows. The greater the sense of intimacy, the more likely it is that a couple will decide to wed. But once a couple does wed, their verbal exchanges are in for some changes.

While heart-to-heart talks still occur with some regularity in the first year of marriage, many newlyweds notice that they happen far less often than they did before. They may find that their discussions now have more to do with day-to-day details than with serious soul-baring. Instead of asking probing questions about each other's childhood or what they want out of life, they may often find themselves posing such comparatively mundane queries as "Have you been using my blow dryer?" and "Do you think it's okay to put the wok in the dishwasher?" Rather than staying up all night jointly pondering the immortality of the human soul, they may find their liveliest debates frequently center around whose turn it is to go to the dry cleaner's or to pick up the kids at their mom's.

Just as the *nature* of couple talk changes after marriage, so does the *amount* of time couples spend talking to each other. Now that they've agreed to be partners forever, newlyweds commonly find that the sense of urgency that accompanied their premarital dialogues tends to dissipate. Though research shows that couples in their first year of marriage speak to each other more than they will later on (some studies indicate that long-married men and women talk to each other for an average of thirty-seven minutes a week!), newlyweds still spend far less time involved in intimate tête-à-têtes than unmarried lovers.

As for those romantic declarations and whispered sweet nothings that men and women shower upon one another when courting, a study by University of Texas psychologist Ted Huston shows that they fall off at a rate of about 50 percent during the first marital year. Intense expressions of emotion, psychologists say, thrive on uncertainty and interruption. To marry is to lower the uncertainty factor in a relationship and to do away, for the most part, with relationship interruption, so it's not all that surprising that the intensity and frequency of affectionate talk is likely to decline. Still, there are times when newlyweds may find this and other natural phenomena of postmarital communication unsettling.

In the early months of marriage, the slacking off of serious and romantic talk may escape notice. Honeymoon-phase couples often don't feel the need to say much of anything. In fact, their sense of merger and oneness can be reinforced by their feeling that they don't need words to communicate. But as the honeymoon glow wears off, along with the feeling that each partner can read the other's mind, it's not unusual for newlyweds to grow a little dissatisfied with the level of talk. Because they haven't yet figured out how to communicate with maximum effectiveness within the framework of marriage, they may even find themselves feeling a wee bit bored.

Do not despair: experiencing a tinge of boredom at this stage of the game is not at all uncommon. Once couples begin to develop and learn to appreciate their own special marital communication styles, post-honeymoon ennui tends to be replaced by feelings of comfortable familiarity. It's only when newlyweds overreact to the communication blahs that they risk driving wedges into their relationship.

Remember Eddie from the movie *Diner?* Not long before his wedding day, he and his buddy Laurence "Shrevie" Schreiber have a heart-to-heart chat about married life. Shrevie, married the year before, complains that he can talk the night away with his pals at the diner but can't have a five-minute conversation with his wife. The two friends shrug and sigh, then console each other. "Well," they say, "we've always got the diner." But abandoning one's spouse night after night in favor of the company of others is hardly a way to get a marriage off on the right foot.

Another newlywed who coped less than wisely with feelings of boredom was Gustave Flaubert's Emma Bovary. Not long after her marriage to country doctor Charles

Bovary, this notorious nineteenth-century bride grew weary of her husband's conversation, which she perceived as being "as flat as a sidewalk," and tired of his romantic raptures, which "had settled into a regular schedule." Madame Bovary's malaise definitely got the better of her. It wasn't long before she started down the wayward path that eventually led her to adultery, bankruptcy, and suicide. I think it's fair to say that such responses are hardly a formula for success in marriage.

Perhaps the best way for newlyweds to combat feelings of boredom is to think of their marriage as an unfolding mystery and to think of themselves as detectives. No matter how much each partner revealed during courtship or even during cohabitation, each is sure to reveal infinitely more, in infinitely subtle ways, in the course of the first married year. Though there may be less *overt* verbal self-disclosure and less sheer talk than there was during courtship, new spouses give each other hundreds of clues each and every day as to who they really are, what they really expect, what they really need from each other, and what they are and are not willing to do on behalf of the marriage. The clues come from what is said and how it's said, but they also come from what is not said. They come through gestures, posture, facial expressions, and the way that partners touch each other. They come through laughter, through sighs, and through silence. Learning to interpret these clues and understand your mate's marital messages not only helps enhance the relationship and facilitate its growth, it makes the first year of marriage feel like the great adventure it is.

Paying Attention

In his inspirational book *The Road Less Traveled*, psychiatrist M. Scott Peck writes that "true listening, total concentration on the other, is always a manifestation of love." Family therapist W. Robert Beavers writes that a spouse's self-esteem is greatly increased when he or she feels heard and understood. But research shows that most of us listen with about a 25 percent rate of efficiency. Instead of really paying attention, we fake it. Now, faking attention may be a useful skill in many areas of life, and listening with a quarter of one's attention to a high school oral hygiene lecture, a Sunday sermon, or a TV sitcom probably never killed anyone. But your partner deserves better. Listening to your spouse this haphazardly can lead to serious marital misunderstandings.

Whenever spouses start talking, they are opening a door, and the best way to keep that door from closing is to make them feel that their words are being received by someone who takes them seriously. Maintaining eye contact with your spouse is one way to keep your attention where it belongs. It's harder to "space out" when you're looking directly at someone who is speaking than it is when you're gazing out the window, staring at your shoes, or examining your fingernails for hanging cuticles. Another way to keep your listening response sharp is to be aware of your own threshold for receiving information. If your spouse is talking a mile a minute and you find yourself feeling overwhelmed and unable to keep up, don't hesitate to ask for the pace to be slowed or for something to be repeated. Perhaps the most important factor involved in effective listening is to stop yourself from worrying about how you're going to respond to a statement or a question until you're sure you've *understood* it.

We're often too preoccupied with formulating responses to really hear what is actually being said to us—and that's especially true if we perceive ourselves as being on the receiving end of a grievance or complaint. If one spouse begins a conversation by mentioning that the other never checks the oil in the family car, the "accused" typically begins to mentally prepare a "defense." Your mind races along, coming up with rationalizations, excuses, or counteraccusations. Like: "I don't know anything about cars so you should take care of that." Or: "I don't have time to do that because I'm too busy doing everything else around here while you never do anything." Or: "Maybe I don't check the oil, but you never get the car *washed,* and it's so dirty I could write a dissertation in the dust on the hood. So there!"

But while all this internal formulation is going on, you've totally tuned out the rest of what's being said. Maybe you've missed the entire point of the communication. Like: "It makes me nervous to think of you driving around in the car when it's likely to break down." Or: "My 'ex' and I used to fight about this all the time and I don't want that to happen to us, so please humor me and learn to use a dipstick or go to a full-service gas station." Had you really *listened,* you might well have felt completely different about the message and responded to it more appropriately.

Paying attention to words is important, but newlyweds must also learn to pay attention to each other's nonverbal communications. We humans are so language-oriented that it can be hard to get into the habit of paying attention to nonverbal signs. In fact, as Desmond Morris points out in *The Naked Ape,* when it comes to interpreting such signals, there are many animal species that put us to shame.

A horse, an elephant, or a chimp is often far more responsive to subtle changes in a human's body posture than is another human. If someone is afraid or means them harm, they know it at a glance. If someone feels comfortable around them, they sense that too. And, as any number of dog owners will attest, "man's best friend" seems to possess an uncanny knack for reading and responding to its owner's moods. Compared to Fido or Patches or Spot, you and I are body-language illiterates.

Yet although most of us, unfortunately, will go through life unaware of many communications that others send to us via their movements and expressions, marriage is one situation in which we have the opportunity to observe and study a person with such regularity that interpreting such messages can become second nature. Long-married couples are often so attuned to each other's body language that they can communicate entire paragraphs to each other with a particular shake of the head, a wink, or a wave of the hand. They may well engage in overt talk for a mere thirty-seven minutes a week, but if we were to add up all their body-talk shorthand, we might well find that they were actually engaged in a great deal of dialogue.

Though learning about your mate's body language gets easier as the years go by, newlyweds can begin to unravel some of the mysteries of marital communication from the very start if they make a conscious effort to alert themselves to the way their spouses grin and pout, shrug and slouch, tap their toes, scratch their heads, or nibble their nails. If your partner rubs his temples or shuts her eyes just before announcing a concern about paying this month's bills or beating a deadline at work, it won't be long before you begin to associate these signs with the fact that your spouse has something worrisome on the brain. If your mate typically shreds a paper napkin into tiny strips just before insisting that it's time to leave a drawn-out dinner party, you'll begin to make the connection between this sort of fidgeting and your partner's boredom or impatience. Of course, one of the most common ways married people communicate nonverbally is through gestures of affection, but everyone—I hope—recognizes without much teaching that a tickle, a hug, a peck on the cheek, or a friendly "goose" is a spouse's way of saying "Hi, there. I love you."

Another kind of communication you'll want to pay attention to is the *paraverbal* kind. This has to do partly with tone of voice. If you don't think it's important, consider the possible variations on this exchange:

> *Question:* Do you love me?
> *Answer:* Sure, I do.

These three little words of response, "Sure I do," can communicate any number of messages depending on *how* they're spoken. Said warmly and resonantly, they can convey reassurance; spoken automatically and perfunctorily, they will have a very different effect. Spoken with a terse and chilly edge, they can be downright unnerving.

Paraverbal messages are also contained in all the sounds we make that aren't part of speech per se. One newlywed assured me that her husband can communicate an entire repertoire of opinions just by saying "hmm, hmm." "Whenever I bought a new outfit I would come home and model it for him," she said. "I'd ask him if he liked it, and the response was always 'hmm, hmm.' It drove me to distraction until I began to figure out that one kind of 'hmm, hmm' meant that he loved it, another kind meant he thought it was okay, and a third kind meant he thought I ought to get my money back."

What does your spouse mean when he or she says "hmm, hmm"—or "mmppff" or "feh!" or, as Ricky

Ricardo used to say, *"aye, aye, aye, aye, aye"*? If you don't know, it's time to put on your detective hat and try to find out. Once you're tuned in to your partner's para-verbal messages, a whole new realm of communication will open up. Is your mate laughing? Well, what kind of laugh is it? A short, brittle, nervous chuckle? A lascivious giggle? A happy and heartfelt guffaw? Is your partner sighing? Is it a sigh of exasperation, meaning "Gee, I wish I could balance this checkbook"? Is it a sigh of relief, meaning "Whew, I've balanced it"? Is it a sigh of fatigue, meaning "Wow, it's been a long day"? Maybe it's a sigh of longing, meaning "I wish you'd pay some attention to me tonight." How will you know unless you *pay attention?*

While you have your detective hat on, remember it's also crucial that you do some investigating into your own way of communicating. As important as it is for new-lyweds to observe each other, self-knowledge is equally crucial. Try to "step outside yourself" from time to time and develop an objective awareness of your own messages. Be as alert as you can to your own speech patterns, your gestures, and your facial expressions. In the first year of marriage, your job is not only to understand your mate but to help your mate understand you. The more you are able to examine your own communication behavior and use what you learn to get your messages across clearly, the better the chances that your feelings, beliefs, experiences, and attitudes will be understood, and the greater the odds that your needs will be met.

Try especially to notice and deal with any repeated re-sistance that keeps getting in the way of your being able to express clearly what you need and want. Remember that communicating to someone else what makes you happy and what makes you uncomfortable is something you ac-tually began doing as soon as you were born, and you surely don't want to stop now. You wouldn't be here today if you hadn't educated your mother very early on, through your cries, your coos, your wiggling and squiggling, as to when you were hungry, when you were full, when you were wet—or worse—and needed to be changed, and when you needed to be rocked or held.

Communication Confusion

Even with both spouses doing their best to stay alert to their own and each other's communication nuances, there are times when clear dialogue gets interrupted by static and when trying to understand each other becomes an insoluble puzzle. It's estimated that, even in long-term marriages, one-fifth of all communications are falsely given or falsely received. New marriages offer even more potential for confusion.

In the first year of marriage, many couples are not yet attuned to each other's characterological defenses, those unconsciously acquired attitudes and postures that profoundly color the way we present ourselves to the world. Everyone employs defenses when communicating with others, sometimes to preserve self-esteem, to "save face" or "put up a good front"; sometimes to deny certain anxiety-provoking realities. Since defenses are part of our very personalities, they ought to be respected.

"When Jack and I first got married," Sandy Farrell told me, "he was unhappy at the construction company he worked for. He'd often tell me he was going to quit his job and travel around the country, and he'd explain how I should quit my job and go with him. At first it was really frightening. We certainly couldn't afford to quit our jobs and travel, and, besides, I *liked* my work. But the harder I tried to point out how irrational he was being, the more involved he'd get with his fantasies. Then, as time went on and Jack didn't do anything drastic, I began to see that he just needed to blow off steam. After that, whenever he talked about packing it all in, I'd just let him go on for as long as he needed to without contradicting him."

Sandy was wise to let her husband blow off steam when he needed to. We all feel the need to "talk through our hats" every now and again. What's said isn't always what's meant, and, as anyone who's ever announced an intention to go on a diet "tomorrow" can tell you, people don't always act on their spoken intentions. What's more, we all have certain blind spots (cognitive psychologists call them "lacunae") when it comes to the way we perceive reality, and, as psychologist Daniel Goleman writes, "there is increasing evidence that in certain situations the ability to deceive ourselves may be helpful." So, if your mate uses a little self-deception now and again to help get through the day, don't push the panic button. Sometimes you just have to be patient and let your spouse's actual long-term behavior speak for itself.

Another way in which spouses can misunderstand each other is by engaging in "selective listening," i.e., hearing only what they want to hear and ignoring the rest. Selective listening can sometimes take the form of attributing too much significance to any one isolated message, as it did in an instance Mark Howard recalled. "Claudia has a girlfriend named Phyllis, who I'm not really wild about because she's a big gossip," he explained. "Usually Claudia would defend her because they're very old pals and have been through a lot together, but one time she suspected that Phyllis had been gossiping about *her* and she said, 'You're right, that Phyllis is a creep. I never want to speak to her again.' I thought that was the end of Phyllis, but was I wrong! Within a few days their relationship was back to status quo. When I asked Claudia why she didn't stick to her guns and get Phyllis out of her life, she became really annoyed. She said, 'I can't believe you believed me when I said what I did. I thought you knew me better.' Well, at the time, I guess I really *didn't* know her better.''

Mark's story shows how giving too much credence to a one-time communication can lead to false perceptions. But "selective listening" can also take a different form. It's not unusual for newlyweds to block out *repeated* messages from each other when those messages don't fit in with their idealized views of their partners. If you like to think of your spouse an an emotional Rock of Gibraltar, your natural tendency may be to ignore messages that indicate your partner is feeling vulnerable or scared, no matter how many of those messages come your way. If you take pride in having married a paragon of decisiveness, you may block out any messages that convey uncertainty and confusion, regardless of how "obvious" those signals may be. Even the most "together" of spouses is bound to come unglued under certain circumstances. When that happens, you have to *let yourself hear* your mate's desire to be helped, comforted, or simply understood.

Of course, not all communication confusion is a result of faulty listening. If the messages one spouse *sends* to the other are mixed, befuddlement is bound to result. First studied in the mid-1950s by psychologist Gregory Bateson with regard to parent-child interactions, mixed messages have the potential to cloud communication in any intimate relationship, marriage being no exception.

Mixed messages are communications that embody contradiction. They're sometimes the result of incongruent words and phrases (as in, "Honeybunch, have you met my mistress?") but they are even more frequently the result of conflicting verbal and nonverbal signals. If someone were to say "I can't live without you, my precious dove" while swinging a meat cleaver at your throat, that would certainly qualify as a mixed message. And if someone were to give you a gift certificate for plastic surgery along with a card that reads "I love you just the way you are," I think it would be fair to conclude that the communication you're getting is double-edged.

Though most mixed messages are somewhat more subtle than these examples, *all* mixed messages have one thing in common: they place those receiving them in what Bateson described as a "double bind." When the surface context of a message is contradicted by a subliminal context, listeners are understandably conflicted and confused. They are placed in a no-win situation. They have no idea what kind of response is expected of them. While they can't respond effectively to two contradicting messages at once, responding to only one seems less than adequate.

Many of the husbands and wives I spoke with recalled feeling bothered and bewildered by mixed messages early in their marriages. One husband complained that his wife used to chastise him for not being nice enough to her mother, then make distracting "funny faces" at him whenever he tried to have a pleasant phone chat with his mother-in-law. One woman remembered that her husband would admonish her to spend less money, then lavish her with gifts they couldn't afford. And another woman recalled her husband asking her to instigate lovemaking more often, then "tensing up and turning off" whenever she made the first move.

It's unlikely that any marriage will ever become totally free of mixed messages, but ambiguous signals are probably sent out more often in the first year of marriage than later on. Mixed messages can stem from ambivalence, which, as we've already seen, is an important aspect of the post-honeymoon phase. If you're at the stage where you unconsciously conceptualize your partner as a "good spouse" or a "bad spouse," it's likely you're sometimes going to send out conflicting signs. Mixed messages can also spring from transference issues. If you're relating to a spouse partly as a parent figure, or if you're involved in a complicated "dual transference," relating to your spouse partly the way you did to your mother and partly the way you did to your father, *voilà*, you've got an instant formula for confusion.

When marital communication is fraught with mixed messages, the result can be a lack of mutual trust. With contradictory signals flying this way and that, newlyweds may feel insecure in their relationships, as though the rug is repeatedly being pulled out from under them. You'll want to keep an eye out for any mixed messages you may be sending. If you sense that your gestures, posture, or tone of voice don't jibe with your words, you may want to halt your communication long enough to figure out what you really mean to convey. Your spouse cannot possibly know what it is you want until *you* know what it is you want. What's more, if you're uncertain about a message your partner is giving you, don't suffer in silence. Ask him or her some questions that will help you clarify things.

One final note about communication confusion. Though the *how*'s of talking and listening to each other are significant, don't underestimate the importance of the *when*'s. In matters of communication, there are, in the immortal words of Sly and the Family Stone, "different strokes for different folks." Some people wake up clear-headed, loose-lipped, and ready to say what's on their minds, while their mates may wake up foggy and oblivious to anything they hear at the breakfast table except "snap, crackle, pop." Some people seem to come alive late in the evening, talking a blue streak when their weary partners may feel ill equipped to process anything more demanding than a

"Tonight Show" monologue. It's small wonder that messages may be misheard, half heard, or not heard at all when one partner is operating in high gear and the other in low.

If you don't feel up to a heart-to-heart dialogue, say so. If you don't feel up to hearing a recap of your partner's day on the job, day at the beach, adventures at the supermarket, or triumph on the tennis court, say that too. There's nothing wrong with suggesting postponing a conversation until you feel you can handle it, provided you do so kindly and tactfully (e.g., "I'd love to hear more about X but I've got so much on my mind. Will you promise to tell me more later?" or 'I know it's important that we discuss Y and I wish I wasn't too tired to do a good job of it. Can we try tomorrow?'').

As long as you manage to make the point that you don't want to cut off communication, just postpone it a little, you'll be doing yourself, your spouse, and your relationship a service. Conversely, if your spouse lets you know that the moment is not right for a cozy chat, don't take offense, take instruction. Find a time when each of you can give the other the attention you deserve, and make a date to communicate.

Honesty, Secrecy, and Little White Lies

We grow up learning from our parents, teachers, and our Boy or Girl Scout troop leaders that "honesty is the best policy." But is such a policy a wise one in marriage? Well, sometimes yes and sometimes no. Certainly those new husbands and wives who share very few of their thoughts, feelings, and experiences with each other will find that too much reticence creates too much distance in their relationship. But newlyweds who share too *many* of their innermost thoughts and feelings may face even bigger problems. Getting to know and be known by a spouse is fascinating, facilitating, and often just plain fun, but saying everything that's on your mind all of the time can be unconstructive, unkind, and just plain dumb.

Though much of what we hear and read about marriage nowadays might lead us to believe that complete openness is the cornerstone of connubial bliss, the best and most pithy advice on the subject of marital honesty is perhaps summed up by a twelfth-century maxim from a "code of love" compiled by the ladies of the court of the countess of Champagne. "Whoever cannot conceal a thing," it reads, "cannot love." Well said, ladies. Anyone who cannot conceal a thing will probably not be happily married for long.

For one thing, telling your spouse "the truth, the whole truth, and nothing but the truth" can make you feel vulnerable and overexposed. As D. W. Winnicott writes, each of us is a permanently communicating being, but each of us is also permanently noncommunicating—secretive, mysterious. Keeping part of ourselves *to* ourselves is a right we all have, even when we're married. Giving up that right is unwise.

As psychoanalyst Hyman Spotnitz writes, "The right of human beings to privacy of thoughts is not abrogated by the marriage contract." Without retaining some reserves of privacy, it's easy to lose a sense of who we are, and when that happens any relationship we share is at risk.

While you ought not to keep from your spouse information that directly affects your marriage, such as the news that you have just cleaned out the joint checking account or agreed to father your secretary's child by artificial insemination, you may justifiably choose to refrain from sharing certain parts of your past history that really have little to do with your married life. If you don't feel comfortable discussing intimate details of a past romance, there's no reason to feel you have to, even if *requested* to. If you're still embarrassed to talk about the time you got caught snitching a candy bar when you were nine or when you got suspended from high school for "streaking" through the auditorium, there's no need to feel compelled to confess it to your mate. And if you feel that certain of your fantasies or secret wishes are just too personal to share even with the one closest to you, you can still enjoy them privately.

But leaving certain things unsaid, and certain messages unsent, is more than a way of protecting yourself; it's also a way of protecting your partner. Let's face it: if we told our spouses every thought we ever had about them without imposing any kind of self-censorship, we would hardly be performing a good deed.

While newlyweds must ultimately decide for themselves the specifics of what to say and what not to say to their mates, and target for themselves the "touchy areas" in their relationships that should be approached only with the utmost caution and tact, there are some good rules to follow when communicating with your spouse: try to say things that will help the relationship instead of things that will harm it, and try to send messages that will make your spouse feel loved, rather than ones that will make him or her feel threatened or rejected.

Although some people may feel that monitoring and screening their marital messages is somehow a "false" or "dishonest" way of relating, it is, in fact, mere good sense. If you're trying to get your boss to give you a raise, you don't say, "This is a lousy place to work and you're a tyrant. I deserve combat pay for doing this job, so give me more money." Likewise, if you want your spouse to think well of you and act accordingly (and that *is* what you want, I trust), you won't be doing yourself any favors by announcing what a disappointment she is to you, or wondering aloud why you married him, anyway. As couples therapist Joan Ormont says, "If you want a better relationship, don't say anything that will make it worse."

Of course, there are times when simply screening out your negative comments is not sufficient. Now and then, your positive comments to your spouse have to be, well, *embellished.* One of the things married people want most from their partners is praise, and a little exaggeration or "white lying" in the service of praise won't hurt. In fact, flattering white lies are as important to the smooth functioning of a marriage as they are to the smooth functioning of society as a whole. Just as people who expect to live in harmony with their next-door neighbors say things like, "What a sharp-looking new car you have there" and "What a cute little baby you've got," instead of, "That car looks like a lemon" and "Your child looks like a turnip," people who want to live harmoniously with their spouses often choose to revise their private opinions before making them public.

Saint Augustine taught that all lies were sins, and that there was no justifiable reason for even the whitest, smallest, and most inconsequential fib. As Sissela Bok writes in her book *Lying: Moral Choice in Public and Private Life,* Augustine's philosophy that all liars endanger their souls "left no room at all for justifiable falsehood." But had the saint had a wife, you can just imagine the kind of trouble he would have gotten himself into:

"Augustine, do you like my perfume?"

"Why, no, my dear. It smells like a goat."

"Augustine, do you think I've lost weight?"

"Frankly, my darling, you look as large as a camel."

"Augustine, I want a part-time job. What do you think?"

"I think a woman's place is in the home."

"Augustine, this just isn't working out."

Constructive Criticism

The more ways you can find to praise, compliment, and flatter your spouse, the better. But if you feel you must make an occasional criticism, remember that even messages that are essentially negative can be packaged so they are helpful, not hurtful. Constructive criticism is a subtle art, and mastering it can be especially difficult for newlyweds who are still shocked to find any imperfections at all in their mates. But there are some nifty little techniques that can take much of the sting out of criticism.

Couples therapists generally agree that the most caring and considerate way to deliver a critical appraisal is to use the pronoun "I" and steer clear of the pronoun "you." "You" messages often end up sounding something like this:

You forgot to turn out the porch light last night. You're running up the electric bill. You're wasting money and driving me crazy. You'd better remember to turn it out tonight.

An "I" message serves to soften what amounts to the same communication:

I noticed the porch light was left on last night. I'm sure that runs up the electric bill. I get so anxious when money is wasted. I hope you'll remember to turn it out tonight.

If you were the porch-light culprit, which version would you rather hear? Beginning statements with "you" is provocative. Beginning them with "I" is a way of reporting what's on your mind without making your partner feel badgered. It conveys the impression that you're not out to blame, but to mend fences.

You'll probably feel most like criticizing your spouse when he or she does something that you perceive as being destructive to your overall relationship. When that's the case, a good way to criticize is to avoid statements altogether and ask questions. Asking "Are you aware that it isn't helpful to our relationship when X happens?" or "Do you know that we might get along even better if Y wasn't coming between us?" can help refine your informal contracts with each other and help remind your partner of the existence of your "third person." Your spouse may be more willing to rethink his or her behavior if it's clear that doing so may result in long-term benefits for you both.

Another way of criticizing without attacking is to suggest alternatives. Psychoanalyst Hyman Spotnitz advises, "If you see your wife wearing a dress you hate or your husband sporting a tie you loathe, saying 'That looks lousy on you' isn't going to facilitate your relationship. But if you say, 'You have a beautiful dress (or tie) in the closet that I'd love to see you wear tonight,' that's a helpful and constructive message. You're not criticizing one piece of clothing, you're simply saying you prefer another."

The ultimate test of constructive criticism in marriage is whether it makes your partner feel loved and inspired, or whether it makes him or her feel embarrassed and ashamed. Naturally everyone has a different tolerance level for criticism, but even if your spouse seems like the sort who can take a certain amount of it in stride, the first year of marriage is no time to test the limits of how much he or she can stand. Because just about every newlywed is more fragile and insecure than usual, even the gentlest of rebukes may give offense. Before you venture to make any kind of criticism at all, make sure it's really justified, and that you are prepared for its consequences.

Laughing and Playing Together

One of the greatest joys of the first year of marriage is discovering that you now have a permanent playmate. When newlyweds engage in baby talk, funny faces, private jokes, and intimate comedy routines, they are strengthening their secret and special bonds. Virtually every couple I spoke with told me they felt extremely close to each other whenever they shared moments of laughter and of good old-fashioned goofiness. When two people feel comfortable enough with each other to be a bit zany, that means that they not only trust each other but they genuinely *like* each other. And when two people laugh at the same thing, they're acknowledging that they're on the same wavelength.

Affectionate play is a big part of our lives practically from the time we're born. When our mothers played clap hands or peek-a-boo with us, or when our fathers bounced us on their knees, tickled our toes, and swung us high up in the air, they made us feel pampered, adored, and, of course, amused. When spouses make jokes or perform silly antics for each other's benefit, they can give each other the same kinds of feelings. When our parents invented playful pet nicknames for us, we felt pleased and flattered in the same way that married people do when their mates address them by whimsical terms of endearment.

Many people I talked to described favorite funny routines that their husbands or wives entertained them with in their first married year, and they told me also how charmed they were by their partners' special ways of clowning around. Claudia Howard was delighted to find that Mark had a limitless repertoire of animal imitations, and his impression of their cat having a hairball attack was enough to bring tears to her eyes. Dave Brown said Megan's wonderful sense of humor really blossomed at home after their marriage. He enjoyed most of all his wife's flawless mimicry of messages left on their telephone answering machine. Barbara Simon found her husband's impromptu limericks hilarious, and Ron Clarke was given to fits of hysterics over his wife's spoofs of California "Valley girl" lingo.

As for pet names, just about everyone came up with one or more spousal sobriquet, some of which stuck for just a few weeks or months, others of which became a lasting part of the couple's life. The pet names the couples I interviewed called each other ranged from the fairly common ("Sugar lips" and "Sweetie pie") to the more unusual ("Tofu," "Kangaroo," and "Moonwalker") to the truly esoteric. One woman called her husband "Zorro the Zero" because he invested so much money in zero-coupon bonds, and one man referred to his wife as "Sixela," which is "Alexis" backward. "I started calling her that because she struck me as just the opposite of Joan Collins' 'Alexis' character on 'Dynasty.' Alexis goes out of her way to cause trouble, but my wife is a perennial do-gooder who goes out of her way to help people."

Clearly, marital play is a great way to add fun, zest, and greater intimacy to your relationship. It's a way of showing your partner how much you appreciate him or her and it's a way of encouraging your mate to appreciate you. But play does other things as well.

Bruno Bettelheim points out that when children play they are often able to express thoughts and feelings they might be unable or reluctant to reveal under other circumstances. Play helps children work through problems in their lives and give vent to certain aggressive impulses (as in, "Bang, bang, you're dead!"). In a marriage, play often serves the very same functions.

William Betcher, a Boston psychologist and psychiatrist who has for many years studied the role of play in marriage, says that play is a time when partners give up many of their standard defenses, take some risks, delve into unexplored territory, and broach subjects that might otherwise be *verboten*. If, for example, a couple has a hard time talking about whether or not to have children, they might gradually begin to get comfortable with the subject by making jokes about whom their child might resemble, what kind of parents they might be, or how much it costs to build up a college tuition fund. Once they can kid about such things, serious discussion may be easier to cope with down the line.

According to Betcher, play is also a way in which couples can safely act out some of their negative feelings toward each other. As he writes in his book *Intimate Play*, "Playful exaggeration and caricature provide a constructive outlet for your frustrations about a partner's behavior." He also writes that "play encourages without insisting on change." The experiences of couples I talked with certainly back him up on both scores.

When Ron and Carol Clarke were in conflict over whether she would give up junk food for vegetables, Carol decided to act out her dislike of "those leafy green things" by cooking her husband a meatless meal that included no vegetables at all. "I served him a dinner of cheese soufflé, potatoes, and biscuits. Starch city! It was my way of saying, 'Okay, if you really don't want meat, let's try my kind of alternative.' Ron not only got the joke, he went me one better. He started doing an imitation of a creature he called the Killer Broccoli. He chased me around the kitchen holding a plant on his head and yelling, 'I'm going to inject you with my poison Vitamin A darts.' '' Though the Clarkes ultimately learned to live with their divergent eating habits, they still remember their "favorite food fight" fondly. They think it was a big step in helping them resolve their dietary dilemmas.

Robin and Charlie Turner were also able to resolve one of their differences through play. It seems that Robin always assumed that she and Charlie would have a dog, even though she never specifically asked him about it before marriage. "After a while, Robin nagged me so much about getting a puppy that it began to get on my nerves. We're both out of the house so much that it would be impractical to have a pet that demanded a lot of attention. I decided I should buy her a dog, so I did—a stuffed, battery-operated one that barked when you clapped your hands. Then I started nagging *her*. When she was all comfy at night watching TV in her bathrobe I'd say, 'Hey, honey, it's time to take that dog out.' When it was a cold, rainy morning I'd say, 'Well, I guess it's your turn to walk the dog.' Then I'd clap my hands and make it bark. 'See? It wants to go out!' Now Robin thought all of this was pretty funny, but after a while she also got the point I was trying to make, which was that having a dog is a lot of work, and it's not always very convenient.''

Just as play can be instrumental in instigating compromise without inciting argument, it can also be used to express anger in nonthreatening ways. It's not at all unusual for married couples to smilingly trade mock insults with each other, to engage in a little good-natured teasing or pseudo–sumo wrestling, or even to stick out their tongues or thumb their noses at each other now and again. While this kind of behavior can certainly be classified as "regressive," like most play it's really a healthy kind of regression. Unless they're carried to obnoxious extremes, joking insults don't convey the message "I hate you"; they convey the message "I love you, even though you're sometimes a little weird, Sweetie pie."

Until recently, the benefits of marital play have been underestimated; but researchers who study relationships are recognizing more and more that couples who play together, stay together, while the absence of fun and games in a relationship can signal some latent problems. Before you start worrying that you might not be spending enough time just fooling around with your spouse, however, it's worth noting that play often becomes so natural a part of marital communication that you may not even realize how much you and your mate actually engage in it.

Chances are that if you really stop and think about it, you'll find that you and your partner have already discovered many of your own special ways of laughing and playing together. But if you do feel your marriage could use a bigger dose of frivolity, giving yourself permission to indulge in a little inspired nuttiness couldn't hurt. Marriage may be a serious business, but it certainly doesn't have to be a somber one. Of course, it's always important to make sure your humor is tempered by empathy and affection. If your partner displays a staunch unwillingness to joke about a particular topic, pay attention to that message. And never forget the difference between harmless kidding and hurtful sarcasm or ridicule.

As for getting your mate to feel freer about play, the best thing you can do is be responsive. If your partner tries to make you laugh, try to show your appreciation. People are apt to feel rejected when their humor isn't responded to. As Betcher says, laughing at your spouse's jokes is a way of offering a kind of applause. But don't expect your partner to be a regular laugh riot all the time. As Honoré de Balzac wrote, "It is easier to be a lover than a husband, for the simple reason that it is more difficult to have a ready wit the whole day long than to say a good thing occasionally."

Marriage and Manners

When couples are courting, they are, perhaps more than ever, mindful of their manners. Once they marry, their mutual politeness may begin to evaporate. For many newlyweds, figuring out what constitutes rudeness to a spouse is tricky. Obviously, we shouldn't be expected to behave at home as we would at a garden party or an afternoon tea, and it's natural to treat one's spouse with somewhat less deference than, say, the Queen Mother. But "letting it all hang out" is not always such a hot idea either.

As a marriage progresses, each partner will learn from experience what kinds of actions cause the other to take offense, but in the first year of marriage, keeping your eyes open for that little wince or keeping your ears attuned to that little sigh that signals "Gee, I wish you wouldn't do that" is especially important. At the beginning of marriage, you are dealing with someone who is probably used to your being on your best behavior most of the time. If you change overnight from a model of mannerliness to an insensitive boor, your indiscretions may make your partner feel as if you don't respect or admire him or her as much as you did before.

Interestingly, many of the newlyweds I spoke with told me they were annoyed not so much by their partners' abandonment of certain courtship amenities after marriage as they were by the abruptness with which those amenities were cast aside. One woman complained that her husband stopped opening doors for her while they were on their honeymoon and never resumed the practice; another said, "I think the last time my husband helped me on with my coat was when we were on our way to church to get married."

Of course, women aren't the only ones with manners grievances. One man I talked to said that his wife, whom he had lived with for two years before marriage, began *after* marriage to change television channels without consulting him when he was in the middle of watching a show and to grab sections of the newspaper out of his hands before he'd finished reading them. Another complained that, once wed, his wife showed no compunction about using expletives that he'd believed her incapable of uttering during courtship. "I didn't even know she knew those words," he said, "let alone used them."

Now, some of these spousal appraisals may be somewhat exaggerated. Once married, people do tend to be more observant of their partners' peccadilloes than they were before. But, even allowing for such perceptual adjustments, it seems clear that some newlyweds do throw courtesy to the wind rather quickly once they've formalized their relationships.

Many complaints I heard about married manners centered around somewhat delicate issues. Some newlyweds, for example, expressed irritation at their spouses' barging in on them while they were in the bathroom. Others were annoyed that their mates never felt obliged to say "excuse me" after expelling gas from either end of the digestive tract. These issues can be especially difficult to resolve if one spouse is more squeamish about bodily functions than the other. As one notorious bathroom-barger said, "I don't understand why this bothers my wife. After all, what has she got to hide?" And as another newlywed who came down in favor of "doing what comes naturally" put it, "If you can't belch in front of your husband or wife, who *can* you belch in front of?"

What, exactly, constitutes good manners within the framework of an intimate relationship and how much "loosening up" is permissible after marriage depend, of course, on the sensibilities of the people involved. If your spouse doesn't particularly mind if you drink milk straight from the carton at the dinner table, feel free to chug away. If your mate doesn't care if you forget to say "please" when you ask for the ketchup to be passed, or neglect to mitigate the grumbling of your stomach with an "oops, pardon me," you're lucky. But if such behavior instills in your spouse the urge to thumb through the "divorce" section of the Yellow Pages, you might want to consider polishing up your act. Preserving even a few of the mannerly rituals of courtship in a marriage can convey the message that you still think enough of your spouse to resist being guided by some of your more basic urges.

In addition to being mindful of how much politeness you evince toward your spouse in private, you'll want to take care never to display bad manners by embarrassing your mate in public. It's the height of rudeness to pick on your partner or to call attention to his or her faux pas in front of other people. Jack Farrell recalled being hurt, for example, by Sandy's tendency to correct his grammar in public. "Sometimes she'd point out the same mistake over and over again in the course of an evening," he said, "and the result was that I'd clam up and stop talking altogether." Claudia Howard became irritated when Mark revealed in front of his parents that she had a mental block against setting the dinner table with the silverware in the right places. "Big forks, little forks," she said, "I mean, who cares? I grew up in a much less formal environment than Mark. We just didn't think much about that kind of stuff, but that's no reason to make me look silly in front of people who I want to have a good opinion of me.''

Newlyweds who find themselves behaving as Sandy Farrell and Mark Howard did might well heed the advice of Miss Manners, who writes: ''It is admittedly difficult to arrest the pleasure of correcting and advising long enough to ask oneself who will feel better after the correction is administered—the person issuing it, or the one who gets it full in the face? But it is well worth the effort, not only for kindness' sake, but because it is a law of nature that he who corrects others will soon do something perfectly awful himself.''

It can be bad manners, too, to interrupt your spouse's version of an anecdote with your version of ''what really happened.'' Though scholar Phyllis Rose is essentially correct when she writes in her book *Parallel Lives* that good marriages seem to be ''those in which two partners agree on the scenario they are enacting,'' I believe that partners must also acknowledge the truth that no event is ever perceived, or remembered, in *exactly* the same way by any two people and therefore resist the temptation to bring the other's concept of reality in line with their own.

As anyone who has ever watched the popular television show ''The Newlywed Game'' has doubtless witnessed, people in the first year of marriage are especially likely to disagree about what happened and when, and who said or did what to whom. Though it may be very entertaining to watch the wacky contestants on this show hit each other over the head with their cardboard answer cards when one spouse's recall of ''facts'' is at variance with the other's, your own mate is probably not going to be amused if you indicate, in front of *any* kind of audience—friends, relatives, or the general public—that he or she is an absent-minded airhead.

Butting in while your spouse is telling a tale is not only counterproductive, it's counterinstructive. Holding your tongue while your partner relays an anecdote gives you an opportunity to learn something, if not about the nature of reality, then certainly about the nature of your mate—and that, after all, is a lot of what first-year communication is about.

5

First Fights

ROBERT LOUIS STEVENSON once wrote, "Marriage is one long conversation chequered by disputes." That's a pretty cynical way of looking at marital communication, but the truth of the matter is that all married couples fight from time to time—yes, even the ones who tell you that they *never* do.

In the first year of marriage, fighting can be frightening because it's unanticipated. Despite the fact that many couples quarrel before they marry, especially when the details and dilemmas of planning the wedding take their toll, researchers have found that most courting couples tend to write off these premarital spats as unusual detours on the path of true love, odd black clouds on an otherwise sunny day. Lovers, it turns out, actually don't expect to argue much after marriage. But even though newlyweds may surprise themselves by the amount of arguing they do, first-year fights are pretty hard to avoid.

Obviously enough, differences in opinion can stem from the differences in tastes, temperaments, and backgrounds with which all newly married couples must grapple. Used to doing things one way, newlyweds may balk and bicker when they realize they have to change some of their deeply ingrained habits. But newlyweds quarrel for other reasons as well, some of them primal.

Zoologist Desmond Morris points out that "animals fight amongst themselves for one of two very good reasons: either to establish their dominance in a social hierarchy, or to establish their territorial rights over a particular piece of ground." Before they've discovered the rewards of sharing power and finding the right balance between closeness and distance, newlyweds, too, may find themselves involved in disputes over issues of power and territoriality.

Newlyweds may also quarrel for the simple reason that, in the post-honeymoon phase, partners run a high risk of finding themselves in bad moods at the same time. The routine stress that accompanies new and unknown circumstances, the strain of having to make many far-reaching decisions in a short span of time, and the pressure they may feel to conform to other people's ideals of cooing lovebirds can all serve to make newlyweds edgy and irritable. So does the dawning realization that certain of their expectations aren't going to come to fruition. It stands to reason that when two people in close proximity are both in a grumpy frame of mind, a few spats are bound to ensue.

It's not hard to see that early marital quarrels are normal and natural. What may be more difficult for newlyweds to understand is that their fights can often be beneficial. Without a long and stable joint history to draw on, newlyweds may view every argument as the possible "beginning of the end." If they're still engaged in "splitting," they may look upon even relatively minor squabbles as evidence that their partners don't love them anymore, or as proof that their own decision to wed was ill conceived. But these assumptions about early arguments are erroneous. In many ways, first fights are a part of any married couple's growth. If you can't make an omelette without breaking eggs, neither can you build a strong relationship without stirring things up once in a while.

As psychoanalyst Hyman Spotnitz writes, and as many happy long-married couples doubtless understand, "An occasional battle of the wits in which differences are explored rather than concealed can help safeguard love." Here are some of the ways that quarrels in the first year of marriage can be especially useful in getting and keeping love on the right track:

They can help partners develop trust in each other, as they learn to understand that their commitment is strong enough to withstand occasional angry remarks or lapses in good behavior.

They can help spouses to recognize their separateness and establish healthy boundaries.

They can help make husbands and wives aware of the unconscious expectations and hidden agendas each of them brought to the marriage.

They can provide valuable experience to newlyweds, enabling them to set ground rules for future arguments.

They can train partners to distinguish between constructive criticism and nagging, blaming, and carping.

They can bring about practical solutions to immediate problems and compromises that will enhance the relationship.

Without some healthy confrontation, a relationship is doomed to remain superficial and characterless. Even though some newlyweds may feel guilty about displaying any sort of aggression toward their mates, aggression is, in fact, an important part of the glue that holds relationships together. Seminal studies on the subject by Nobel scientist Konrad Lorenz prove that aggression and bonding are inextricably intertwined. Where aggression is nonexistent, feelings of love and attachment are nonexistent, too.

In all fairness, though, it should be said that learning how to engage in healthy confrontation in a marriage is often more difficult than learning how to appropriately express anger and aggression in other areas of life. In the movie *The Joker Is Wild*, Frank Sinatra, portraying a nightclub comic, quipped, "Without marriage, husbands and wives would have to fight with strangers." That's a funny line, but in fact fighting with a stranger is infinitely easier than fighting with a spouse. The closer we are to someone, the more intense our anger toward him or her is likely to be. And since frustrations in domestic life typically engender more regression than do frustrations encountered while working, socializing, driving your car in heavy traffic, or waiting in line at the post office, marital anger can be somewhat irrational as well as enormously potent.

Some of the men and women I spoke with told me they entered their marriages without any real notion of how to handle the delicate art of postnuptial combat. In their first married year, they found their way through trial and error, and in retrospect many of them felt that error had the upper hand. Others said they began their unions with very definite philosophies about expressing anger, but quickly discovered that what worked for them in any number of less intimate situations did not work in their marriages.

Claudia Howard was one newlywed who embarked on her marriage thinking she knew all about how to fight. As a child she was frequently praised by her father for her outspokenness and her "spunk." As an adult, she chose a career in law and became an assistant district attorney, known for her impassioned arguments in the courtroom and her many successes there.

"I'd always believed in speaking my mind," she said. "I was taught that if you didn't stand up for yourself people might take advantage of you, and that having an honest confrontation was better than stewing in anger. The way I was used to operating when I was angry was that I would get things out in the open and convince the other person that I was right and he was wrong, no matter how much I had to hammer away at my point."

In her marriage to Mark, Claudia was determined to be faithful to her habitual style of dealing with anger. When Mark did something that upset her, she immediately and eloquently summarized what was wrong with his behavior and why it ought to change. Unfortunately, she found she couldn't resist also telling her husband what was wrong with *him* and why *he* had to change—right away. Needless to say, Mark did not appreciate her style of honesty, and as long as she persisted in it, he did not feel inclined to change at all.

"During our first fights, I felt Claudia wasn't just criticizing my behavior," said Mark, "she was criticizing my character. If I said I wanted to spend the weekend skiing, I was selfish. If I said I didn't like opera, I was a Philistine. If I gave in to my ex-wife on some minor matter regarding the kids, I was a pushover. If I left a wet towel on the floor, which I did *once,* I was lazy and sloppy. I found myself not even trying to be flexible. I wasn't going to give her the satisfaction of doing things her way when she was so insensitive."

With two and a half years of marriage behind her, Claudia admitted to me that when she was first married her anger tended to spread uncontrollably and that her criticisms were, for the most part, exaggerated and unfair. Now, Claudia is not a naturally nasty person, just a strong-willed one. Her feistiness may have pleased her father, and her relentlessness in the courtroom may have swayed some judges and juries, but in the marital arena her way of expressing grievances just wouldn't play. She lost her sense of proportion and her angry words seemed to take on a life of their own.

In behaving as she did at the start, Claudia was falling into one of marital anger's most common traps. In voicing all of her complaints all of the time, she lost the ability to distinguish between being assertive and being insulting. Because she didn't take the time to consider her anger, or edit it, she frequently let it get out of hand. Fortunately, Claudia was wise enough to change her tactics when she saw not only that they didn't get her what she wanted, but that she and her husband both felt awful after her tirades.

Ron Clarke had a different view of anger when he married Carol. Ron was raised by parents who argued, as he put it, "perpetually and professionally." Their quarrels never seemed to resolve anything; they made matters worse. Priding himself on the "easygoing nature" he had cultivated in conscious contrast to his parents' volatile temperaments, he promised himself that his own marriage would be a model of domestic harmony.

Ron spent the first half of his first year of marriage *avoiding* quarrels. When annoyed, he sulked, moped, and was silent for what Carol considered maddening lengths of time, but when it came to outright fighting—forget it!

"The way he acted was much worse than if he'd just come out and said he was mad at me," said Carol. "I knew there were things I did that bothered him. For example, when we first got married I was a terrible driver. It seemed as though every time I tried to back out of our narrow driveway, or navigate one of those labyrinthine Los Angeles parking garages, I would scratch the car. Ron never complained when that happened, he just touched up the paint and refused to talk to me for the rest of the day, or else he just talked in monosyllables. Then he started making little 'jokes' about my driving in front of his friends. I was mortified. Why couldn't he just tell *me* what he was thinking? You know, sometimes I think I was subconsciously trying to damage the car just to get a rise out of him.''

Finally, and fortunately, one scratch too many did the trick. Ron told his wife how reckless he thought she was being and how angry he was at the condition of the car. He suggested she take some lessons and learn to drive more carefully or buy herself a smaller second car.

Much to his surprise, this communication did not result in the verbal Armageddon he had feared. Both he and Carol began to feel less tense. He stopped poking fun at his wife in public, and her driving, slowly but surely, improved. Having just celebrated his fourth wedding anniversary, Ron now knows that an occasional private expression of displeasure on his part, or on Carol's, for that matter, is not going to do irreparable harm to their relationship. In fact, quite the opposite.

Claudia Howard's and Ron Clarke's initially misguided behavior patterns are typical of the most prevalent schools of thought regarding the expression of anger. School number one is the Getting It Off Your Chest school. Its proponents, like Claudia, may start out as champions of honesty, but they face the danger of overreacting to every little slight. In a marriage, such behavior can make a spouse feel underestimated, unappreciated, and, worst of all, unloved.

School number two is the Peace at Any Price school. Its subscribers, like Ron, will do almost anything to avoid the uncomfortable feelings that accompany verbalizing their anger. But in attempting not to battle with their partners, such people are fighting losing battles with themselves. Their negative feelings have a way of expressing themselves in other forms—in Ron's case through petulance and sarcasm; in other people, through more subtle but equally hurtful ways. Sooner or later, their spouses will sense their untold anger and become alienated, perhaps even deliberately provocative.

For all the differences between the two schools of thought, they do have one thing in common: they don't work. When it comes to expressing anger effectively in marriage, it's a bad idea to say too much and an equally bad idea to say too little. A good emotional balance can be achieved only by finding a middle ground.

It is possible to learn how to verbalize angry feelings without damaging a partner's ego or one's own self-esteem, but in order to do that one must understand the fundamental ground rules for fighting in marriage. Though each couple must contend with its own unique circumstances and problems and with the partners' individual temperaments and styles, most marital therapists agree that certain strategies work best to keep a healthy difference of opinion from deteriorating into a mutually destructive interchange. What follows are some general guidelines for fighting fair and for keeping matrimony free of acrimony:

Remember the "I's." As discussed in Chapter 4, criticisms that begin with "I" are far less provocative than those that begin with "you." In the midst of an argument, it's especially important, though admittedly somewhat harder, to stick with "I" messages. In the heat of anger, a natural tendency is to blame and accuse, but saying "You do this to me" and "You do that to me" is apt to incite tit-for-tat rebuttals and create vicious circles. The more often you can manage to say instead, "I feel angry because this-and-that has happened," the better your chances will be for preventing a minor quarrel from escalating into a major battle.

Stay in the moment. A good way to keep a disagreement from turning into a global dispute is to stay in the present, rather than dredge up past incidents and behavior. If you have a legitimate complaint about something your spouse has done, try phrasing your grievances in terms of a "now" message rather than an "always and again" message. A now message might say:

> It's very chilly in the living room and I feel uncomfortable. I know you like this room kept colder than I do but I'd like you to shut the window now.

The "always and again" version might be:

> It's very chilly in here again. You always keep the living room too cold. You always have to have things your way. Well, you better shut the window and keep it shut.

If the second message is the one put forth, chances are the living room won't be the only thing that's chilly—your spouse may well give you the cold shoulder. Reminding someone of past misbehavior is not only provocative, it's futile. What's done is done and can't be undone, no matter how much you argue about it.

Count higher than ten. In her book *Anger: The Misunderstood Emotion*, social psychologist Carol Tavris compares marital anger to an onion because it so often consists of layers within layers, causes within causes. Knowing why you're angry with your spouse is not always easy, especially in the confusing early phases of the union. Before venting your anger, though, it's sensible to try to comprehend it as best you can, since doing so will often lessen its intensity.

Our mothers often told us to count to ten before speaking when we were angry. The impulse behind this kernel of wisdom is solid but (sorry, Mom!) the specifics are wrong. Ten seconds is not nearly long enough to process such a potent emotion. Instead, try waiting an hour or two, or even a day. If you take this kind of time to decide *why* you are angry, you may well find that your reasons are not pressing enough to justify a full-scale, full-speed-ahead confrontation. Perhaps your outrage is even somewhat silly. At best, you may decide that laughing at yourself is a more appropriate reaction than lashing out at someone else. At worst, you may decide that your anger is completely justified, but having made use of a cooling-down period, you now may be able to present your complaint less aggressively than you might have otherwise—perhaps in the form of a suggestion or a question.

Consider your timing. One advantage of holding off from acting on your feelings until you interpret them is that time becomes your ally. It's up to you to choose the right moment to say your piece. If you're wise, you'll choose a moment that is opportune not only for you but for your partner. Don't introduce a potentially volatile topic just as a horde of in-laws is about to arrive for dinner, or when your spouse has just come home from a grueling day at the office. What you want to find is a time when both you and your mate are in a relatively placid frame of mind and have the opportunity for a little prolonged privacy.

While you're waiting for the appropriate moment to present itself, though, don't make the mistake of exacerbating your angry feelings by rehearsing what you plan to say over and over in your head and anticipating your part-

111

ner's responses. As Tavris points out, there's a difference between examining anger and rehearsing it. The former can make you calmer while the latter, studies show, often only serves to make you angrier.

Hands off emotional push buttons. Everyone has certain Achilles' heels, sensitive spots that are especially vulnerable to attack. When we say that So-and-So "really knows how to push my buttons," we usually mean that someone knows how to zero in on our points of vulnerability, make us feel bad about ourselves, and trip off a kind of automatic anger alarm.

If someone's emotional push buttons are pressed during an argument, a run-of-the-mill quarrel can suddenly escalate beyond all reason and expectation. New husbands and wives all too often are dangerously unaware of the particular remarks that may trigger disproportionate reactions in their spouses. Like drivers on unfamiliar roads, they don't know when to slow down or swerve to avoid potholes or bumps.

One doesn't need a Ph.D. in psychology to know that it's unwise to call a weight-conscious woman "Tubby" or a short man "Tiny," but many of our vulnerable spots are not so obvious. Emotional push buttons are often triggered by remarks that are all too familiar to us, hurtful comments that echo those we heard repeatedly from significant people in our past—especially parents and siblings.

If a wife complains that her husband is lazy, she may unwittingly remind him of all the times his mother told him he was not competitive enough in Little League, not ambitious enough about schoolwork, not much of a go-getter when it came to soliciting subscriptions on his paper route. If a husband says his wife is vain, he may unknowingly call up all the times her sister reproached her for hogging the bathroom mirror or using the last bit of hair spray.

New spouses have three tools for learning how to steer clear of their mates' psychic jugulars. The first is *observation*—and here's where you'll want to don your detective hat again. Noticing how your partner and his or her family interact can provide some valuable clues. Does your husband sigh and groan when his brother teases him about the time he nearly blew up his first car when tinkering with the engine? Chances are this man has already heard enough about his dubious mechanical abilities. Does your wife flinch and flush when her father recalls her "two left feet" in the third-grade ballet extravaganza? This woman has no desire to have her clumsiness remarked upon further.

The second tool is *experience*. It's practically certain that a rookie husband or wife will occasionally push a button he or she honestly didn't know was there. If a certain remark detonates an emotional explosion, that should be enough to warn you that you are playing with dynamite. Be pragmatic—don't light that fuse again.

The third useful tool is *intuition*. In many ways, married people "guess" about their spouses more than they really know on a conscious level. The unconscious is a vast reserve of knowledge, so trusting one's instincts to make certain gut-level guesses makes good use of a finely tuned receptor. If you have a strong sense that certain things are better left unsaid, you're probably right.

Know whose emotions are whose. Projective identification can be a prime source of misunderstanding in marriage. In first-year fights, before couples have resolved certain issues of oneness and separateness, this mechanism can play an especially large role.

Projective identification, you'll recall, is when we deny

some of our own unwanted traits and ascribe them to others with whom we are close. Since projective identification is the source of many unfair criticisms, its use can be inflammatory. When the pot calls the kettle black, the kettle feels unjustly accused. When a parsimonious husband calls his wife tightfisted, or an uncommunicative wife calls her husband withdrawn, it's easy to see how angry confusion can ensue, how feelings can be hurt, and how resentment can build. When you recognize and criticize your own faults in your spouse, your mate becomes a scapegoat, doomed to bear psychic burdens that are really yours to deal with.

"If you could eliminate projective identification," says psychoanalyst Benito Perri, "you could eliminate the vast majority of marital problems." Unfortunately, this unconscious process is difficult to vanquish completely. But while you may not be able to rid yourself entirely of projecting, just knowing the process exists may help you to better understand your feelings and your behavior.

Projection is yet another factor to take into account when trying to discover why you're angry and whether the target of your anger should rightly be your spouse. Perhaps the person you're really angry with or disappointed in is yourself.

Another unconscious mechanism you should be aware of is something called "emotional contagion." Emotional contagion is a first cousin of projective identification. It occurs when you accept your spouse's projections and unwittingly take on his or her emotions. Becoming aware of this mechanism can help you distinguish your own anger from anger that you may be acting out on your partner's behalf. Taking action on feelings induced in you, and attitudes projected *onto* you, by your mate can lead to many a marital *folie à deux*.

Example: A husband tells his wife that their next-door

neighbor's dog has just dug up the flowerbed he's spent the last three weekends planting. The wife senses her husband's wrath, becomes enraged at the neighbors, and wastes no time in calling them up demanding apologies and restitution. In jumping on the anger that is really her husband's, she's denied him the opportunity to deal with the situation himself. Oddly enough, even if he unconsciously intended to make his wife the "designated screamer," her husband may not be consciously grateful to her. Since he's left holding on to a lot of unexpressed rage, he may aim some of it at his all too cooperative spouse, whom he'll perhaps accuse of being rude or unduly hysterical. Think what a complicated quarrel might then occur!

Before acting on a feeling, it's important to live with it long enough to know whom it belongs to. There's a real difference between empathy, which allows us to *understand* someone else's emotions, and emotional contagion, which tempts us to steal them away. It may be hard to let your mate fight his or her own battles in the world, but it's necessary. After all, your partner is a grown-up, just like you.

Take turns with big-league anger. Regardless of how hard couples try to fight fair and to find constructive ways of expressing displeasure, there will be times in every marriage when one person or the other lets loose an uncensored storm of anger. If the partner at whom the blow-up is aimed responds by blowing up too, the high-decibel result may raise blood pressures and irk the neighbors, but it won't solve anything at all. If, on the other hand, one partner can resist what may well be a natural inclination to respond *to* yelling *with* yelling, chances are the storm will blow over without causing too much damage.

If your mate is unable to resist an occasional temper

tantrum, your job is to refrain from joining in and throwing one right back. By staying calm and speaking softly, by countering accusations with neutral phrases like, "That's an interesting point," "I hear what you're telling me," or "I need time to think about that," you're not sacrificing the opportunity to speak your mind, you're just postponing it.

Taking turns with anger may sound easier said than done. Anger stokes its own fires, and its power can be seductive. Who can blame you for wanting to get in on the action? You've got your grievances, too. But look at it this way: a child in the throes of a temper tantrum is, whether he knows it or not, counting on the fact that his parents will not react in kind. If Mom and Dad started wailing and stomping every time Junior did, Junior would never learn what it means to grow up. If husbands and wives do too much simultaneous ranting and raving, their marriages may never grow up.

Those who are beginning a marriage may find it difficult to wait for a future time at which to vent their anger. When their loving mates are busy erupting like volcanos, they wonder whether there *is* a future for the two of them. The chances for that future are greatly enhanced, however, by the ability to resist fighting fire with fire.

So far, the guidelines here have dealt with the how-to's of coping with anger in marriage, but the how-*not*-to's of anger management are at least equally important. If you don't want always to remember the occasions of your first fights as your worst married times, you should probably keep the following caveats in mind:

Don't use threats or "cry wolf." Newlyweds often are all too quick to threaten divorce or other drastic measures in the heat of anger. Threats don't work unless you mean them (and chances are you don't). Even said half jokingly, they can scare your partner and provoke him or her into making retaliatory threats, resulting in what psychiatrist M. Scott Peck calls the "I'll desert you before you desert me" syndrome (otherwise known as "you can't fire me, I quit"). Your quarrel can easily become reminiscent of the taunting fights you used to have in your elementary school playground, except here the stakes are higher. You especially don't want to have your threat perceived as a dare. Some people just can't resist a dare.

Don't blackmail your partner. Some of the people I spoke with recalled instances of their partners' refusing them sex or other "favors" if they didn't give in on certain issues. Extortion is not only extremely provocative, it's simply not nice. What you've got here, after all, is a marriage—not organized crime.

Don't be a brinksman (or brinkswoman). Some newlyweds test each other's degree of commitment by seeing just how far they can push their spouses during an argument and still have someone to wake up next to in the morning. In the long run, there's only one answer to the question of how far you can go with such dangerous experiments: just so far and no farther. Do you really want to walk that fine a line?

Don't blame your spouse for problems you had before marriage. Many newlyweds haven't experienced a domestic argument since they left their parents' homes. Some of their early marital spats may, in fact, be little more than continuations of the arguments they stopped having with their mothers, fathers, sisters, and brothers. If they lost these quarrels before, they may be especially determined to win them now. Reenacting outdated battles with your mate is just another manifestation of transference and of the "compulsion to repeat." The first year of marriage will afford you plenty of real opportunities to get angry at your mate for reasons anchored in the present; there's no sense in getting angry for reasons rooted in the past.

Don't interpret your mate's unconscious aloud. Using your unconscious to pick up clues about your partner's reasons for anger is all fine and good. Telling your partner what you think you've learned, however, can make him or her feel exposed, embarrassed, and highly defensive. Using such phrases as "What you're really afraid of is . . ." "What you're really trying to say is . . ." or "The real reason you're angry is . . ." during a quarrel is always a mistake. If our partners wanted us to interpret their hidden fears and motives or label their lingering neuroses, they would have engaged us as shrinks, not spouses.

Don't bring third parties into an argument. It's unfair to blame your spouse for the behavior of his or her family or friends. If you've suffered a slight at their hands, you may have a legitimate grievance that merits calm discussion at another time. But bringing up such complaints during a fight practically ensures that your spouse will defend their behavior to the bitter end.

Partners with children may be partially responsible for *their* behavior, but if the fight is not about them, leave them out of it. If it *is* about them, keep your complaints specific rather than branding them as incorrigible demons who should be sentenced to several years at hard labor.

Don't fight in front of others. Making a scene in front of strangers is embarrassing enough. Doing so at your best friends' dinner table is even worse. No one quite knows what to do when a couple starts bickering in their company. They may say, "Ahem, would one of you please pass the salt," but they're probably thinking, When are these two going *home?*

If you have children, quarreling in their presence is especially inadvisable. All kids become upset when their parents fight, even if they try not to show it. Often they imagine *they're* responsible. Children who have been casualties of a divorce are especially likely to think they are the "real problem" and to envision yet another supposedly stable environment coming apart at the seams. You need not always agree with your partner when the kids are around, but if you're going to disagree ardently, wait until they're not.

And last, but definitely not least, for those who are remarried:

Don't ever compare your present spouse unfavorably with your ex. For reasons so obvious they need no explanation, no matter how mad *you* are, this tactic is 100 percent guaranteed to make your spouse even madder.

Making Up

No discussion of marital quarrels would be complete without considering how couples reinstate peace in their households. Marriage is no place to carry grudges. Making up after a fight is a wonderful opportunity to reaffirm your love for and your commitment to your spouse. What's more, as most newlyweds have probably learned before marriage, making up can be a lot of fun.

Despite the now-famous trope "Love is never having to say you're sorry," saying they're sorry after a fight is just about the best thing married people can do for each other and for their relationships. In the aftermath of an argument, it's far less important to figure out whose fault it was, or who was "right," than it is to get things back on an even keel. Besides, the odds are good that both partners are partially responsible for starting a fight and that both were partly right and partly wrong in the positions they took. It generally takes two to tangle.

There are, of course, many ways of saying "I'm sorry." Many of the husbands and wives I talked with developed their own rituals for doing so. Some brought flowers, some cooked their partners' favorite meals—or their partners' kids' favorite meals—and some thought of ways to make their mates laugh, dispelling the tension between them. However you get the message across, the idea is not to grovel, belittle yourself, or swear that you will never ever behave badly again. If you're like every other married person on the planet, you probably will. The point is simply to let your partner know that you still feel affection and are willing to let bygones be bygones.

Perhaps the most important thing to keep in mind about making up is not to let too much time go by before you do it. "Don't go to bed angry," a piece of advice that is heard often enough to seem a bit shopworn, is actually a very wise policy. It's always nicer to wake up in the morning with a clean slate than it is to wake up carrying a lot of leftover psychic baggage. But whether you are more comfortable making up before bed or *in* bed (one newlywed said she and her husband referred to their bed as "Little Switzerland," a neutral ground on which they could always find a way to reach accord), or at breakfast or *before* breakfast the next day, you should never let more than twenty-four hours go by without making a move toward reconciliation. If you do, you risk deepening and "setting" your own and your partner's negative feelings and creating a chasm between you that will be harder to bridge later on.

Of course, your partner isn't the only one you have to help feel better in the wake of a fight; you have to take care of yourself as well. In the twenty-four hours following a quarrel, it's not a bad idea to work through your residual emotions. Examine how you felt during the argument and how you feel now. Try to recall how the fight got started and what it really was about. If the quarrel taught you anything about yourself or your spouse, now would be a good time to make a mental note of it; if the argument got out of hand, now would be a good opportunity to think about ways of minimizing the chances of its happening again.

One thing you shouldn't do during this time, however, is to let yourself dwell on feelings of guilt. Family therapist W. Robert Beavers has a rule of thumb about guilt: "It is useful if it doesn't last more than five minutes and if it produces a change in behavior." That's a wise rule, indeed. If you think you acted like something of a jerk during your marital spat, it's fine for you to try to correct your jerklike propensities next time around, but beating yourself up about what you've just done isn't going to help you *or* your partner. Just because you're not perfect doesn't mean you're unlovable or impossible to live with. It only means you're human.

Once you've given yourself a full day to process your feelings, the next thing to do is put the argument behind you. To ruminate too long over any quarrel is to live in the past. Your unconscious will be happy to mull over any unfinished business, leaving you to get on with the business at hand—living in the present with the person you love most.

Two First-Year Fights

Having looked at the dynamics of quarreling and reconciling, let's now look at some specific arguments that took place in the first married year of two of the couples I spoke with. What caused these fights to take place? How were they handled by both husband and wife?

The following quarrel occurred between Charlie and Robin Turner in their sixth month of marriage. By the time I interviewed the Turners, a full year later, they laughingly referred to this incident as their "Diet Cola War." But they weren't laughing when it happened. They were too busy discovering that sometimes the smallest things can set off a marital tempest.

One morning Robin said she had to work overtime and would be home late. Charlie volunteered to stop by the supermarket on his way home and do the grocery shopping. Robin told him what they needed from the store and asked for some diet cola for herself.

When Robin returned home she noticed that Charlie had purchased several of the wrong items, including some nondiet soda. She announced, somewhat irritably, that she was going to the delicatessen a few blocks away to get the right kind of soft drink. Charlie said he didn't understand why someone as slim as Robin wanted diet soda anyhow, and that going out at that late hour to get it bordered on the fanatical.

Robin left anyway, and when she got back she found a very irate husband. "What's really the matter?" he asked. "Nothing," she replied. "I was just thirsty.'' Charlie pressed her, asking again what was *really* wrong. Robin told him he'd neglected to buy several things they needed and that she would have to make another trip to the supermarket.

"Oh, I see,'' said Charlie. "And do you have any other complaints? You must have other reasons why you think I'm such a terrible husband.'

At that point, Robin let loose a barrage of grievances. Charlie never took out the trash and he always forgot to empty the dishwasher. She had to do everything. He didn't care about the house and he didn't care about her. *And furthermore,* he never let her listen to classical music because *he* disliked it, he lost too much money playing poker with his friends, and his mother had neglected to send her a birthday card.

Charlie countered with a list of his own. Robin dieted all the time when she didn't need to. There was never anything in the house for him to eat. She bought too many clothes and took up too much closet space. She hogged all the bedcovers at night. *And by the way,* his mother might send her birthday cards in the future if Robin would only call her "Mom'' as requested.

Robin said she was too tired to listen to any more of this nonsense. She announced she was going to sleep on the living room sofa so Charlie could have all the bedcovers to himself. And she did.

It was several days before the Turners shared a bed or even a tension-free conversation.

What happened here? How did something as trivial as diet cola come between two people who cared deeply for each other? In looking back on this quarrel, Robin and Charlie were able to describe some of the hidden motives that lay beneath its surface.

Charlie felt his attempt to be a good husband and take on the chore of grocery shopping was undermined by Robin's nitpicking. Since childhood, he'd been sensitive to criticism that he was inattentive to his chores. Whenever he raked the leaves or cleaned out the garage, his father scolded him for not doing it right, then insisted on doing it over himself.

Charlie also admitted that early in his marriage he had felt threatened by Robin's constant dieting because he feared she was doing it to make herself attractive to other men.

Robin said she never wanted the argument to happen, even though she was annoyed by her husband's carelessness when buying the groceries. She thought that by going to buy her own soda and taking care of her own immediate needs she would avoid a confrontation. But she was egged on by Charlie's persistent provocations, and finally she couldn't resist giving him what he seemed to be asking for: an all-out assault. She was actually surprised when he responded in kind.

As for her habitual weight-watching, she said she had behaved that way throughout her courtship with Charlie, indeed all through her life. Her mother and sisters were seriously overweight and she feared she would end up that way too unless she was careful. She thought Charlie should have been more sensitive to her concern, since she'd explained it to him many times.

The Turners' Diet Cola War is typical of many early marital arguments. Though its origins lay partly in the circumstances of the moment, the fight was greatly exacerbated by the bugaboos of the past and the insecurities that both husband and wife brought with them to the marriage.

Charlie might have avoided a scene altogether if he'd apologized for buying the wrong items, or if he had simply let Robin express a little annoyance and be done with it. Instead, he became overly defensive and actually goaded Robin into attacking him. Still angry with his father for labeling him a thoughtless and inattentive son, he baited his wife into chastising him for being a thoughtless and inattentive spouse.

Under other circumstances Robin might have known better than to cooperate with Charlie's unconscious attempt to have her re-create his father's role. She might also have realized, from Charlie's extreme reaction to her initial minor annoyance, that she had unknowingly pushed the wrong emotional button. But this was one quarrel that was clearly ill timed. After an exceptionally long work day, she was not at her best.

Though she was indeed provoked into scolding her husband, Robin went overboard. Giving vent to frustrations that apparently had long been brewing, she threw everything but the kitchen sink into her catalogue of complaints. And by attacking her mother-in-law, whose behavior was completely irrelevant to the issues at hand, she practically assured that Charlie would take his mother's side.

Some of Robin's reactions were understandable. Since Charlie knew about her fear of weight gain he should not have questioned it at such a tense moment. In doing so, he too pushed an emotional button. Robin's irritation about the shopping errors also seems justifiable, but by telling Charlie what he "always" did wrong and "never" did right, she turned a here-and-now skirmish into a historic tug-of-war. And by sleeping on the sofa, thus implying there would be no reconciliation or lovemaking until Charlie straightened up and flew right, she only prolonged the couple's stand-off.

There was no hero in this fight, and no villain—just two newlyweds trying to come to grips with the ghosts of the past and the quandaries of the moment. Both parties, though, could have spared themselves and each other a good deal of hurt if they'd been more aware at the time of the many layers of this argument and the ways in which they were feeding the flames of each other's anger.

This next quarrel took place between Dave and Megan Brown eight months after their wedding:

It was New Year's Eve. Dave and Megan had long-standing plans to have dinner with another couple at a quiet French restaurant near their home. Dave had specifically requested that they keep their celebration low-key. He'd always disliked this particular holiday—too much noise, too many crowds, too much drinking and driving.

A few hours before their planned departure, the phone rang. Megan answered. When she hung up she told her husband that one of her public relations agency's most important clients had insisted that she and Dave stop by his New Year's Eve party after dinner. She couldn't refuse, she said, because it might be bad for business. Would Dave mind going for just a little while?

Dave said he would mind very much. Their plans had been set for months. He didn't want to run out early on their dinner companions, and he didn't want to drive to a party several miles away late at night. He complained that his wife was being thoughtless and self-serving. He said she always put her clients and co-workers before him, and that ever since they'd married she'd acted like she should call all the shots in their relationship because her work was more glamorous and better paying than his teaching job.

Megan was aghast. She offered to call back her client and make excuses. But Dave said no, he didn't want to be accused of ruining her "golden opportunity." "We'll go to the party," he said, "and then we'll talk about the divorce."

"Fine," said Megan. "Who wants to be married to a stick-in-the-mud, anyhow?" Dave wasn't outgoing enough, she said, and he didn't know how to have fun. Furthermore, if he felt his profession wasn't as exciting as hers, that was *his* problem.

The Browns went to dinner and then to the party, though they had a pretty miserable time at both. The next morning they both felt ashamed of themselves and sentimental about the holiday. Over a champagne brunch, they each made promises that were virtually impossible to keep. Dave vowed never again to resist attending any function that would help his wife professionally. He further promised to be the life of the party at them all. Megan swore she would never let a client's wishes take priority over her husband's wishes and that the demands of her job would never ever again interfere with her marriage.

Again, neither party involved in this quarrel wore a white hat or a black hat. Both Dave and Megan were trying to reconcile their individual priorities with their commitment to each other.

Megan was thoughtless in agreeing to attend the party without consulting her husband, but Dave overreacted to her slight. He also missed an opportunity to let his wife make immediate amends by not taking her up on her offer to back out of attending the party. He *said* he didn't want to risk her resentment, but instead he threatened divorce, albeit partly in jest, and frightened her into taking a toughminded stance of her own when she didn't get the "joke."

In trying to repair the damage done, both parties made the mistake of bending over backward to appease each other and making unrealistic pledges out of a disproportionate sense of guilt. Their way of making up was as melodramatic as their way of arguing.

The Browns' quarrel unearthed some serious issues: professional envy; the balance of commitments to work, to friends, and to the marriage; and differences in how each partner liked to socialize. Trying to eradicate issues as complex as these overnight is like trying to treat a compound fracture with a Band-aid.

In reminiscing about this fight nearly two years into their marriage, Dave and Megan agreed they would have been wiser simply to kiss and make up and then think for a while about how they might work toward some reasonable compromises rather than pave the way for future letdowns by promising instant changes in their personalities and priorities.

If You Fall Off the Wagon

It should come as no surprise that the Browns and the Turners, as well as all the other couples I talked with, said that they continued to argue throughout their first year of marriage and beyond it. The good news is that most of these couples felt their first fights taught them a good deal about the ins and outs of marital quarrels and about their own and each other's ways of coping with conflict. Now they find that much of the time they are able to disagree in constructive ways and avoid the sorts of anger traps they unwittingly fell into early on. The not-so-good, though not-so-shocking, news is that every once in a while they temporarily forget what they've learned.

As virtually every person who has considered anger from a psychological or philosophical perspective knows, this integral human emotion is one that simply cannot always be gotten under control. As Montaigne said, "There is no passion that so shakes the clarity of our judgment as anger."

Where anger is concerned, big people sometimes act like big babies. We give in to impulse and forget to heed the voice of common sense. We say things we wish we hadn't said, we do things we wish we hadn't done, and we often feel more than a little foolish for having said and done them. But that doesn't make us harpies or ogres or even emotional nincompoops. Anger is a natural outgrowth of our fundamental aggressive drive, a drive without which we could not live or love. But the kind of learning that enables us to rein in so basic an instinct is the hardest kind of learning there is.

In your marriage there will almost certainly be times when bad temper gets the best of you and your spouse and when your mutual anger results in the kind of quarrel that creates more heat then light. But just because that happens once in a while doesn't mean you have to make a habit of it.

Learning to express angry feelings appropriately is something like going on a weight-loss diet. You vow that this time you're going to stick to your guns and eliminate junk food from your life. For weeks you keep the promise you made to yourself, turning up your nose at Cheez-its, Twinkies, and Ding-Dongs and eating nothing but fruits, vegetables, and poached fish. One night, though, in the grips of an overpowering urge, you wolf down two fudge brownies and half a pint of rum raisin ice cream. Now what? You can either abandon all your good efforts and continue to eat everything in sight or forgive yourself, put a halt to your binge before too much damage has been done, and go back to dining on salmon and salads.

The same holds true for an anger binge. You can throw in the towel after "falling off the wagon" and convince yourself it's useless ever again to try to express anger in a more restrained fashion. Or you can grant yourself and your partner amnesty for your intermittent indiscretions and move along. Occasional failures to be paragons of self-control and restraint don't make you or your spouse a failure, and there's absolutely no reason why they should make your relationship a failure. So, if you find yourself unable at times to obey the "rules" of marital combat, don't despair. A few food fests won't spoil a long-term diet if you're really committed to getting rid of your extra pounds, and a few shouting matches shouldn't spoil a long-term love if you and your mate are really committed to each other.

6

The "M" Word

"WE BARELY DISCUSSED IT when we were dating or even when we were engaged," said one newlywed. "Believe it or not, the subject hardly ever came up," said another. "I guess you could say we talked *around* it, but not really *about* it," said a third.

What are these recently wed men and women referring to? What subject could possibly be so volatile that it is skirted with such astonishing regularity during courtship? Sex? Old flames? Politics? Religion? Uh-uh, no sir! A widespread reticence when it comes to dealing with *m-m-money* before the wedding bells chime assures that many newlyweds have a great many postnuptial surprises in store and economic quandaries to solve.

As startling as it may seem, many of the husbands and wives I spoke with said they entered their marriages with vague, imprecise, or even completely erroneous notions of exactly how much their spouses-to-be earned, owned, or owed. Their blissful obliviousness when it came to money matters was, apparently, not unusual. In *American Couples*, a book based on an extensive ten-year study of the impact of finances, work, and sex on relationships, authors Philip Blumstein and Pepper Schwartz call money "the last frontier of self-disclosure." "Money," they write, "is often a more taboo topic of conversation than sex, and courting couples may discuss their prior sex lives while never raising the question of their economic histories."

That money matters are often a largely, if not entirely, neglected topic of conversation between two people falling in love is certainly understandable. It's not very romantic to provide your beloved with a detailed account of your pension benefits, charitable contributions, or child support payments, nor is it terribly entertaining to spend time explaining to the object of your affections why you've chosen to balance your portfolio between tax-free bonds and aggressive-growth mutual funds.

People so much want to be loved for themselves that they often look upon revealing the extent of their wealth or indebtedness as a risky business. Those fortunate souls with oodles of money may not want to *say* they have lots of it for fear that prospective mates will be impressed for all the wrong reasons. Those people with money problems may fear their predicaments will make them less viable candidates for a trip to the altar. Either way, a lack of complete prenuptial candor when it comes to the black or red ink in one's ledger books is not a deliberate deceit so much as it is a bit of discreet prewedding editing.

On top of all this, most of us consider our own ways of handling dollars and cents a deeply personal and private affair. Justifying our fiscal methodology to a loved one before marriage can go against the grain, reminding us— when we may not want to be consciously reminded—that marriage will mean giving up a certain degree of autonomy in this area, too! And divulging our individual financial eccentricities and superstitions can make us feel embarrassed.

Of course, asking about a loved one's financial state can be even more embarrassing than revealing one's own. Regardless of the fact that our mothers may have told us, "It's just as easy to fall in love with a rich person as a poor one," and despite the old English proverb that warns, "He who marries for love without money hath merry nights and sorry days," many people consider it intrusive and even a bit vulgar to inquire about a lover's bank balance or the contents of his or her safety deposit box. In the old days, parents may have made such indelicate inquiries in negotiating a marriage contract on their children's behalf, but today, as Blumstein and Schwartz point out, "the matchmaking that currently takes place—on college campuses, at parties given by friends, in singles bars—operates less openly on the gold standard."

Certainly not all newlyweds are completely in the dark when it comes to each other's monetary situation. Couples who have executed prenuptial agreements, for example, know more than most. But even those couples who know something of each other's financial assets may marry without knowing much about each other's financial attitudes. An enormous number of couples find themselves forging full speed ahead into matrimony without first having discussed such nuts-and-bolts issues as how—or whether—they will budget, who will be responsible for paying what bills, and whether or not money will be pooled. They may have *assumptions* aplenty about how such matters will be dealt with, but, once wed, they may quickly learn their assumptions are diametrically opposed to those of their partners.

Yet such a lack of realistic planning is also easy to understand. When people are marrying for the first time, they may not realize how many significant decisions about money have to be made jointly. When people are remarrying, they may simply expect to handle financial details approximately the same way they did the last time around. And when couples live together before they wed, one or both parties may anticipate—often incorrectly, given the way marriage can alter people's perceptions and priorities—a more or less routine continuation of the arrangements they already have. What's more, couples courting under any of these circumstances may deem in-depth discussions of future money strategies mundane. During a time when both partners are rhapsodically focused on the wedded bliss they hope to find ahead, no one wants to be the first to introduce such tedious topics as who is better at balancing a checkbook and who does or doesn't believe that revolving credit is the greatest invention since the wheel.

The long and the short of it is that when it comes to the "M" word, most couples take the attitude that they will, somehow or other, deal with the logistics of it after marriage. There's nothing fundamentally wrong in adopting this position—and even if there were, saying so would probably not dissuade most people from taking it—provided both spouses do indeed make a determined effort to address the subject of money fairly soon after taking their vows.

In reviewing studies going back several decades, Blumstein and Schwartz found that "between one quarter and one third of all married couples ranked money as their primary problem." Clearly, the way you and your spouse can keep yourselves from joining the ranks of couples plagued by financial discord is to communicate with each other. The more candidly and objectively you and your mate can state, right up front, what your financial status is, what your philosophy regarding money is, and what your financial priorities are, the better your chances will be of avoiding future monetary struggles and the kinds of accumulated resentments that result from them.

Though everyone's approach to money is bound to be somewhat different, a meeting of the minds will never be possible unless each partner knows something of how the other's mind works—and this applies to all couples regardless of how much money they have. Wealth undeniably can help cushion some of life's frustrations, but even if you're a Du Pont married to a Rockefeller, you will still have to contend, in your first year of marriage, with the sticky issues of day-to-day money management. Besides, as psychoanalyst William Kaufman writes in his essay *Some Emotional Uses of Money*, "most people, rich or poor, are more or less continually concerned—consciously or unconsciously—with the solution of their private money problems." When people marry, the fact that their private money problems aren't private anymore is all the more reason for addressing them openly.

While the transition from courtship to marriage usually causes newlyweds to realize that the time has finally come for putting their financial cards on the table, it does not necessarily make them terribly eager to do so. In fact, as Blumstein and Schwartz note, "games for avoiding communication on the subject are ingenious and widespread." Even those exceptional few who suddenly find themselves ready, willing, and able to engage in straightforward postnuptial talk about the "M" word may be stymied by a mate's refusal—or inability—to do the same, or by their own unconscious refusal to *listen* to what their partners are *really* saying on the topic. Money is certainly one area where many of us tend to hear only what we want to hear and ignore the rest.

There's simply no getting around the fact that money talk is hard for lots of people under any circumstances. Jim Polos, a certified financial planner and a vice president with a major brokerage firm, put it succinctly: "Even people who are entirely rational about almost every other aspect of their life can be irrational, totally unpredictable, or even completely careless when money comes into the picture.''

According to Polos, ''One of the most important things newlyweds can do is to try and understand their partners' emotional profile in terms of their ability to handle money, to undertake risk, and to understand the uses of money, including how it can work for you and against you.'' The key word in this savvy piece of advice is ''emotional,'' for many of our attitudes toward money are motivated a lot more by such psychological factors as fear, desire, jealousy, and even guilt than they are by logic, objectivity, and the profit motive. And internal realities, such as how much we like or dislike ourselves, how much security we crave, and what significant people in our past we identify with (not to mention how we've been influenced by our cultural and religious backgrounds and how susceptible we are to mass-media messages that instruct us to buy, buy, buy!) often have a lot more impact on our saving and spending decisions than external realities like whether interest rates are up, whether inflation or deflation reigns, or whether bulls or bears control the stock market.

Whatever your emotional reactions to money may be, one thing is for sure: you didn't develop them overnight. In fact, people probably begin developing at least some of their financial attitudes when they are very young.

As Kaufman points out, the first sense that most of us have about money is that it is a magical thing. As small children, we see our parents put their hands in their pockets, withdraw paper or shiny round objects—from what we perceive as an inexhaustible supply—and trade them for food, clothing, toys, a ride on the bus, a ride on a pony, or—if we grew up in Beverly Hills or Shaker Heights— perhaps a pony itself. By the time we are allotted a meager amount of cash and coins to handle on our own, usually somewhere between the ages of five and nine, we already have implanted in our minds the notion that money leads to gratification.

Some children act on this belief by impulsively spending their allowance as soon as they get it on whatever will bring them the most immediate pleasure. Despite their parents' admonitions that money doesn't grow on trees, they are loath to let go of the belief that there will always be more of it. Such children are very much like—and might possibly grow up to be—the type of adult who spends lavishly and indiscriminately, running up debts and ignoring, or attempting to ignore, the consequences.

On the other hand, children with different kinds of personalities and predispositions may react in an opposite fashion to the finite weekly sum doled out by Mom and Dad. They may not only recognize the limitations imposed by their allowance but react to them by hiding and hoarding their small bit of capital. For them, gratification comes from *holding on* to their precious currency, not in letting it go. Their sense of security and control that comes from a full piggy bank is akin to that of certain grown-ups who feel weak and vulnerable unless they have a cache of cash in reserve. In fact, some of these frugal little tykes may end up with a lifelong habit of parsimony and a tendency to save compulsively.

Most children, however, fall somewhere in between these two extremes. They grow to recognize money's potential as a source of both pleasure and frustration, and they develop an ambivalent attitude toward it. Most of us adults, too, react to money with ambivalence. We act out that psychological fact by developing ambiguous and enigmatic spending and saving habits. We may spend money on certain things happily, on other things guiltily, and on yet other things grudgingly. We may sometimes save prudently or, like bargain hunters who spend five dollars in gas driving from store to store to save a few pennies, we may confuse saving with squandering. We may vacillate between unjustified splurging in order to reward ourselves and unwarranted scrimping in order to punish ourselves.

The fact that most money-related behavior embodies so many contradictions makes it difficult to get an exact handle on one's own emotional-financial profile, let alone a mate's. But by applying observation, experience, and intuition, newlyweds should be able to unearth at least some clues to why their mates feel the way they do about money and how their feelings affect their reactions. Noticing how spending money or refraining from spending it makes your partner feel may not give you a foolproof method of predicting his or her every financial move, but it will give you some general understanding of your mate's predominant patterns; and paying attention to your partner's money quirks may not get you to endorse the way he or she allocates dollars and cents, but it may help you to empathize more with your mate's sense of priorities.

Of course, to complicate matters even further, you'll have to pay attention in order to figure out, as best you can, how marriage itself has affected your partner's—and your own—feelings toward money matters. Unfortunately, even people who managed to develop a reasonably well-balanced approach to money when they were single may evidence some unreasonable attitudes toward money after becoming husbands or wives. Considering that couples at all economic levels may find themselves overextended in the aftermath of throwing a wedding party, taking a honeymoon trip, moving, buying furniture, and the like, a certain amount of postnuptial pecuniary angst may be natural. But some newlyweds exhibit peculiar financial behavior in their relationships that has little to do with such immediate practical concerns.

Some newlyweds may equate money with love, and demand their spouses provide for them as proof of affection.

One women I spoke with said her husband tried to "test" her love shortly after marriage by announcing he was leaving his medical practice to pursue a graduate degree in philosophy, which he hoped she would finance. "The strangest thing," she told me, "was that I knew deep down he didn't really want to do this at his stage of his life. He just wanted to see if I would flee or stand by. Ultimately he 'changed his mind' and decided to stay where he was." By the same token, some new spouses may be overgenerous toward their partners in order to express loving emotions they have trouble putting into words. Another woman said, "My husband bought me a lot of jewelry in our first year. That may sound like a nice 'problem' to have, but his extravagance made me really nervous. I would have been much happier if he'd told me how much he valued *me* rather than giving me valuable things."

Newlyweds with stepchildren may even go overboard in spending money on their new sons and daughters, in an attempt to prove to their partners how much they love and accept their kids. As one man said, "When my wife and I first married, I bought her two-year-old son a new toy or stuffed animal almost every day. There were pandas, giraffes, and whatnot all over the house. I think he was pretty oblivious to most of them, but it was my way of saying to *her* that I cared about them both. Finally, my wife told me enough was enough. She said I'd spoil the boy silly and go broke in the process."

Other newlyweds may tend to employ money in their early power struggles. Some spouses who have more money than their mates may think that gives them the right to be in charge. One man I talked to said, "When I first got married I tried to dictate to my wife exactly how we should decorate our new house. Since I had put up most of the money for the down-payment, I thought that naturally entitled me to set everything up just the way I liked."

But, as we already know about marital power struggles, it's not always the person in the "strongest" position who necessarily wins out. As this gentleman further explained, "It wasn't too long before my wife started acting as though she were losing interest in the house altogether. She said I *should* make all the decisions because she obviously wasn't smart enough to have a job that paid as much as mine and so probably wasn't smart enough to pick out wallpaper or floor tile. I felt so guilt-ridden that I gave her a big pep talk and turned all the swatch samples right over to her. From then on, it was she who had the final say."

Some couples express their belief that money equals power by using it almost as if it were a weapon. They may make purchases on a tit-for-tat basis, on the grounds that if one spouse buys something the other considers foolish or unnecessary, "retaliation" is in order. One wife recalled joining "a ridiculously expensive health club" in her first year of marriage just because her husband bought "a big, ugly rowing machine that he never used." And although Dave and Megan Brown lived together for a year before marriage, Dave said he quickly developed a post-marital habit of buying a new sport coat or shirt each time his wife bought a new dress. "I wasn't interested in clothes much," he said. "I guess I just wanted to prove that I had as much of a right to pamper myself as she did."

In a marriage, confusing money with love or power can have some rather unpleasant consequences. It can cause you and your spouse to go broke in a hurry. Couples who feel the need to equal or outdo each other's spending sprees, or who consistently buy each other expensive trinkets in lieu of ever saying "I love you" out loud, may soon find themselves dodging phone calls from collection agencies. Or it can cause you and your partner to have endless fights—the kinds of fights that are so emotionally charged that they may repeatedly get out of hand.

Now, unless you and your spouse are real odds-beaters, it's virtually inevitable that you are going to have some fights about money. As Blumstein and Schwartz write, married people "are intimately connected to each other's financial future" and that fact alone is motive enough for locking horns occasionally. But if you want your financial fights to be constructive and fair, you'll have to try as hard as you can to refrain from letting such quarrels spread to issues such as who loves whom more, or who has the right to tell whom what to do.

Ideally, what should emerge from your first-year talks and spats about the "M" word is some kind of overall plan for dealing with finances and a mutual determination to stick to that plan and make it work. Under the best of all possible circumstances, newlyweds might even find that the process of discovering their partners' financial perspectives and methodologies helps them to refine their own problem-solving abilities and modify some of their more extreme monetary habits. As one of Aesop's fables shows, a grasshopper can learn from an ant how to save for a rainy day. But, as Aesop neglected to point out, an ant can also learn something from a grasshopper—like how to loosen up and enjoy life a little.

Of course some couples won't be quite so lucky and may find that, despite their best efforts, they seem to be locked into a series of postnuptial financial feuds that go round and round with no resolution in sight. If you and your spouse are one of those couples you may want to enlist some help from a professional financial planner.

Consulting a trained expert whose *job* it is to deal with money can sometimes help couples de-emotionalize their financial issues. It is often easier and less nerve-racking—not to mention safer—to take driving lessons from a calm, cool, and collected driving instructor than from an inwardly terrified and outwardly hysterical family member who threatens to disown you every time you change lanes without signaling. Just so, financial advice solicited from a well-trained and neutral third party is often more palatable than the kind of fiscal "advice" overwrought spouses might offer each other all too freely (e.g., "I think you'd better stop buying sixty-dollar sneakers, unless you're planning to use them to outrun our creditors, darling" or "I'm going to have this marriage annulled if you keep on buying stock in companies that are trying to convert lawn fertilizer into gasoline, dear heart").

A good professional planner will be able to determine your own and your mate's level of financial sophistication and help you both to work through your money-related "blind spots." With this accomplished, the planner can help you explore options and alternatives and formulate a future-oriented game plan tailored to your needs. In rare instances, though, consulting even the most skillful financial planner might prove futile. Where one or both members of a couple are unbudgeably set in emotionally extreme attitudes toward money—spending recklessly or being self-punishing with miserliness—some therapy (see Chapter 10) might have to be undertaken before they can even begin to address the realities and ramifications of bottom-line figures.

But whether you enlist any sort of professional help or decide you can deal with your marital money quandaries on your own, there is no getting around the very real fact that you and your partner are ultimately going to have to face certain important decisions about finances.

Joint or Separate Accounts

These days most people who marry already have their own checking accounts, and some have their own savings tucked away as well. The question of whether to merge checking and/or savings accounts will inevitably crop up in the first few months of marriage, and it will doubtless provoke anxiety in many newlyweds.

Pooling funds can be a scary prospect for many, because it implies giving up exclusive control over what has long been one's own domain. But the thought of continuing to keep completely separate accounts can make some newlyweds nervous as well. Some couples fear they're not really behaving as married couples ought to if they forgo the traditional step of merging their money. When trying to decide between maintaining "his" and "hers" accounts, or putting everything into a big communal pot marked "ours," newlyweds should consider the practical and psychological advantages and disadvantages of both systems.

For some couples, opening joint accounts can be a way of enhancing both partners' sense of being joined to each other, of making each spouse feel "richer," both financially and emotionally, and helping them to make decisions for the long-term good of the relationship. For other couples, though, pooling can hurt a developing relationship by engendering stress, discontentment, and even mistrust. Partners who bring larger assets to the marriage, or who bring home bigger paychecks than their mates, may feel it's unfair to grant their partners unrestricted access to their money. Those who have less or earn less may fear their comparatively small contributions to joint accounts will get lost in the shuffle.

On the practical side, merging individual accounts may cut down on administrative fees. Theoretically, it can cut down on paperwork too, although some couples find that keeping one joint checking account for two people who write lots of checks can be a paperwork nightmare. As Charlie Turner, who tried such an arrangement with his wife, Robin, explained, "The two of us each wrote twenty or thirty checks a month and forgot to enter about half of them in the joint checkbook we kept at home. Whichever of us would try to balance the account at the end of the month would be faced with a sky-high pile of indecipherable check stubs. We'd almost always end up accusing each other of being irresponsible, and we both felt really sheepish about having to go to the bank and have them decode our statement for us. It wasn't long before we went back to separate checking."

What the Turners found out the hard way is that joint accounts tend to work best, at least on a pragmatic level, when one member of the couple takes care of all the hands-on managing of them. If such an arrangement just doesn't fit into your marital situation, or if neither of you can bear the thought of being the person who doesn't get to *do* the managing, total pooling is clearly not the way to go. If, on the other hand, you are like the newly married man who told me, "I would rather stick pins in my eyes than balance a checkbook or even write checks," and if, like this lucky fellow, you have a spouse who adores such chores, pooling may be an ideal solution.

The practice of keeping all funds in separate accounts has its pros and cons, too. On the negative side, some couples may fear that financial separateness will make their relationship more tenuous—easier to dissolve and perhaps, therefore, more likely to *be* dissolved at some future time. And even newlyweds who don't subscribe to this theory themselves may be reluctant to suggest such an arrangement for fear their mates may take it as a sign that they don't put much stock in the relationship's longevity.

On the positive side, though, the practice of keeping separate accounts can alleviate the financial tensions that may arise when one spouse is far more finicky about record-keeping than the other or when one partner routinely spends money in ways that the other doesn't condone. Jack Farrell found that separate accounts worked best for him and his wife. "Sandy is terrible about keeping track of money and she knows it. She's always misplacing her checkbook, her credit card receipts, and even her wallet. She's been known to carry her money around in little plastic sandwich bags. She'd no more keep a running balance in her checkbook than she'd keep a pet python in the basement. Having separate accounts was the only way I could keep from having daily anxiety attacks." Keeping funds separate helped keep Robin Turner sane, too. "Once Charlie and I went back to separate accounts, I stopped nagging him so much about the money he lost in his weekly poker games—usually about twenty or thirty dollars—and about how much he spent on gadgets for his favorite hobby, photography. It turns out I'm happier not knowing where his every dime is going."

In addition, separate accounts are often favored when one partner pays alimony or one or both spouses have financially dependent parents or children from a previous marriage. Some newlyweds cringe at the thought of having part of their pooled money siphoned off to support their mates' kids, no matter *how* much they love and care about them. They may want to save their money for their own children, whether they already exist or are planned for the future. Or they simply may want the freedom to decide exactly how and when they will contribute to their step-children's support. One woman who pooled her money when first married woke up with "the cold sweats," imagining that all the money she had laid aside would end up in the hands of her twelve-year-old stepdaughter's orthodontist. Such fears are far from uncommon, and keeping money separate is a good way of heading anxiety and resentment off at the pass.

Individual accounts are also a common choice when one or both partners come to the marriage with substantial accumulated debts, such as student loans. Though there's no need to do this for legal reasons—according to marital attorney Raoul Lionel Felder, no one can hold you responsible for debts your spouse took on before you were wed—it does give some newlyweds greater peace of mind. (By the way, in nineteenth-century England, a man *did* become automatically responsible for a woman's debts as soon as he married her. This law inspired some strange goings-on, such as women marrying convicted criminals who were about to be executed, so that these unfortunate grooms would take their brides' debts with them to heaven—or wherever else they were bound.)

If knowing the pluses and minuses of joint and separate accounts only seems to make your decision about how to handle your money more difficult, keep in mind that it's possible—and, according to many marital therapists, desirable—to structure your finances so that you have the best of both worlds. By pooling a little of your money and keeping the rest in individual accounts, you can enjoy the satisfaction of functioning separately and together. Mark and Claudia Howard tried such a plan and found it to their liking. Said Claudia, 'We liked the idea of pooling because it made us feel 'really married,' but we liked having our own money, too, so we could buy little indulgences for ourselves and gifts for each other without having to justify their cost. We have checkbooks coming out of our ears, but for us it's worth the trouble.''

The ultimate criterion when it comes to deciding whether to pool or separate your accounts should be figuring out which system makes you and your mate feel most comfortable. If you do consult a professional planner, remember that his or her responsibility is, in the words of financial planner Eric Riedman, ''to point out the pitfalls and pluses of each method as they apply to your situation, not to dictate your choice.'' (One thing Riedman and many of his colleagues will strongly—and sensibly— suggest, however, is that each of you keep at least a few credit cards in your own name in order to preserve your individual credit ratings.)

Once you and your mate decide which system you prefer, you will better be able to address other pressing financial matters.

The Budget Blues

All married couples, even those who keep their accounts completely separate, have to make some joint spending and saving decisions. The first year of marriage is a time when many couples try to figure out how much money they need to allocate for necessities, how much they can afford to spend on luxuries, and how much they want to tuck away for the future. In the process of doing so, they must also decide whose money should go toward what. That's enough to give any couple the budget blues.

The question of which spouse will cover what living expenses may have been comparatively easy to tackle in times when many new couples had only one breadwinner in the family, but nowadays, with two people winning a significant share of the bread in so many households, it can be especially tricky. Of course, most everyone wants to be fair when it comes to this issue, but what exactly is "fair"?

If two working spouses earn approximately the same salaries, they may well think that splitting expenses fifty-fifty is reasonable and just, but a social worker married to an investment banker may have other ideas. So might a spouse who has a large income but is paying alimony, putting three children through school, and supporting an aging grandmother and her dog. It might indeed be more fair to divvy up household expenses by coming up with a formula that takes such extenuating circumstances into account.

Working out such a formula, of course, can be threatening to a lot of newlyweds' egos. Some don't feel right about paying less than half the expenses—even if they can't really afford to—because they don't want to be too dependent or feel like a burden to their partners. Some don't like paying more than fifty percent of the expenses—even if they really *can* afford to—because of the responsibilities entailed in being cast in the role of "chief provider." (This can be especially true if a couple has lived together before marriage as financial roommates, sharing all costs equally, regardless of what each partner earned.) Some very traditional husbands may not want their wives to contribute anything at all to overhead expenses—even if she is CEO of a *Fortune* 500 company—and feel that the money she earns should be put aside and invested, used only for luxuries, or allocated for her personal expenses.

Given all this, you shouldn't be surprised if hammering out a method of paying the bills leads to a few disagreements. But you'll have to *keep* hammering until you reach some kind of workable compromise. If you and your spouse are careful to take each other's psychological as

well as financial needs into account and to remember your
"third person," the one who thrives on give-and-take, you
should be able to come up with some sort of formula that
makes you both at least fairly happy. If you don't manage
to compromise on a viable plan, you'll find yourself em-
broiled in disputes whenever your rent or your car payments come due, and that's a prospect guaranteed to make
any couple entirely unhappy.

Whatever formula you arrive at, it's important to keep
in mind that no one's rights in a marriage should be determined by how much money they pay toward expenses.
A person who contributes 25 percent of the grocery money
has just as much right to say what he or she wants for
dinner as the one who contributes 75 percent. And someone who puts up a third of the rent money shouldn't have
to make do with one third of the closet space.

Deciding how you want to pay your bills early on is
smart, not only because it will clear the air, but because
it can help you begin planning for long-term financial objectives. Though the urge to build up a serious nest egg
may not hit every couple in their first married year, marriage has a way of making many folks, including some
who have lived their entire lives thinking of budgets as the
"B" word and meeting expenses on an ad-hoc basis (as
in, "Whoops, I need a new typewriter; I guess I'll eat mac-
aroni and cheese for a month"), begin to think about long-
range goals like buying a home or planning for retirement.
Such goals, obviously enough, require big bucks, and so
does raising children. According to financial planner Jim Polos, raising just one child from infancy through college can
run into several hundreds of thousands of dollars!

If nest-egg fever does hit you and your partner, Polos
says, a good way to build a savings plan into your budget
is to start by determining your goals and then working
backward. "Ask yourself where you want to be in five years

or ten years," he advises. "Do you want to own instead of rent? Do you want to own a second home if you already have one? Do you want to work part time instead of full time? Once you know where you're heading, you can begin to figure out how to get there. Decide how much money you have to put aside every month in order to meet your goals on schedule. Then look at your expenses and see where that money can come from."

Of course, the first thing you may imagine when you look at your expenses is that there's no place to get the money from. But don't give up too quickly. If you and your mate look hard enough, chances are you will be able to spot the cracks through which your money may slowly be leaking. One couple I talked with said they found they were spending too much on vacations. Several found they were going overboard when it came to eating out, even though they frequented restaurants euphemistically listed as "moderately priced" in dining guides. As one man said, "My wife and I were regularly spending twenty-five dollars apiece on meals we could have eaten at home for a fraction of that. When we stopped to really figure out the cost, it was staggering. Fifty dollars times four meals a week came to two hundred. That's eight hundred a month, or almost ten thousand dollars a year! We cut back to eating out once a week, or twice if we were splurging, and saved a small fortune." Some couples discovered they could save a bundle in interest charges by cutting back on credit card use, and others opted to forgo some name-brand products in favor of generic ones. One woman said, "At first we felt a little silly loading up our shopping cart with those plain black-and-white packages. We thought the savings would be small potatoes, but they added up to big potatoes."

It may take a while to get into the habit of cutting corners, especially if both partners are novices not only at joint housekeeping but at denying themselves certain immediate pleasures and practicing thrifty tactics. But saving money can be easier as a twosome—you see results more quickly, for one thing—and it can also be more fun. You might even try making a game out of budgeting by seeing which of you can come up with the most ingenious and least painful savings methods, or keeping a scoreboard showing how much closer you're getting every month to that house down-payment or whatever goal you're aiming for.

Of course, once you've got some capital, you'll have to decide where and how to invest it, and that can present yet another opportunity for butting heads with your mate. If you feel uncomfortable with anything riskier than a passbook savings account and your spouse likes to buy stocks on margin, you're clearly going to have to do some negotiating. Financial planner Eric Riedman says, "If it's agreed that one spouse can save up separate money for an individual goal that the other spouse isn't particularly interested in, like a sailboat, then that savings should be invested his or her own way. But where there's a joint goal in mind, couples have to come to grips with investment policy compromises. There are a lot of options available and every couple should be able to come up with some investment system they can live with."

The "D" and "T" Words: Death and Taxes

Even though marriage vows commonly include the phrase "until death do us part," few newlyweds feel comfortable contemplating what will happen should the Grim Reaper indeed part them from their spouses. Establishing life insurance policies and drawing up wills in the first year of marriage can create deep anxieties, reminding people of their own mortality at a time when they least want to think about it. Nevertheless, such practices are eminently sensible and should, ideally, be a part of any new couple's financial plan.

According to attorney David Larsen, an expert in estate planning and author of the book *Who Gets It When You Go?*, 70 percent of all Americans die without a will. The reason you probably don't want to be one of them is that dying "intestate," as lawyers say, can leave your spouse largely unprotected. Says Larsen, "Each state has rules and regulations which will 'write a will' for you if you die without one. Those rules and regulations rarely, if ever, leave the surviving spouse with everything you had when you died." Larsen points out that those rules, which affect all assets held in your name alone, will result in your property being distributed partly to your spouse, but partly to your parents and/or your children. If that's not what you and your mate want to happen, the only way to prevent it is to bite the bullet and see an attorney who will help you make sure that your property ends up in the hands *you* have chosen.

Another way to make sure your spouse doesn't get left out in the cold is to take out a life insurance policy. A lot of people are covered by group life insurance through their jobs, and if you're one of those you should check to see exactly how much your death benefits—now there's an oxymoron for you!—are worth. Are they enough to allow your partner to carry on more or less the same living standard you're already living as a couple? If so, great; if not, you may want to get a supplemental policy. Of course, if you're not insured through work and you want coverage, you may have little choice but to take out an individual policy.

If, like many newlyweds, you're already saddled with more than enough bills, you may not relish the thought of adding insurance premiums to your monthly tally. But, as Eric Riedman points out, there are all kinds of life insurance policies, and with a little research just about any couple can find one that fits their budget.

"Let's say you and your spouse are both in your twenties and each making twenty-five thousand dollars a year," Riedman hypothesizes. "And let's say you're carrying a mortgage and require three hundred thousand in insurance. Policies which cover you for your whole life and which double as a sound investment could wreck your budget, but you can take out something called renewable term insurance which covers you for a few years at a time." You won't get back any of the money you put into renewable term insurance—unless, of course, you are unlucky enough to die, in which case your beneficiary will receive full payment on the policy—but it's an inexpensive way to buy peace of mind, and you can usually convert it to another sort of policy later on if you wish.

There's certainly no hard-and-fast rule that says you *must* deal with wills and insurance in your first married year. But look at it this way: the sooner you deal with these pieces of business, the sooner you can stop feeling guilty for ignoring them and the sooner you can stop dreading having to deal with them in the future. And if you're more willing to face up to these matters than your partner is, you might try stressing that you're motivated by love and concern for his or her well-being, not by some ghastly premonition that you're going to be hit by a bus or come down with a fatal disease the day after tomorrow.

Interestingly enough, some newlyweds I spoke to confided that they had to resort to some rather crafty methods in order to get their mates to face up to the "D" word. Charlie Turner was one of these. "Robin was completely appalled when I told her I wanted to take out life insurance. She actually said, 'Don't do it. It's betting against yourself.' So one night I had an insurance agent drop in by 'surprise.' He managed to calm her fears a little, and she did end up changing her mind.'' Claudia Howard had a similar problem with her husband. ''Mark completely froze up if I even mentioned drawing up wills, but as a lawyer I knew how crucial they were. So I had some fellow lawyers over for dinner and managed to steer the conversation around to the subject. I could tell from the look on Mark's face that he knew what I was up to, but after an hour of hearing some of the horror stories my friends told about families of clients who died without wills, he threw up his hands and said, 'Okay, okay, you're right!' ''

Charlie's and Claudia's tactics were far from subtle, but the moral of their stories seems to be a sound one. If you're the sort of person who won't rest easy until these important issues are taken care of, and you're married to someone who feels differently, you may just have to use your wiles before you do your wills, and you may have to do a lot of reassuring before you can do any insuring.

Having dispensed with death, let's move on to a topic that is equally unavoidable and that many find equally unnerving: taxes.

The nice thing about death is that it happens to each of us only once. Taxes, on the other hand, have to be paid up annually. Sometime during your first year of marriage, April 15 is bound to roll around, and when it does you may find yourself even more confused as a married taxpayer than you were as a single one.

Will filing jointly save you money or cost you? How will a joint return affect your allowable deductions? How about your tax bracket? Are there any financial advantages to filing separately even though you're part of a couple? Riedman suggests that the easiest way to find out the answers to these perplexing questions is to have an accountant run figures for both cases—i.e., filing jointly and separately—and then make bottom-line comparisons. Riedman does predict, however, that most couples will find that they do get a break by filing joint returns.

If you do decide that filing jointly is your best option, you may find your habitual IRS-inspired anxiety doubling as tax time approaches. As hard as it is for one person to gather up and make sense out of all those W-2's, 1099's, expense receipts, and the like, this process can be even more taxing, as it were, when two are involved.

Some people may be driven to distraction by a spouse who thinks that being organized means scribbling tax data on the backs of matchbooks, cramming piles of indecipherable records into shoe boxes, or filing receipts according to color. Others may be equally irritated by a fastidious mate who can recall with complete accuracy exactly how much you each spent on business-related costs on any given day of the year. ("First of June? Ah yes, twenty-six dollars and forty-two cents.") And some couples might be terrified at the possibility of being audited together, correctly deeming such a prospect less fun than a second honeymoon on Bora-Bora.

Once again, if you find it hard to contend with the emotional side of this financial matter, you might want to consult a professional whose expertise may well enable you to be calmer and more objective. Even if you've prided yourself on filling out your own tax returns for decades, it could be that after marriage you'll discover that the benefits of third-party advice are well worth the fee.

A few of the couples I spoke with went even a step further in their determination to avoid April angst. Even though they determined they could save money by filing jointly, they opted to file individual returns instead. In each case, these newlyweds felt their styles of record-keeping and preparing returns were so radically different that any attempt to merge their efforts would result in certain and severe discord. Though many might consider their choice unorthodox and unnecessarily costly, these couples felt that preserving the harmony of their relationship was worth more than the extra money they had to hand over to Uncle Sam. They balanced their emotional priorities against their financial ones and took what was, for them, the right path.

Dealing successfully with money, especially in the context of marriage, is more of an art than a science. It's not a matter of dollars and cents so much as it is a matter of dollars and sense. If, in your first year, you are willing to overcome your resistances to talking about money, and if you are able to apply trust, tolerance, flexibility, pragmatism, and optimism when it comes to financial matters, chances are high that money will not prove to be the "root of all evil" in your relationship.

Money is a conduit by which you can reach some of your goals, and as such it must be paid attention to. But as nice as it is to have, money is a means, not an end. The quality of your married life hinges far more on your ability to deal with each other lovingly and rationally than it does on how many riches you have in your coffer or the color of your American Express card. As one long-married woman of relatively modest means told me, "My husband and I may not be worth millions as far as the bank is concerned, but we know we are worth a lot because we have a lot. We have each other." If you hold on to that thought, it should be somewhat easier to take the "M" word in stride.

—————— 7 ——————

Systems, Schedules, Work, Work, Work

GONE ARE THE DAYS when the average husband went off to work each morning, leaving his average wife at home to contend with unsightly floor wax build-up and ring-around-the-collar. Sweeping economic and social changes have made two-career couples the norm, and their numbers are rising all the time.

Today, with fewer than one third of all married couples in America fitting the traditional man-as-wage-earner/woman-as-homemaker mode, a great many newlyweds are faced with figuring out how they will balance their responsibilities to their jobs with their responsibilities to each other and their children or children-to-be, how they will reconcile their professional identities with their personal ones, how they will manage to find time for work as well as time for love, and, of course, how they will divide up the obligatory chores that keep their households running smoothly.

Cooking, Cleaning, and Complaining

Throughout the ages, the allocation of household tasks was, for the most part, a pretty simple business. They fell to the woman. In fact, according to the *Oxford English Dictionary,* the very word *bride* is thought to stem from the verb root "brü," meaning to cook or make broth, and according to *Samuel Johnson's Dictionary, wife* originally was used to denote a woman of humble employment.

In many cultures, a woman who married knew that her inescapable fate was to keep the home fires burning. If she had any doubts about her proper role, there were ceremonies especially designed to remind her of it.

In ancient Greece, brides customarily indicated their zeal and facility for attending to household duties by arriving at their bridegrooms' homes bearing vessels filled with poached barley. In Poland, after a wedding ceremony, the bride was blindfolded, veiled, and conducted to each door of her new house in turn. As she kicked each door with her foot, her companions threw rice, wheat, oats, and beans at the threshold, while crying out that this lucky lady would never want for foodstuffs so long as she performed her domestic functions well.

In this country, until quite recently, one of the hallmarks of marriage was the drastically differentiated household functions assigned to each partner. Because child-rearing kept women at home, wives did the bulk of cleaning, cooking, shopping, washing, ironing, and mending. They also served as family social secretaries, sending out birthday cards, thank-you notes, dinner invitations, and the like. Husbands, charged principally with bringing home the bacon, were, by and large, uninterested in frying the bacon, serving it, or washing the pan in which it was prepared. They could usually, however, be found carrying out the bacon fat along with the rest of the trash and performing Saturday-afternoon-type chores such as servicing the family car or mowing the lawn.

There was a time when such a division of labor was considered efficient. When only one partner was out in the world earning money, the other naturally was more available to tend to household matters. What's more, the wife who made her husband's homelife as relaxed as possible was generally looked upon by society as making a valuable contribution to the couple's overall well-being.

But many things have happened to change all this. Since the 1940s more and more women have joined the nation's work force, of which they now make up a whopping 45 percent. Today, with almost everyone busy earning a dollar, the constraints of time often make both spouses feel disinclined to take on the majority of the housework. When Betty Friedan's *The Feminine Mystique* was published in 1963, many people who once viewed housework as an exclusively female domain radically revised their opinions. Now that the women's movement has been a driving force in our society for over two decades, few people have failed to recognize, at least on a theoretical level, that to expect wives to contend with the overwhelming bulk of the housework is simply unjust.

Yet despite the relatively enlightened attitude that many contemporary newlyweds hold toward housework, this is one area where a couple's informal marital contracts often need refining. Even men and women who before marriage vowed to each other and themselves that they would split all chores equitably, or even be willing to take on more than their share when circumstances required it, may find afterward that such idealistic policies can be difficult to put into practice. When it actually comes to divvying up household duties, new spouses sometimes come up with ingenious reasons for why they simply *can't* do this or that.

A favorite justification for shirking a particular task is often "I'm not good at it." People don't like doing things at which they don't feel competent, and indeed there's little sense in bullying a spouse who trembles at the sight of a wrench to be the designated family handyperson. However, some people who maintain that they don't have a flair for certain domestic tasks may simply never have tried them. But that doesn't mean they might not be able to acquire some new skills if they *did* try—and who knows, they may even discover they get enjoyment out of doing so. Dave Brown, who took up cooking in his first year of marriage, said, "I found I liked unwinding at the end of a workday with a little kitchen creativity. It's easy to put your work-related problems out of our mind when you're busy separating eggs or making sure the onions don't burn." And Claudia Howard, who took to tinkering around the house when her husband, Mark, was away on business trips, found that "a little nail-pounding goes a long way when it comes to getting rid of tension."

Of course, what some men may really mean when they say "I'm not good at such and such" is that they consider a particular task too feminine for them to take on, and what some women may mean is that they view a particular chore as too masculine. That a reluctance to part with lingering sexual stereotypes can be found even in the most "liberated" newlyweds should come as no surprise. Many people marrying today were raised by parents who ran their domestic lives according to traditional roles.

On top of that, the concept of "man's work" versus "woman's work" has long been reinforced by the mass media. It's hard to find a television commercial that features a man lamenting the fact that he can't see himself in his dishes or a woman praising a new brand of motor oil. And witness the popularity of the endless re-runs of "The Honeymooners" episode where "the boys," outfitted in frilly aprons, try cooking a meal only to end up turning Ralph's kitchen into a disaster area, or the "I Love Lucy" romp where "the girls" try building a backyard barbecue that ends up looking like a piece of abstract sculpture. The not-so-subtle message of such divertissements: Look how botched-up things get when men and women swap their rightful duties, ho, ho!

While it's certainly true that women may have more *experience* with "woman's work," and men with "man's work," it's hard to believe that females are born with a gene that predisposes them to take up sewing, or that the male Y chromosome contains a strand of DNA that specifically enables men to operate power drills. Although anthropologist Claude Lévi-Strauss has postulated that the heterosexual bond depends on a distinct division of labor into male and female activities, a number of men have become handy with sewing kits, and a lot of women have become adept at using tool kits; and despite such social sacrileges, heterosexuals still seem to be bonding left and right.

Another reason given for dodging certain chores is "I don't have the time." Clearly, if one partner's work schedule makes it impossible for him or her to get to the dry cleaner's before it closes or to get home in the evening in time to prepare an elaborate meal consisting of the four major food groups, he or she cannot realistically be held responsible for such tasks. But a job that demands long hours shouldn't be used as an excuse for one spouse to dump *all* household responsibilities in the other's lap. Perhaps the person who can't prepare dinner can be responsible for picking up take-out food several nights a week, and perhaps a spouse who can't make it to the cleaner's can take time out for a phone call to arrange for pick-up and delivery.

In these career-oriented times, some couples may find that both partners are genuinely too busy with their jobs to do very many domestic chores at all, and if that's your situation, you have to examine your options. Some couples find they can let numerous chores go by the board and still manage to live a fairly comfortable existence. As one recently married woman said, "My husband and I both grew up in homes where one could literally eat off the kitchen floor. You wouldn't want to try that in our kitchen. I don't mean to say our house is a mess, but I don't think we'd pass the white-glove test, either. We'd rather spend our precious time at home together relaxing and talking than scrubbing and dusting. Every few weeks we buckle down and do a major dirt purge, but in between, we figure we can live with a little comfy chaos. In fact, we've even come to like it that way."

If comfy chaos is not your style, you may want to get yourselves a little help. Many couples with two incomes find their domestic life is made a lot more tranquil by hiring a cleaning person, and they consider the dent this makes in their budget well worth it. Busy couples who can't afford that kind of professional help, or who are philosophically opposed to having a stranger sort through their dirty laundry, may find that taking a few short cuts helps. Using a microwave oven or eating off paper plates occasionally can be wonderful ways to avoid chores that neither spouse can cope with—not to mention the resentment that may accompany them.

Short cuts and professional help are two ways of avoiding some of the quarrels about housework in which newlyweds may find themselves all too deeply involved. But the best way to keep the number and intensity of such spats to a minimum is to put more effort into compromising about housework than you do into complaining about it. Some couples compromise by dividing up tasks based on each partner's talents and temperament and taking turns with chores that neither of them relishes. This can be a good strategy, provided both partners also take care to remain somewhat flexible. If you're not scheduled to wash the dishes but your spouse gets called away on some work-related emergency—say, the delivery of quintuplets—you can at least *soak* the dishes that night. And if it's not your night to cook but you notice a pot boiling over, you can prevent your mate from boiling over too by getting up and turning off the stove, as opposed to sitting in your favorite easy chair yelling, "Hey, honey, you've got a problem there."

Some couples compromise by taking on some chores as a twosome rather than individually, and some of those who do find that certain tasks wind up seeming more like play than work. Ben and Barbara Simon, for example, never liked cooking alone, but when they merged their culinary skills they produced some pretty spectacular meals. "Incredibly," said Barbara, "we now cook for fun." Jack and Sandy Farrell overcame their aversion to grocery shopping by concocting their own version of "Supermarket Sweep." "Jack is six foot two," Sandy explained, "and I'm five foot one. Whenever we go to a crowded store on Saturday afternoon—which is the only time we have to shop—he plucks the items we need from the top shelves and I make a dive for the lower ones. We often get done so fast that we have time to stop and treat ourselves to ice cream afterward."

In addition to compromising about housework, there are two other ways to help keep it from becoming a sore spot in your marriage. The newlyweds I spoke with said they

felt annoyed when their partners didn't express appreciation for the things they did. No one likes being taken for
granted. Saying "thank you" to your partner, even for
routine things he or she does around the house, can certainly do no harm. Another cause for complaint is when
one partner seems to be deliberately, needlessly helpless—
i.e., lazy—around the house. The heroine of Nora Ephron's
hilarious novel *Heartburn* is understandably irked when
her husband asks her, "Where's the butter?" One woman
told me that *her* husband even topped that by asking her
where she kept the ice cubes. Her admirably good-
humored reply: "Up the tap. In liquid form they're easier
to hide."

Back to the Grind

The way new couples handle domestic work can have
an important impact on the first year of marriage, but the
way they deal with the work they do for a living can have
an even greater one.

During the fervor of courtship, it's not unusual for men
and women to devote less time and energy to their jobs than
they normally might. Smitten lovers are, quite naturally, more
interested in spending time with each other than they are in
crunching numbers, building bridges, filling cavities, or doing whatever else it is they do that earns them a paycheck.
And since planning a wedding itself can be nearly a full-time
occupation, engaged couples are frequently more caught up
with flower arrangements and table-seating charts than they
are in writing memos, attending meetings, or exceeding their
last month's sales quotas.

A kind of on-the-job dreaminess may also persist well
into a couple's honeymoon phase, but when that blissful
period comes to an end, reality tends to rear its head with

vengeance. If newlyweds' consciences don't tell them, their bosses probably will: it's time to get back to the grind.

In many ways, reapplying themselves to their jobs can have a positive effect on newlyweds. Work often serves to reinforce our egos, reminding us of who we are and what roles we play in the grand scheme of things. As psychologist Dorothy Dinnerstein writes, "The joy of enterprise serves to console us for the inexorable loss of the infant sense of omnipotent oneness with the world."

Newlyweds may find that rediscovering satisfaction in their work can help them reestablish their personal boundaries, enlarge their perspectives, create a sense of healthy distance between them and their mates, and lessen the disappointment that often accompanies the realization that they and their partners are not, after all, one and the same person. Since work can be a great way of enhancing self-esteem, spouses may find that it makes them less dependent on their partners for emotional gratification. Since work also provides a good way to sublimate aggressive energy, newlyweds may discover that getting back to work helps them control the negative feelings they may have toward a spouse whom they perceive as sometimes being "bad."

Yet, although focusing outward and displacing some of the feelings we have toward a mate onto other interests, other things, and other people can help a relationship grow, sometimes this process can be taken too far. As David Rice points out in his book *Dual Career Marriage*, work life is generally filled with more certainties than domestic life, and consequently some newlyweds may bury themselves in work in order to escape coping with marital ambivalence and resolving power struggles. They may begin to ignore their partners and start taking their relationships for granted. Others may overinvest themselves in their careers, not because they seek to avoid the issues of first-year marital adjustment, but because they are consumed with the desire to build a better future for themselves and their spouses. The trouble is, they can become so obsessed with the years ahead that they forget to stop and savor the present.

In an age when many jobs demand an inordinate amount of time and attention, some newlyweds may get over-involved in their careers not because they choose to but because they feel powerless to set reasonable limits for themselves where their jobs are concerned. Instead of finding themselves in their work, they lose themselves in it. They can easily increase their own stress levels to the point where they are, quite simply, not much fun to be around. Whenever newlyweds let their involvement in work become the overriding focus of their lives for any significant length of time, some very real problems are bound to ensue.

One way to help keep your work in perspective and to keep your spouse from feeling resentful and left out is to share with your mate some of what's going on at your job. While you don't want to bore your partner with the endless, intricate details of what you do from 9 to 5—or 9 to 9, as the case may be—keeping that part of your life a complete mystery is not a good idea either. It's hard for someone to offer you empathy, encouragement, or sound advice about your work if they don't understand what doing your job entails, what kinds of demands are being put on you, and how you feel about them.

Many newlyweds I spoke with found that chewing over work-related problems with their spouses not only enhanced their sense of intimacy but also gave them a better handle on those problems. As is so often the case, discussing a dilemma with someone who is not as subjectively involved as you are can be a wonderful way of achieving fresh insights.

Claudia Howard, for example, said that discussing some of her court cases with her husband, Mark, helped her realize when she was becoming too emotionally involved in a case to do her best work. Mark, an architect who designs private homes, found that Claudia's opinions of his early rough sketches often helped steer him in the right direction. "While she can't give me technical advice," he said, "Claudia's aesthetic advice can sometimes be right on target. I found that when I described my clients' personalities to her, she could often zero in on what would suit them. She wasn't always right, of course, and I wouldn't let her advice guide me against my own instincts, but I came to really value her input."

Charlie Turner, who designs software for a large computer manufacturer in the Silicon Valley, found that although his wife, Robin, knew nothing about disk drives and microchips, she was able to help him improve his relationship with his boss. "When we first got married," he explained, "I was working for someone I didn't really get along with. He wanted me to write so many detailed memos that I had little time left during the day for the part of my work that was creative. I got to putting in an incredible amount of overtime to get everything accomplished—and that frustrated me *and* my wife. But after talking about this with Robin and finding out she'd once worked for someone who also had an excessive penchant for paperwork, she helped me figure out ways of placating my boss while still managing to get what I considered the meaningful part of my job done without burning the midnight oil."

Charlie did a wise thing in discussing his interpersonal work problems with Robin. If he hadn't, he not only might have failed to come up with a viable solution to them, he may also have begun to transfer some of the negative feelings he had toward his boss to his wife. People who feel anxious or irritated all day long and who keep those feelings bottled up for fear of jeopardizing their employment may, understandably, find it hard to shut those feelings off at quitting time. Once home, they may aim some of their pent-up anger toward a spouse who—they hope—isn't going to hand them a pink slip.

While discussing work-related problems with a spouse can be a positive thing, reenacting them is bound to have just the opposite effect. If you've had a particularly trying day on the job, for whatever reasons, and feel incapable of leaving your wrath and frustration behind or discussing your emotional state calmly with your partner, you might be better off heading out for a walk, a jog, or a good game of racquetball rather than heading straight home to unload the chip on your shoulder. Your mate will probably be happier to have you arrive a little late for dinner—provided you phone ahead, of course—than to have you spend the entire evening sulking, stewing, or being in a snit.

Everyone Needs a Cheerleader

Many of the new spouses I talked with said their partners often were very good at lending an ear or providing a shoulder to cry on when things were going less than swimmingly with their work. Jack Farrell was glad that Sandy allowed him to gripe about the construction management job he had when they first wed—a job he didn't care for at all. As he said, "The fact that she let me talk about and complain about my situation as much as I did really helped me figure some things out. I think it was because of her support that I was able to stay with that job until I realized what my options really were. When I finally did leave, it was for a much better job with a big general contracting outfit.''

Carol Clarke, who, after moving to Los Angeles to marry Ron, spent nearly eight months hunting for a position with an advertising firm like the one she'd left behind in Boston, said it was her husband's "constant optimism and encouragement" that saw her through. "Interviewing for jobs day after day can be awful," she said. "You start to wonder if anyone is ever going to think you're a valuable commodity. But Ron kept me going by reminding me that he knew how valuable I was and telling me he was absolutely sure things would come together for me. They did, eventually, but I might have crumpled before anything good happened if my husband hadn't been pulling for me.''

But sometimes it's easier to be a sympathetic listener to a partner for whom things are going badly than it is to cheer on a mate for whom things are going well. Should your spouse's career really take off, you might feel threatened. You may wonder if success will change your partner, if he or she will become too swell-headed, too independent, or simply too preoccupied. Since career advancement is often accompanied by such accouterments as a pay raise, a grander office, a larger staff, or increased business travel, husbands or wives who see their mates accruing such trappings might well feel envious and competitive.

Having all of these feelings, to a certain degree, is completely natural, and if you acknowledge to yourself that you are having them, you'll probably find them easier to contend with than if you go out of your way to deny them. The important thing to remember is that even though you may be resentful or envious of your partner's work-related triumphs, you don't have to act on those feelings. Because success is often accompanied by problems of its own, such as a sense of added pressure or fears about whether one can live up to one's new exalted role, people who are blessed with success need as much support on the home front as those who are less fortunate.

Even if they don't like to admit it, successful people need cheering on if they're going to continue being successful, and focusing on the bright side of your partner's accomplishments can help get you in the proper frame of mind to do that cheering. If your partner suddenly begins earning a lot more than you, you might try thinking of all the ways that extra income can be useful rather than worrying that your own monetary contributions may seem smaller by comparison. After all, you did marry each other "for richer, for poorer." If your beloved is taking off for an important business trip, you might try considering the advantages of having a little time to yourself. Take the opportunity to eat crackers in bed or read trashy novels you wouldn't be caught dead with in front of your discriminating mate, rather than dwelling on the fun you imagine your partner to be having on his or her glamorous out-of-town mission. Chances are that a mate who is hanging around airport lounges, eating on the run, and sleeping in strange hotels is not having a terrific time. What's more, your spouse is probably missing you a great deal, particularly if he or she was sent off with a smile instead of a scowl.

Of course, if *you* are the partner that fortune has smiled upon, or the one whose work society deems more "important," you'll want to be sure to continue to respect your spouse's work, whatever it may be. No one enjoys feeling that the job he or she does day in and day out is not admired or not taken seriously.

Barbara Simon, for example, managing editor of an up-scale interior decorating magazine, became more than a little perturbed when, in her first year of marriage, she perceived her husband, Ben, as being insensitive to the demands of her job. "Ben is an obstetrician," she explained. "Needless to say, he sometimes has to dash off at the oddest hours to perform a delivery. But when I had a crisis at the magazine, which sometimes meant I had to work around the clock to put an issue to bed on time, he wasn't very understanding. I think he felt my work was frivolous compared to his, and while I'm not saying that getting a magazine out on time is as important as bringing a new life into the world, it's certainly important to *me*, not to mention my advertisers." Ben ultimately became more tolerant of Barbara's occasional all-nighters, but like many people who love what they do for a living and are engrossed in it, he took a while to come to grips with the fact that he had married someone who found her work as meaningful as his was to him.

Even if you're a high-level diplomat married to a plumber, it would behoove you to keep in mind that your mate's work is also valuable. While it may be easy to convince yourself that a leaky pipe or a stopped-up toilet is not a major emergency, someone whose home sweet home is filled throughout with three feet of raw sewage will surely disagree. And those who have partners who stay at home with the children or attend school should remember that although they do not earn any money, they are doing something that requires as much, if not more, concentration, dedication, and energy as a "real" job. Such vocations merit cheering too.

The Name Game

Before leaving the topic of work, it's worth mentioning that professional women who decide to change their surnames to their husbands' may have some special on-the-job dilemmas to deal with upon marrying.

Attorney Una Stannard points out in her book *Married Women v. Husbands' Names* that a woman's last name is not, as a matter of law, changed to her husband's when she weds. Thanks to the tenacity of feminists who began challenging the confusing and conflicting case law surrounding this issue in the late nineteenth century, there is now no state in the union that compels a woman to identify herself as Mrs. So-and-So should she choose otherwise. Even Hawaii, the last hold-out, declared in 1975 that: "Upon marriage each of the parties to a marriage shall declare the surname each will use as a married person. The surname chosen may be the person's own, that of the person's spouse alone, or that of the person's spouse placed before or after the person's own surname and separated by a hyphen." (Whew!)

Though many women are quite content to keep their own names, often out of a reluctance to part with their sense of independence and personal identity, others opt for the more traditional route, and they, too, have many sound personal reasons for their choice.

Some feel that taking their partners' names gives them a firmer feeling of solidarity with their mates; some want to make as public a statement as possible about their change in marital status; and some women, for the sake of harmony, may give in to the wishes of a spouse who feels espccially strongly that a name change is desirable.

172

Some women change their names with an eye toward the future. They may dread the complications and confusion involved in raising children whose surnames will be different from their own, or, like one particularly future-oriented woman I spoke with, they may even dread the thought of being buried in a multi-name family plot. "If I'm going to be married for forty or fifty years," this lady laughingly explained, "I don't want anyone forgetting about that significant achievement."

But whatever the reasons for changing one's name, leaving a job as Miss X and returning a week or two later as Mrs. Y has caused some newly married women several months' worth of hassles. Laura, a forty-year-old executive, is one example: "Although I was happy to be changing my name, I really didn't give much thought to how much time and paperwork was involved. Not only did I have to explain my name change to my company's payroll department, to our travel department, and to the head of Office Services, who had to provide me with new business cards, stationery, and even a new name plaque for my office door, I also had to take time off from my job to go to the Social Security office and the Bureau of Motor Vehicles. Just when I thought everything was done, I had to go abroad on business and found myself with airline tickets in my new name and a passport in my old one. That meant yet another afternoon waiting on line."

Annie, a thirty-four-year-old social worker who deals with dozens of families through a county social services agency, complained of a different complication. "It took me a long time to get my colleagues used to calling me by my new name," she said. "And then the inevitable happened. New staff members would come in and be introduced to me as Mrs. Bauer. When clients I hadn't seen since before my wedding and who still knew me as Miss Bradley called up and got one of those new employees on the phone, they were told that no Miss Bradley was employed there. You can imagine how long it took to straighten everything out.''

Trying to mitigate some natural mix-ups by transforming oneself from Ms. X into Ms. X-hyphen-Y can also have its pitfalls. As many woman who tried this seemingly simple compromise strategy have discovered, a lot of folks are resistant to such composites. Considering them too long or too difficult to remember, they insist on dropping one name or the other. On top of that, credit card companies often limit the number of characters that can appear on a card to twenty or so and stipulate that hyphens and other symbols cannot be used. Thus, a married woman who goes by the name of Ms. Margaret Worthington-Mulchwater may have no choice but to do away with part of her name on the pieces of plastic with which she pays her tabs. As far as her creditors are concerned, she can be a Worthington *or* a Mulchwater, but not both. If this woman is using her cards to pay for business-related expenses, it's just another source of confusion.

Some women try to minimize their on-the-job identity crises by using two different names—their husbands' at home and their own in the workplace. But that system also has its drawbacks. One woman said it took her nearly a year to get over what she called the "Who-Am-I-Where-Am-I?" syndrome. "I kept correcting myself in mid-introduction whenever I met someone," she recalled. "I would say, 'Hello, I'm Ms. This—oops, I mean Ms. That.' I wonder how many people thought I had some sort of split personality.''

Unfortunately, there seems to be no ideal solution to the name-change problem. Women who choose to alter their surnames are simply going to have to muddle through a minor avalanche of paperwork and tolerate the unavoidable moments of disorder that are almost certain to occur until the period of transition comes to an end. On the other hand, wives who *don't* change their names may have to buck resistance from in-laws, stepchildren, even their own parents. They also have to deal with the logistical snafus that will doubtless ensue when they are traveling with their spouses, dealing with merchants or repairmen (*"Whose* car did you say you were picking up, lady?"), and so on.

What husbands should bear in mind is that, either way, they may have to put up with some griping on their wives' parts as the name game unfolds. Your wives' lamentations don't mean they regret having married; they probably are just wishing, as most members of both sexes do, that life were a little less complicated.

Taking Time Out

Though there's no doubt that newlyweds can strengthen their bonds by helping each other contend with the rewards and frustrations of the workplace, there's also no doubt that, as David Rice writes in *Dual Career Marriage*, "all work and no play makes for a dull marriage." No matter how hectic their lives, newlyweds simply must find ways of calling "time out" now and again if they want to keep their relationships from going stale. Though spontaneous silliness and brief moments of fun and frolic around the house are wonderful, they should serve more as a supplement *to,* rather than a substitute *for,* longer stretches of leisure time spent in each other's company.

A lot of overworked people may feel they simply can't find enough time to spend relaxing with their partners, but if they tried applying some of their business-related time-management skills to their private lives, they might be pleasantly surprised by the results. No matter how busy they are on the job, dedicated workers always seem to be able to find some time to spare for an extra meeting, a last-minute brainstorming session, or a working lunch. If they try hard enough, those equally dedicated to their marriages can probably also find time for a romantic dinner or weekends out of town.

Everyone has favorite ways of unwinding, but newly married couples may find that their ideas of what constitutes relaxation are worlds apart. Spending Friday night with the "Miami Vice" squad or the gang from South Fork may be one person's idea of the perfect way to put the cares of the week behind; but if such a person has a spouse who wants to burn off the week's accumulated tension by disco-ing till dawn, well, the problem seems vivid.

Many of the couples I spoke to said that when they began their marriages they had vastly divergent tastes when it came to leisure activities. These days, with so many people of disparate backgrounds marrying, it's not unusual for a balletomane to team up with a jazz buff who wouldn't know a *plié* from a *relevé* or for a baseball fanatic to join forces with an avid chess player who has no idea who won last year's World Series. One of the nice things about being part of a couple, though, is that it often gives you both reason and opportunity to explore new activities. You may ultimately find unexpected delight in doing things to which you were formerly indifferent.

Claudia Howard, who found she loved skiing after finally giving it a try, said, "Even though my learning to ski was like a Neil Simon comedy, I'm really glad I did it. My only regret is that I didn't take it up sooner." Jack Farrell, who spent his whole life avoiding movies with subtitles until he married Sandy, now scours listings of revival houses, hunting for Bergman and Truffaut classics. And Carol Clarke, who didn't know a basketball from a beach ball before she wed, now can think of no better way to spend a fun evening with Ron than cheering on the Los Angeles Lakers.

It's certainly no sure thing that all of your spouse's preferred pastimes will magically begin to appeal to you as time goes by, but the important thing is that you be willing to sample enough of your spouse's pleasures to find at least a few that you want to share. Married couples frequently find that taking up new activities together is a way of growing closer. In fact, sociologist Francesco Alberoni writes that trying new things as a twosome is one of the ways of re-creating the state of falling in love. If you find that you and your mate have a pretty limited repertoire of leisure pastimes—say, watching TV with your shoes on and watching TV with your shoes off—making a joint foray into the unknown may do wonders for you both. Whether it's flying a kite, flying a plane, or chasing fireflies in the backyard, a little something different can add pizzazz to your life together. Vacations, too, can provide couples with a sense of renewal and a fresh perspective, and they don't have to be expensive to fulfill that purpose. If you and your mate can afford to take the Concorde to Paris for a two-week fling and some three-star dining, terrific. But even a two-day stay at a campground or a country inn can serve to get you reacquainted with each other.

Where work is concerned, the adage "time is money" is often right *on* the money, but where marriage is concerned it's more often the case that time is love. However you choose to get away from it all, spending what's come to be known as "quality time" together is a way for couples to reassure each other that they still value shared intimacy, that their commitment remains strong, and that they still genuinely enjoy each other. What's more, it's a way of maintaining the passion component of the relationship, which, as the next chapter will show, can undergo some changes after marriage.

8

Someone Is Sleeping in My Bed ... Forever

IN TIMES GONE BY, newlyweds frequently found themselves in some rather awkward sexual predicaments. Some tribal societies made the consummation of a marriage more a public than a private affair, and a newly married couple might be expected to perform "the act" in full view of their clan before their union was considered valid or to consummate their marriage in the semiprivacy of their hut while a throng of boisterous well-wishers gathered outside to sing, dance, and shout happy cries of encouragement. In certain Mediterranean cultures, "morning-after" inspections of the nuptial bedsheets for hymeneal blood were considered routine, to assure the couple's friends and neighbors not only that the groom had successfully executed his manly duties but that the bride had "saved herself" for her husband.

Such practices, now happily out-of-date, doubtless contributed to a high degree of performance anxiety for the couples involved. But even after newlyweds began to be allowed to conduct their lovemaking without benefit of onlookers, cheerleaders, or Monday-morning quarterbacks, there was no lack of opportunity for postmarital sexual anxiety.

In Victorian England, where premarital sex was considered taboo—at least where the middle class was concerned—newlyweds' sexual inexperience and ignorance were the source of a good deal of pre- *and* postnuptial angst. And though terrified brides who sought advice from their mothers about how to conduct themselves during the dreaded wedding eve were frequently advised to "lie back and think of England," women were often not the only ones who entered their marriages ill informed and unprepared.

Writer John Ruskin, for example, wed in 1848 to an attractive young lady named Euphemia Gray, was shocked and dismayed to find, upon removing his bride's nightgown, that she did not resemble the classical statues of hairless and small-breasted women that were the only representations of female anatomy with which he was familiar. Concluding that Effie's body was "not formed to excite passion," Ruskin began to extol the merits of postmarital chastity. His marriage, not surprisingly, ended in annulment.

In America, the Victorian legacy remained alive and well for a very long time. Our society placed a high value on premarital abstinence, and, although not everyone practiced what was preached, as late as the early 1960s a fair number of newlyweds—especially women—readied themselves for their wedding nights by reading marriage manuals, which attempted, in the most genteel language imaginable, to grapple with such questions as "What is a hormone?" "What exactly is an orgasm?" and "Is it really possible to have sex with the woman in the upper position?" Such manuals often recommended that brides-to-be undergo surgical dilation of the hymen as "an aid to early marital adjustment."

Most Americans nowadays accept premarital sex as a fact of life, and a vast majority of couples become sexually acquainted with each other before they tie the knot. Ironically, however, it is precisely *because* sex per se is no longer thought of as a frightening and unknown territory that sexual dilemmas of an altogether different nature arise.

Accustomed to having sex with their partners when they were single, many newlyweds are caught somewhat off guard by the very significant ways in which marriage can affect lovemaking. Though just about all sex therapists agree that lovemaking in the context of a good marriage can provide the greatest possible pleasure, the first year that a couple spends as husband and wife inevitably involves some sexual readjustments. Indeed, many couples find that this period is a kind of bridge between premarital sexual thrills and the later enrichment that stems from a growing sensitivity to each other.

The "Honeymoon Effect"

Nearly every couple I spoke with, including many who lived together before they married and many who did not, said that the frequency with which they made love declined during their first wedded year. Their situations, it turns out, were anything but unusual. As Carol Botwin notes in her book *Is There Sex After Marriage?*, figures from the Kinsey Institute and other credible sources show that the frequency of sex falls off by an average of one half by the end of the first year of marriage. What's more, the research Philip Blumstein and Pepper Schwartz conducted for their book *American Couples* shows that unmarried couples who live together have sex more frequently than couples who wed.

Though many newlyweds told me that before marriage they had anticipated that such a fate would *never* befall them, they had to admit that they were not exceptions where this "rule" was concerned.

Charlie Turner recalled that shortly before his own wedding he had, during an evening of "guy talk," asked his married male friends how often they and their spouses made love. "Every one of them," he said, "gave me answers I found, well, *pitiful*. Some said once a week, and some said two or three times a week. I felt sorry for them, and I had to resist the temptation to tell them how unlucky I thought they were. You see, at that time Robin and I were likely to have sex once or twice a day!"

Sandy Farrell said, "My married girlfriends tried to prepare me for the fact that my sex life with Jack would just naturally become less frenetic, but I never thought it would happen to us. I thought we were 'special,' you know, that rare one couple in a million." And Megan Brown said, "I had read lots of statistics about lovemaking and marriage, but who wants to think of herself as a statistic? I figured if Dave and I were still having a lot of sex after living together for a year, it was silly to think that a piece of paper would have any impact on that."

Apparently, however, that "piece of paper" does indeed have an effect on couples' sex lives, so much so that, according to Botwin, some sex researchers have dubbed the phenomenon of postmarital sexual cool-down "the honeymoon effect."

Now, not all couples who find themselves in the throes of the honeymoon effect are particularly upset by it. Some actually are very good at accepting their curtailed sexual timetables as a fact of married life. A number of newlyweds I spoke with felt that the new sense of intimacy they were experiencing in other areas of their relationships more than compensated for the fact that they made love less often. Others said that, because marriage added new dimensions to their feelings for their mates, the quality of their sexual encounters improved even though the quantity declined.

Nonetheless, many newlyweds may feel confused and insecure when sexual passion begins to undergo this natural transformation. They may take a decline in lovemaking to mean that their partners don't care for them as much as before. They may anxiously keep track of the length of intervals between sexual encounters and even make a mistake of comparing themselves to mythical married couples who they imagine engage nightly in endlessly gratifying intimacies. Such couples might well be less befuddled and anxious if they understood the reasons *why* the honeymoon effect takes place.

During courtship, lovemaking tends to have an urgent quality about it. Since the bond between the two people involved is somewhat tenuous, sex is used as a way of continually reinforcing it. With the permanency implied by a marriage license, many newlyweds begin to think about lovemaking less in terms of "now or never" and more in terms of "sooner or later." They may begin to siphon off some of the extra time and energy they devoted to sex before their marriages and devote that time and energy instead to other pursuits, from working harder, to paying more attention to their finances, to socializing. They may give up, at least to a certain degree, some of the sexual "good behavior" they routinely practiced during the initial stages of their relationships, feeling freer to postpone lovemaking if they are too pooped, too frazzled, too preoccupied with work, or too worried about their child who is flunking math.

In short, instead of being eternally "in the mood"— which is, alas, an abnormal state—newlyweds may find that their sex drives simmer down to a more, shall we say, realistic level. Dr. Gayla Margolin of the University of Southern California points out in Botwin's book that this simmering-down process can be harder for newlyweds who were involved in numerous intense relationships before marriage and therefore used to a string of "initial sexual highs." If one has known many sexual peaks, experiencing a few valleys may make one feel that something has gone awry.

Premarital sex, no matter how widely accepted it has become, always tends to have a titillating air of "naughtiness" about it. Since marriage is the way society *officially* sanctions a couple's lovemaking, some newlyweds may go through a phase in which they think of sex as somewhat less exciting than it used to be. As the popular philosopher Eric Hoffer noted, "Lovemaking is radical, while marriage is conservative." One recently married man I spoke with put it well: "I think my wife and I went through a period of becoming less sexually enthralled with each other because the element of risk was suddenly gone. Since we were raised by rather strict old-world parents, we no longer had that feeling of 'getting back at Mom and Dad.' Before we got married, I think we both took pleasure, on some level, in thinking, Ha, ha. We're doing it and they'll never know."

Speaking of parents, it is amazing how often their presence makes itself known, albeit on an unconscious level, in the marital bed. Because getting married can make us identify with our parents, some newly married couples find themselves more sexually inhibited with each other than they had been previously. Suddenly thinking of themselves as respectable, mature grown-ups, just like their mothers and fathers, newlyweds may feel awkward about engaging in sexual practices at which their own parents might balk. Instead of wondering what lotions, potions, or positions they might try on a given night, they may find themselves wondering if what they have in mind is legal in all fifty states. (Given recent judicial and legislative trends, it's probably not.)

The phenomenon of transference can also alter the nature of a couple's sexual relationship early in marriage. Though the person we wed almost invariably possesses some of the qualities of at least one of our original family members, if newlyweds are at a stage where they think of their mates as being *too* similar to their mothers or fathers—or sisters or brothers, for that matter—it's easy to see how that might get in the way of their romantic urges.

Finally, there's no denying the fact that any nonsexual problems a couple might be experiencing in their marriage are almost sure to reverberate in the sexual arena. Thus, if a newlywed couple is having trouble building a certain amount of healthy distancing into their relationship, their emotional claustrophobia may express itself as a temporary sexual aversion. Just about all sex therapists agree that too much intense and uninterrupted closeness can pack a much bigger wallop than a cold shower. If a couple is having problems reaching agreement or compromise on the many decisions they must share, the resulting tension may serve as a kind of mental anti-aphrodisiac. And if newly married partners are having conflicts over how to accommodate each other's children, they may curtail sexual activity on the grounds that the kids are draining their energy or "barging in" at inopportune moments.

What's more, studies have repeatedly shown that newlyweds who have not yet reached an equitable distribution of power in their relationships report being less sexually satisfied than those who have. In their 1982 article "Equity and Sexual Satisfaction in Recently Married Couples," psychologists Elaine Hatfield, David Greenberger, Jane Traupmann, and Philip Lambert explain that an unequal balance of marital power may make partners who feel ineffective and uninfluential in their marriages respond angrily or passive/aggressively to their mates' sexual advances. On the other hand, the authors note, partners who feel overtly powerful may feel too guilty to enjoy sex, or too fearful that their "good fortune" will come to an end.

With so many factors contributing to the honeymoon effect, it's easy to see why this phenomenon should be so widespread. But a reasonable degree of decreased sexual activity, in and of itself, should not be viewed as a handicap to the marriage or used as an excuse for newlyweds to "blame" themselves or each other. Couples who manage to do a good job of adjusting to the realities of married life, who learn to see themselves and their partners for who they really are, and who can resolve their differences in ways that cause neither party to feel taken advantage of, will soon notice that feelings of true bondedness, empathy, and affection can easily fill the gaps where unmitigated sexual passion used to be. They will ultimately come to realize that their changing sexual patterns represent yet another step along the road to exploring new areas of fulfillment and growth.

It's important, however, that newlyweds don't become so preoccupied with contending with nonsexual areas of marital adjustment or with the parts of their lives that are separate from their relationships—their jobs, hobbies, friendships, and so on—that they let *all* of their sexual activity fall by the wayside.

Satisfying sex is important in a marriage, and not just because it is more fun than, say, enjoying a good game of double solitaire or playing the home version of "Wheel of Fortune." It's also important because it provides an opportunity for couples to transcend their individual boundaries and, without relinquishing their sense of self, experience a sense of oneness with their partners. It is a way of harking back, however briefly, to the joy of symbiosis, but in a healthy rather than a regressive way. In short, it is a source of renewal.

If your sex life has, in your first year of marriage, become slightly less than ultra-hot-and-heavy each and every night, you are simply experiencing a natural transition. However, if you have reached a point where your sex life is totally or near-totally on hold, you may well want to take measures to spice things up again.

Rekindling the Fires

One way to overcome a case of the sexual blahs is to make sure to set aside time for romance. Now, this doesn't mean it's necessary, or even desirable for that matter, to greet your spouse at the door wearing nothing but a loin-cloth, load an X-rated film into the VCR, and announce that you're serving oysters for dinner. While it's true that some people may experience such blatant come-ons as turn-ons, your mate may well be one of the zillions of folks who regard such behavior as more frightening or confusing than arousing.

Instead of setting up a situation that implies "you'd better come across after all the trouble I've gone to," you might simply try to arrange to enjoy some uninterrupted time together in pleasant surroundings and then let nature take its course. Whether you choose to sneak off with your mate for a long walk, a drive in the country, or a night on the town, or whether you stay at home, unplug the phones, and uncork a bottle of bubbly, what's important is that your spouse gets the message that you long to be alone with him or her just as much as you did when you were courting. Flattery is one of the most powerful aphrodisiacs that exists, and what, after all, could be a greater form of flattery than that?

Just because you're married is no reason to stop courting your mate in other ways as well. Newlyweds may fall into the trap of thinking that it's inappropriate, unnecessary, or just plain silly for husbands and wives to engage in any kind of physical affection that falls short of the actual sex act itself. In fact, a lot of people seem to think that petting, fondling, stroking, and flirting are activities that might as well be branded "for unmarried lovers only."

To go back to the movie *Diner* once more, the film contains a wonderfully telling scene where "the guys" are sitting around eating their cheeseburgers and fries and debating whether Frank Sinatra or Johnny Mathis records provide better "making out" music. When it's time for the group's sole wedded member, Shrevie, to add his two cents, he exclaims, "I'm married. We don't make out!" In John Updike's novel *Marry Me,* Sally and Jerry are conducting an extramarital affair. When they find themselves in a public situation where they must pretend to be husband and wife, Sally fears her paramour's affectionate behavior will blow their cover. "She wished Jerry would stop touching her so much," Updike writes. "It damaged the illusion that they were married."

But there's really absolutely no reason why married couples should forfeit the simple romantic pleasures that unmarried couples share. Marriage is no reason to deny yourselves the joys of "making out," dancing cheek-to-cheek, exchanging little love notes, bringing each other flowers or small gifts "for no reason," or simply holding hands and gazing into each other's eyes. Having children around the house is no reason to forgo romantic indulgences either, providing you use good judgment and discretion. Granted, it's not always easy for kids whose parents have remarried to accept the fact that Mom or Dad has a new love interest, but they'll probably get used to the idea more easily if your affectionate feelings for your mate are acknowledged openly—though appropriately—rather than being hidden behind closed doors.

There are endless ways to make love to each other, and not all of them need involve the genitals. Engaging in spontaneous displays of affection and tenderness is not just a way of improving your sex life, it is a very real and important part *of* your sex life.

Another thing people may pay far more attention to during courtship than after marriage is their personal appearance. Once married, people who might never have considered letting their beloved see them looking anything less than their best may feel it's perfectly all right to sit around the house night after night in baggy sweatsuits and tattered tennis shoes. Though such people may still look like a million bucks when they go out in public, at home they are quite content to look more like a bargain-basement version of themselves.

While it would be ridiculous to suggest that you never let your spouse lay eyes on you unless you are perfectly dressed and groomed—everyone is bound to look a little bedraggled sometimes—it would be equally ridiculous to suggest that a good way to get your spouse into an amorous mood is to look as though you've just tunneled your way out of a maximum security prison. As Blumstein and Schwartz's study confirmed, "the appeal of beauty endures long after courtship."

Last, but definitely not least, a good way to improve your sex life is to communicate about it. Experienced married people communicate nonverbally about sex all the time, giving each other subtle signals, but newlyweds may often have trouble interpreting such signals correctly.

Mark and Claudia Howard ran into such a problem early in their marriage, when Mark misread what he thought was a clear message from his wife. "I love to read in bed," Claudia explained. "For me it's the perfect way to wind down from the day. Now, when Mark and I were dating and only spending a few nights a week at each other's place, I very rarely did this, but after we were married and spending every night together I got back into my lifelong habit pretty quickly. Unfortunately, for a time Mark thought that my reading in bed meant I didn't want to make love, but that wasn't true at all. It's a good thing he finally said what he was thinking so I could explain that I was just reading in order to relax and shift gears. For a while there, I thought something was really wrong!"

If you're not sure of what sexual cue your spouse is trying to give you, ask. If your husband says, 'I want to turn in early tonight," he may be indicating that he doesn't want to make love, but he may also be hoping that you are going to turn in early as well, and not for the purpose of catching up on sleep. If your wife decides to sleep in flannel pajamas one night instead of sleeping in the customary raw, she may be expressing a wish to be left alone sexually, but then again she may simply be feeling cold and could use a little extra body heat. If you jump to conclusions instead of exploring the meaning behind the behavior, you may never come to understand what is on your partner's mind.

Talking about your sexual preferences and dislikes is also desirable, but while some newlyweds find such discussions easier after marriage because they feel less shy around their partners, some actually feel more reluctant than ever to make sexual requests. They make the mistake of assuming that their mates have suddenly become endowed with extrasensory powers and therefore should be able to intuit their sexual needs at all times. If they're not getting what they want, they may think it's because their spouses don't choose to give it to them, when the truth may be that their partners are totally unaware of their desires.

One of the best ways to give nonthreatening sexual "instruction" is to stress what turns you on instead of what turns you off, as this avoids making your partner feel criticized or controlled. And one of the best places to engage in sexual communications is in bed, when you're both already feeling bonded and intimate. Far better to curl up against your partner after making love and say, "Gee, I really love it when you do such-and-such" than to sit across the breakfast table and say, "Please pass the Froot Loops, and would you mind not biting my toes ever again."

Couples who find that they are very dissatisfied with their sex lives and cannot manage to resolve their situation on their own may find that visiting a sex therapist will help them address their problems in a constructive way. Sex therapy used to be chiefly a clinical means for resolving physiological "performance" problems, but the field has changed a great deal. As Francine Klagsbrun points out in her book *Married People: Staying Together in the Age of Divorce*, today many sex therapists are experienced marital therapists as well and approach sexual problems from a broad, humane perspective.

If you and/or your partner are experiencing a lack of sexual desire that goes beyond the usual honeymoon effect, and you consult a competent and caring sex therapist (your doctor can probably point you in the direction of a reputable clinic), you should gain more than a list of behavioral exercises and a pair of his-and-hers vibrators. What you should gain, at least ideally, is an understanding of the motives that underlie your diminished sexual longings, as well as the ability to enhance your sexual communication with each other and to feel more comfortable with your own needs and desires.

But please don't go rushing off to a sex therapist the first time—or even the second or third—that you experience a brief lull in your love life. Every married couple experiences normal fluctuations in sexual interest, not only during their first year together but throughout their married life. And don't enlist professional help merely because you suspect that what you and your spouse are doing or not doing in bed differs from the practices of your friends, your neighbors, or the guests of the Playboy mansion. When it comes to sex, there is no hard-and-fast formula for what a "normal" amount of desire is. If you and your partner are content with your sex life, that's all that counts.

The Green-Eyed Monster

No discussion of sex and marriage would be complete without a mention of jealousy. Interestingly enough, marriage seems to affect people's feelings of jealousy in one of two ways: some newlyweds have fewer run-ins with the "green-eyed monster" after they marry, but some have more.

Those who feel more secure of their status and more confident of their mates' affections once their liaisons become official are less apt than others to fear that their partners are going to be tempted to roam. Though they may experience a minimal amount of "healthy" jealousy from time to time—anyone who finds one's own spouse desirable is bound to suspect that others do too—they are usually able to laugh off their fears and put them aside before getting carried away with visions of being abandoned for a steamy, sexy siren or a muscle-bound hunk.

But newlyweds who are insecure by nature or who feel that, now that they're married, they have much more at stake and much more to lose may succumb to "unhealthy" jealousy. If their partners so much as glance at someone of the opposite sex, or vice versa, they may become depressed, angry, and envious: depressed because they dread the loss of their spouse's love; angry because they feel neglected or humiliated; envious because they suspect their mates may be more "desirable" than they.

Whereas healthy jealousy can be a form of flattery, sending your mate the message that you still care, unhealthy jealousy can turn into a form of persecution. If you are constantly suspicious of your mate or hit the roof every time your spouse runs into an ex-lover, has more than a thirty-second conversation with another reasonably attractive human being, or engages in completely routine social or professional behavior that just happens to involve members of the opposite sex, you are, sooner or later, going to damage your relationship.

It's certainly not nutty to worry that one's mate may someday stray. Though monogamy is an implicit aspect of commitment in most marriages, sex researchers estimate that approximately half of all wives and slightly more than half of all husbands commit adultery before age forty. Whether anxiety about sexually transmitted disease will change these figures significantly, no one can yet say, but certainly your jealousy isn't going to change them, and worrying isn't going to change what happens to your relationship down the line. In fact, such worry can only undermine the trust and optimism that you should be cultivating in your marriage.

Unhealthy jealousy sometimes passes of its own accord as newlyweds work through their post-honeymoon anxieties and ambivalence and reach the stage of constancy. Carol Clarke, for example, said that while early in her marriage she experienced an urge to tattoo the word "taken" on her husband's forehead in order to keep him from being targeted by what she described as "carnivorous single females," she calmed down after a few months. "I ultimately realized," she said, "that Ron married me and not someone else because he wanted to be *with* me and not with someone else. Besides, my supervigilant attitude was driving us both a little crazy." Charlie Turner at first agonized over the possibility that Robin would run into her former beau (a realistic fear, since he lived just a few blocks away). But eventually he was able to get such concerns out of his system. "After all, my wife broke up with this guy because they couldn't get along," he said. "So I finally thought to myself, Hey, if they weren't able to get along before, what makes me think she'd want him back? Things were a lot easier after that. I know we were *both* relieved when I no longer felt the need to peek out the window every time Robin went to mail a letter."

But sometimes new spouses need some extra reassurance from their partners before they are able to ease their fears and relax their vigilance. Newlyweds on the receiving end of excessive jealousy should be aware that when spouses feel jealous, they are probably doubting their own uniqueness and special place in their partners' hearts. No one wants to feel easily replaceable. If you don't believe that, here's an anecdote from the animal kingdom that may help you understand what the emotional impact of such feelings might be:

In his book *On Aggression,* ethologist Konrad Lorenz tells a story recounted to him by Professor Ernst Schüz, the director of the Rossiten bird observatory. It seems that a male and female stork, a "married couple," if you will, were in the habit of nesting on Professor Schüz's roof. Though they migrated south separately each winter, the "husband" and "wife" returned to the roof each spring to repair and reinhabit their nest. One year the husband arrived back first and a strange female stork appeared.

Though the professor recognized that this female stork was not the original one because she did not have the same leg bands, Mr. Stork greeted her, in every behavioral detail, as though she were his returning mate.

While Mr. Stork and this feathered femme fatale were busily rebuilding their nest, the real Mrs. Stork arrived on the scene. Less than delighted by what she found, she launched a full-scale attack on the interloper. Though she succeeded in reclaiming her territory and her "spouse," Mr. Stork appeared as impervious to the second change of wives as he had been to the first.

Now if you were in Mrs. Stork's place, how would you be feeling? Resentful? Sad? Anxious? Perplexed? More than a tad annoyed? All of the above? Would you be experiencing a lack of self-confidence and self-esteem? Would you be wondering why you married Mr. Stork, anyway? Well, all of these are emotions that newlyweds may well feel if they fear that their partners view them as ordinary, interchangeable, or dispensable.

The best way to help your spouse get over feelings of jealousy that in the long run will prove detrimental to you both is to convey the message that your mate is still Number One as far as you're concerned. Whether it's through words, or touch, or a wink, or a special smile, such a message should help to take the edge off your partner's anxieties. Indeed, several of the newlyweds I talked with mentioned that they were far better able to contain their flashes of jealousy when their partners reassured them than when they didn't.

Ben Simon explained how this works in his marriage. "I like to think that my wife and I are both attractive people. Naturally, there are times when someone flirts with one of us. At first it was a real problem, but now we've decided that each of us is entitled to 'bragging rights.' We know it's okay to say 'So-and-So seems to have a little crush on me' as long as we follow up a statement like that with a kiss or a hug or by saying something like, 'But you know you're my one and only.' This way, everything is above board, but it gets taken with a grain of salt.''

A Final Word: Fantasy

One of the sexual issues newlyweds must contend with is the issue of fantasy. Question: Should spouses fear their marriage is in trouble if either or both of them harbor secret sexual longings for the likes of Christie Brinkley, Don Johnson, Woody Allen, Cher, Mr. Universe, or the Playmate of the Month? Answer: No! No! No!

No matter how committed one is to monogamy of the body, monogamy of the mind is not only difficult to achieve, it's probably impossible. And even if it were possible, it wouldn't be desirable.

As any sex therapist will tell you, fantasy is not only a routine part of human sexual experience (indeed the mightiest among us have confessed to lust in their hearts), it can often be an invaluable aid to sexual pleasure. In fact, the secret stirrings we may feel toward an exciting, attractive person to whom we are not wed may well enhance our sexual appetite for the person to whom we are. Which may in turn result in more fantasizing. As one recently married man attested, "The more sexually happy I am, the more likely I am to engage in casual fantasies."

Yet some of the newlyweds I spoke with said they went through a period early in marriage when they felt incredibly guilty about having such fantasies. More than one told me they caught themselves making conscious efforts to "censor" such thoughts. Now, while it may be a good idea to be selective about which, if any, of your mental dalliances you choose to share with your partner, it's a bad idea, and usually an unworkable one, to try to control the utterly normal sexual meanderings of your mind.

So, if an evening at the movies leaves you with a lingering passion for Kathleen Turner, if a day at the ballpark instills in you an unmitigated admiration for Keith Hernandez, if a ride on the bus causes a craving for the person sitting two rows ahead of you—well, so what? That just means you're alive and well and that all systems are go.

Though the first year of marriage may require a certain amount of sexual simmering down, it does not require you to play dead. And for that you should feel thankful, not guilty!

9

Congratulations, You're Not Just Gaining a Spouse . . .

SWEPT UP in the joy of discovering each other, courting couples tend to pay less attention than they normally might to their families and their friends. Once married for a while, however, newlyweds not only rediscover the emotional and social obligations they have to their own kin and circle of friends, they also realize, often with something of a start, that they now have a whole new cast of characters in their lives as well.

To marry is not only to form an alliance with one other person. It is to become involved with that person's mother, father, sisters, brothers, cousins, uncles, and aunts—not to mention his or her colleagues and chums. As people remarry, this cast of characters can grow exponentially. With ex-spouses and children from prior marriages being added to the mix, some couples practically need a score card.

Though living out one's married life in a social vacuum would get pretty dull pretty fast, there's no denying that the more a couple's relationship extends to people outside it, the more complicated things can get.

The Ins and Outs of In-lawism

Because in-laws, particularly much-maligned mothers-in-law, are the butt of so many jokes in our society, it's easy to see why some newlyweds fear that their new relatives, as nice as they may seem on the surface, may turn out to be malevolent monsters or maladjusted maniacs underneath. And since most people feel, usually quite justifiably, that coping with their own families is hard enough, it's small wonder that many women and men harbor great trepidation about gaining an auxiliary family once they wed.

Despite such anxieties, most newlyweds really want to get along with their mates' kin. They know in their hearts that things will go much more smoothly in their marriages if they're accepted by their in-laws, but they often fear they will be rejected. What many newlyweds don't stop to think about, however, is that, once married, they too become in-laws, and chances are that their spouses' relations are just as anxious about being accepted as they themselves are.

All of this mutual longing for approval and fear of rejection can have some strange consequences indeed. Newlyweds and their in-laws may be overly critical of each other because they're really a little scared of each other or envious of each other's exalted position in the life of the person they love. Or they may go to the other extreme, trying all too quickly to ingratiate themselves to each other before their relationships have had a chance to develop at their own natural pace.

There's no denying the fact that sometimes the behavior of newlyweds' new in-laws may warrant a little criticism.

In their zealousness to become an important and indispensable part of the happy couple's life, some mothers and fathers of brides and grooms may come on a little strong. Some have been known to offer unsolicited advice on everything from how to boil an egg, to how to make a bed with hospital corners, to how to practice—or not practice—birth control. Some have insisted on being called Mom or Dad by sons- and daughters-in-law who really feel more comfortable addressing them by somewhat less intimate appellations (as one woman I spoke to protested, "I couldn't seem to make them understand I already *had* a mom and dad!"), and some have been so enthusiastic about "keeping in touch" that they have made Aurora Greenway, the meddling mother of *Terms of Endearment* who phoned her daughter, Emma, first thing every morning, seem mellow by comparison.

But while it's annoying when in-laws behave this intrusively, newlyweds may well find that the best strategy is to reserve judgment and put their complaints on hold for a while. Sooner or later, you may have to lay down a few ground rules, like, "Please don't call us before six A.M., at least not on national holidays," or, "Please don't cook us a twenty-pound turkey every Sunday so we'll have something to 'pick on' all week," or, "Please try letting us figure out for ourselves what kind of vacuum cleaner bags to use." After all, you and your spouse are entitled to make your own decisions, and you certainly have the right to privacy. But, if they're simply humored for a while, overenthusiastic in-laws may just calm down on their own.

If your partner's parents felt somewhat edged out of their son's or daughter's existence during the time of your courtship, they may want back in—and want it with a vengeance. But if they get the message that you're both willing to let them be a part of your world, they may not insist on being such a *big* part after all. Holding off justifiable criticism of your in-laws' behavior will allow them the chance to do a little self-correcting, and just about everyone prefers correcting himself to being corrected by others. But what's even more important is to stop yourself from airing *un*justifiable grievances about your new family.

It's not fair, for example, nor is it wise, to find fault with your spouse's relations simply because their lifestyles, philosophies, or priorities differ from your own. Doing so will not only make you less lovable in their eyes, it will almost certainly irritate your mate.

Dave and Megan Brown, in fact, had one of their stormiest quarrels when Megan complained to her husband that his mother and sisters were hopelessly tacky dressers. "I was raised to believe that when it came to clothing, you should buy the best, even if it meant buying less," Megan explained. "My mom and my sister and I would rather have one perfect silk 'little black dress' in our closet than a rackful of polyester ensembles. But the women in Dave's family obviously had a different point of view. They thought it was frivolous to spend money on clothes, and, though it may have been my imagination, it seemed to me they always eyed my wardrobe a little disdainfully, as if I was using my clothes to show off. That made me mad.

"But the capper came one day when I was having dinner at Dave's parents' house. One of his little cousins knocked a bowl of gravy over and it fell right in my lap. I was wearing a suede skirt, which I figured was probably ruined beyond repair. I could have lived with that, but when Dave's mother advised me to go into the bathroom and wash it with soap and water, I was incensed. That skirt *surely* would have been history had I obeyed. I see now I was overreacting, but I felt then that I was being sabotaged. When we got home I told Dave that his mother had probably never even *seen* suede before, and that no one in his family had an iota of taste.''

Needless to say, Dave disagreed—rather forcefully. No one wants to hear that his family members are candidates for the Worst Dressed List, nor do they want to hear that they are, as other newlyweds I talked with accused their in-laws of being at one time or another, "a bunch of stuck-up snots" or "a gang of Archie Bunkers." Such lowly estimations of your in-laws are, without exception, better kept to yourself— especially since they're almost certain to be gross exaggerations construed in the heat of an angry moment.

What's more, no one wants to be told how superior their partner's family is to their own. Even people who like to think of themselves as having traits radically different from their parents' and siblings', and who pride themselves on being apples that fell far from the tree, are bound to take umbrage when you attack that tree. After all, it's *their* tree.

It's also unfair to gripe about your new relations if they practice customs and rituals different from the ones you grew up with. If your family opened presents on Christmas Eve over rum toddies and your mate's family likes to open them on Christmas morning over eggnog, that's no reason to become a Scrooge and spoil everyone's fun. If yours makes an incredible fuss over birthdays, while your spouse's likes to play down the fact that everyone is getting older, you'll age more happily if you just take their habits in stride. And if your mom would never dream of serving anything less than a twelve-course Thanksgiving dinner with all the trimmings, while your mother-in-law favors ordering in Chicken-in-a-Bucket, you'd be smart to give thanks for your own discretion and maturity while you hush up and eat up.

In-laws are just people, and like all people they have their idiosyncrasies, their eccentricities, and, alas, their flaws. If you find yourself dwelling on those flaws you may want to do a little reality testing and figure out why that is so. Some newlyweds may discover that they are using anger toward their in-laws as a kind of smoke screen. They may feel an excess of negative feelings toward their spouses' families because they are denying negative feelings they have toward their spouses. They may even be projecting onto their partners' kin some of the negative feelings they have toward their own families.

Newlyweds often tend to idealize their own families once they are wed. Once psychically separated from their families of origin by the act of marriage, they may begin to unconsciously edit their pasts, "erasing" the difficult times and concentrating on the good memories. Once the stage of premarital separation anxiety is behind them, newlyweds often find that they can enjoy a better relationship with their own parents and siblings, who may treat them with more respect now that they are perceived as more "grown up" and independent.

If they are enjoying new and improved relationships with their mothers, fathers, sisters, and brothers, it's no wonder newlyweds may choose to forget the days when their interactions with their families may have gone somewhat less smoothly. While no one would argue that enjoying a better relationship with one's own family is undesirable, those erased and forgotten negative feelings may just surface in another form, with in-laws taking the heat.

But let's not forget there is another extreme to which newlyweds and their new relations may go. Some of the men and women I talked with said that early in their marriages they rapidly formed a mutual admiration society with their in-laws. And while this might sound like a very fortuitous arrangement, it, too, can have its drawbacks.

If, early in your marriage, you and your in-laws go overboard in accentuating the positive and eliminating the negative from your relationship, you will not give yourselves the chance to experience each other as real and complex people. Rather you will view each other as fantasy objects: "the perfect parents I never had" or "the perfect child I always wanted." Since no one is ever a perfect parent or child, such illusory perceptions can only pave the way for later disenchantment. An even greater danger, however, is that you will cause your spouse to become jealous.

While most newlyweds are pleased as punch if their mates and their families get along, few of them like to imagine that their parents and siblings might actually prefer their spouses to them. One newly married man I talked with complained, "As soon as I got married, my parents attributed everything good that happened in my life, like getting a promotion and even losing weight, to my wife's influence on me. I was glad they thought highly of her, but I couldn't help but wonder why *I* wasn't getting credit for anything." And as one woman lamented, "When I was growing up, my father always spent more time with my brothers than he did with me. They were all big sports enthusiasts, and it seemed like they were always off together at some football game or hockey match. When I got married, the male contingent of my family immediately took my husband under their wing. Before I knew it, it seemed as if he was spending more time with them than he was with me. I felt even more excluded that I did before, and I wanted to say, 'Hey, wait a minute, he's *mine*, not yours.' " The moral of these anecdotes: if you and your new family feel you must get involved in an intense love fest, at least make sure your partner is included.

There's no doubt that striking a balanced relationship with one's in-laws can be a tricky business. Just as you must do with your spouse, you must learn to see your new family in a realistic way and to experience and tolerate both loving and not-so-loving feelings toward them. You must also resolve with them, just as you have with your mate, issues of closeness and distancing, making them a part of your life without becoming overly dependent on them or letting them become overly dependent on you.

Forming a mature, constructive relationship with your new family is crucial, for it will make it easier for you to make the kinds of policy decisions that many new couples must make with regard to their families. In your first year of marriage, you may well have to determine things like how much time you and your partner are going to spend with each of your families, what holidays will be spent with which clan, whether or not you're going to try to get your families to socialize with each other (now don't cringe, *sometimes* it can work), how much financial aid, if any, you're willing to accept and under what terms you will accept it, and how much you are going to tell your families about the private details of your married life.

There are certainly no hard-and-fast rules that govern such personal choices, and every couple must decide for themselves what suits them best. But the first step toward making such decisions wisely is to refrain from making quick judgments about your new family—one way or the other—and, instead, to take things one step at a time.

The Ex-Spouse, the Kids, and You

In her book *Funny Sauce*, humorist Delia Ephron enumerates some common fantasies that stepmothers entertain. Among them:

"My stepchildren will go into analysis and spend the entire time discussing how much they hate me."

"My stepchildren will be in analysis five days a week for five years and never mention me once."

"I will have to pay for my stepchildren's analysis."

With her characteristic cleverness, Ephron has pinpointed some of the major areas of anxiety that almost all stepparents, female *or* male, experience. They worry that their stepchildren will view them as "wicked," will attempt to ignore them completely and shut them out of their existence, or will become unmanageable financial burdens.

Newlyweds who marry mates who already have children, and thus find themselves endowed with "instant" offspring, are almost certain to have such anxieties. In addition, they often wonder if their stepchildren will become unmanageable *emotional* burdens. They fear that their relationships with their partners may become strained if their relationships with their partners' children are less than spectacular.

There's no question that such fears are not entirely ill founded. As children and their new stepparents go through a period of adjustment, all kinds of difficulties may present themselves, and those difficulties are bound to take their toll on the way new husbands and wives get along. Perhaps that is why newlyweds who gain new family members through such "package deal" marriages are afforded an additional 39 points on the Holmes-Rahe stress scale and why the largest proportion of remarriages that culminate in divorce are those that involve children from previous marriages.

It would be impossible to cover here all the significant issues with which new stepparents must cope. There are many fine books devoted solely to the art of stepparenting. If you are a newlywed who fits into this category, you would probably do well to read as many of them as you can find time for, and to concentrate especially on those chapters that focus on the specific age group you are dealing with—toddlers, young children, adolescents, or even adult stepchildren. But today, with more than ten million children living in households with one natural parent and one stepparent, many newlyweds must contend, on top of everything else, with the task of being a novice mom or dad. So it's worth mentioning at least a few of the major dilemmas that you, if you are one of them, will face.

How do you want to be addressed by your stepchildren? Once wed to their mother or father, do you automatically become Mom or Dad yourself? Are you comfortable with being called by your first name instead? What are *they* comfortable calling you?

How are you going to discipline your stepchildren? Are you obliged to filter any complaints you have about your stepchildren's behavior through your spouse, or will you deal with them directly when they misbehave? How much authority do you have when it comes to setting ground rules, enforcing curfews, and the like? Who has the final say when it comes to setting limits for your stepchildren— you or your partner?

How will you handle any feelings of jealousy or resentment toward your stepchildren? A little rivalry between newlyweds and their new children is natural, but will you go overboard in competing with your stepchildren for the attention and affections of your spouse? If you do, you'll probably find your strategy backfiring. Not only are children more legitimately needy than adults, they are also inherently good at upstaging grown-ups when they feel they're being given short shift. Do you want to play one-upmanship games with a three-year-old or a thirteen-year-old?

How will you deal with the fact that they will almost certainly feel a little jealous and resentful of you as well?

Everyone likes to be liked all the time, but if stepchildren sometimes feel resentful of you, trying extra hard to ingratiate yourself to them may only increase their resistance. Time may be the only force powerful enough to help them get over such feelings. Are you patient enough to let it do its work?

How much responsibility will you take for your stepchildren's day-to-day "maintenance"? Will you do their laundry and help clean their rooms? Are you willing to serve as part-time chauffeur and chef? Will you make sure they take their vitamins, brush after meals, and bundle up when it's cold, or do you feel such duties fall primarily to their "real" parents?

How involved will you become in your stepchildren's financial life? Do you feel you have a responsibility to contribute some of your own money to your stepchildren's upbringing and education? Will your spouse feel better if you don't become involved? Will you be able to avoid what is sometimes an almost irresistible temptation to *bribe* your stepchildren in order to win them over?

How involved will you be in their emotional life? Do you see yourself as a "third parent," a surrogate parent, a role model, a pal—or all or none of the above? Will you overextend yourself or hold back too much? Will you communicate openly with your stepchildren, or keep your own emotions bottled up inside? Will you feel rejected if your stepchildren feel that becoming too intimate with you means being disloyal to their "real" mother or father? Will you try to influence the direction of their lives or leave that to their natural parents?

It's possible—even usual—to start out with one sort of relationship to one's stepchildren and develop it into another sort as they grow older. Can you accept a role that is gradually, yet consistently, redefined?

How much will you intervene in the relationship between your partner and his or her children? Will you try to use your influence to improve the relationship between your partner and his or her kids when the going gets rough, or will you take a step back and let them work their problems out for themselves? Do you feel it's all right for your spouse and his or her children to spend a certain amount of time alone together without you around?

How will you deal with the relationships between your stepchildren and their natural parents' families? Your stepchildren are certainly entitled to retain their connections with *all* their grandparents, aunts, uncles, cousins, and so on. How will you handle the endless logistical problems this will entail? Is it all right if the kids see Grandma X at Thanksgiving, Grandma Y at Christmas or Chanukah, and Grandma Z on the Fourth of July? Is it okay if they miss your sister's wedding in order to attend their mother's second cousin's graduation? Will you require a computerized spread sheet to keep track of family events?

How will you cope when your stepchildren "tell on you"? Are the kids going to tell their relations things you wish they wouldn't (e.g., "Daddy's new wife feeds us TV dinners when she gets home late from work" or "Mommy and her new husband yelled at each other last night")? Will you start pulling your hair out if they do, or take it in stride? Will you pump the children for information as well, or be able to resist trying to get them to be "double-agents"?

As Jean and Veryl Rosenbaum point out in their book

Stepparenting, all parenting is stressful—but being a step-parent can be especially so. Although many stepparents may feel self-pity once they realize how much they have to deal with, that is hardly the way to establish a healthy relationship with your stepchildren, let alone with your mate.

Perhaps the best way to get things off on the right foot where your new children are concerned is to bear in mind that the tasks of the first year of marriage can be equally applicable in your first year as a stepmother or stepfather. Trust, tolerance, flexibility, pragmatism, optimism, and, of course, constructive communication are really the basic keys to all good relationships, as is resolving ambivalence by stressing positive and loving feelings over other kinds of emotions.

If *you* are the one who has a child or children, you will have to help your children adjust not only to the changes in your emotional life and day-to-day routine, but quite possibly to a new home, neighborhood, and school as well. You will have to find ways of answering the hard questions they will pose and of making sure they don't feel neglected—even during those times when your spouse demands much of your attention.

You will also have to do your part in facilitating the relationship between your mate and your kids. Sometimes you will need to intervene. Your new partner simply won't know as much about your children's personalities, habits, likes and dislikes, and special ways of communicating as you do. Thus the roles of educator and "interpreter" will often fall to you. But sometimes you will have to stand clear. You can influence, but not *control,* the bonds that ultimately develop between your children and their stepparent. If you insist they become close before they're ready to, you'll only succeed in making yourself frustrated and miserable.

If you and your partner *both* have children, be prepared to iron out even more wrinkles in your domestic life and to test your skills as a consummate diplomat. You'll have to concern yourselves not only with how your offspring relate to their new parent but how they relate to their new siblings as well.

If you think sibling rivalry is tough within one family, try merging two. Which kids get the bigger allowances? Which ones are allowed to stay out later? Which ones have to help with what chores? What happens when your kids root for the Mets and your partner's kids root for the Cubs? And what happens when they announce to each other that "my dad can lick your dad"? Though "The Brady Bunch" may make this all look like a lot of fun, as you can imagine, it's often not so rollicking.

As the Rosenbaums write, children vary in their ability to accept change. If your children or stepchildren accept new situations and new people with aplomb, your job will be easier. If they have difficulty with change of any sort, you may have to do more psychic work. But the pay-off for such work is large, and the cost of ignoring it can be high.

If your spouse has children from a prior marriage, your spouse's ex-husband or ex-wife is no doubt going to remain a part of your mate's life, and therefore become a part of yours. Negotiations will take place about everything from nuts-and-bolts issues like when the children are picked up and dropped off and whether they should be allowed to tint their hair purple, to larger concerns such as where they will go to college. Such negotiations have a way of becoming less than amicable from time to time. Even if you're not directly involved in them, chances are you will be treated to blow-by-blow descriptions, along with lengthy discourses on how unreasonable and uncooperative your partner's ex is being.

In addition, don't be surprised if the children, consciously or unconsciously, force you to compete with the ex. Statements like "My real mom never makes me clean up my room," and "I never have to do my homework before I watch TV when I'm at Dad's house," can be enough to drive any well-meaning stepparent up the wall. You may well find yourself torn between spoiling the children so that you'll be their "favorite" and standing your ground so as not to abandon your principles. If you're not careful and consistent in your philosophy of child-rearing, whatever decisions you make may lead to guilt, insecurity, and endless second-guessing.

But even if no stepchildren are involved in your marriage, even if your mate and his or her ex never speak at all, in fact even if your partner's ex has died or taken up residency on a remote desert island, he or she is *still* going to be a factor in your marriage.

Although it may not be intentional, your partner is bound to make some comparisons between his or her ex and you. When those comparisons are in your favor, like "Boy, I'm glad I have a good sex life this time around," or "I'm glad you don't spend as much time in the bathroom as my ex did," you're sitting pretty. But when the comparisons are negative ones, you could be in for some not-so-great surprises.

Any little annoying thing you do that even vaguely reminds your partner of what his or her ex did may trip off a disproportionate reaction—a kind of *ex*aggeration, if you will. You may not think, for example, that forgetting to water the philodendron or neglecting to file the record albums in alphabetical order is a big deal, but if the exasperating ex committed similar infractions, look out!

While most people tend to remember primarily the bad

things about their former marriages, there is one situation in which they primarily remember the good. If you marry a widow or widower, you may find yourself dealing with what psychologists have come to call "the halo effect."

People find it difficult to allow themselves to think negative thoughts about a loved one who died. A surviving spouse may mentally transform the deceased partner into a flawless being. Anyone with flesh-and-blood foibles is clearly no match for someone who has been elevated to sainthood. Ben Simon maintains that he has to bite his tongue whenever he is tempted to compare his new wife, Barbara, to the wife who died three years before he rewed. If your spouse is not as sensitive as Ben, you may have to point out that it's unfair to involve you in a "contest" that you cannot possibly win.

Ex-spouses, living or not, are always a ghostly presence in a new marriage. Like all ghosts, they can be scary. Just when you least expect it, they can sneak up behind you and let loose a resounding "Boo!" Rather than don your *Ghostbuster* T-shirt, you'd probably be better off accepting an occasional apparition around the house. Your best defense against letting past partners take over your relationship is to focus on the present as much as possible. As your marriage progresses, you may well find that the specters become dimmer and dimmer, though they will never entirely disappear.

Among Friends

When people announce they're getting married, their friends may fear they'll no longer be needed. After Robin and Charlie Turner announced their engagement, one of Robin's friends demonstrated just how prevalent such fears can be: "My old friend Karen, whom I'd known since college, came out from Chicago to spend the weekend with me a few times each year," Robin explained. "Even after Charlie and I started dating seriously, she'd visit regularly, and everything seemed fine. But her visit after we announced we were getting married turned out to be a different story. Karen seemed to be carrying some sort of chip on her shoulder. She was on edge the entire time, and her usual wonderful sense of humor seemed to have vanished.

"Late that Saturday afternoon, when Charlie and I told her we had to run an errand and that we'd be back in an hour or so, she seemed miffed. When we got back she had packed up and left, without even leaving a note. What Karen didn't realize was that she had walked out on her own surprise birthday party, which we'd planned for the following day. The 'errand' we went off on was a trip to the bakery to order her cake."

Karen and Robin ultimately got things straightened out between them, but sometimes things don't work out so well. Some friends of brides- and grooms-to-be become so insecure about their place in their pals' lives that they deliver their good wishes along with a blender or a toaster-oven and then skulk off, never—or rarely—to be heard from again. Assuming *their* companionship will no longer be desired now that their buddies have "constant companions," they prefer to vanish of their own volition rather than risk the rejection they're sure is at hand.

Certainly not all friends of newlyweds react so drastically, especially not the very close ones. But even the ones who feel more secure about their relationships may make themselves somewhat scarce in the months before and after the wedding. They may need a little nudging before they feel free to reenter their friends' orbits.

Once newlyweds begin breaking out of the honeymoon

cocoon, it's often up to them to make the first move in the direction of friends who have backed off, for a friend who seems distant is often just waiting for a signal that he or she is still valued and cared for. Taking action that will get your friendships back on track is important not only because it will make your friends feel better, but because newlyweds need friends as much as anyone else. Perhaps even more.

Friends can help break the psychic suction between newlyweds, a suction that can prove dangerous if it goes uninterrupted too long. They can serve as sounding boards and "reality checkers," helping newlyweds put things in perspective and remember that there is a whole wide world that exists outside their marriage. They will provide good company when a newlywed wants to pursue an activity in which his or her spouse has little interest, be it discount shopping, weightlifting, or a friendly game of Trivial Pursuit.

Newlyweds also have to decide what kinds of relationships they are going to have with their partners' friends. Before the wedding, people tend to be primarily concerned with whether their mates' friends will like and approve of them. Afterward they may become more conscious of how much *they* like—or dislike—their partners' pals. It's at this point that spouses begin to make distinctions between the people who will become friends of both and those who will remain friends of only one. Once such designations are clear, you will, once again, have to make certain policy decisions.

Will you allow your mate to socialize separately with friends you don't like? If you don't, you will almost certainly cause your spouse to feel controlled and resentful.

How comfortable will you feel when your mate spends time with platonic friends of the opposite sex? Such friendships are a remarkably important part of many people's lives, and they often can help a marriage far more than harm it. They afford each partner opportunities for a broader range of friendships, as well as opportunities for "safe" flirtation and the enhanced self-esteem that can accompany it.

Will you try to merge the groups of friends each of you brought to the marriage? Sometimes attempts to do this can prove successful; sometimes they can turn into social disasters. Many couples find that trial and error is the only way to learn.

Which spouse will serve as the couple's "social director," coordinating the hows, the whens, and the wheres of getting together with friends? This is no easy chore when people's schedules are as jam-packed as they are nowadays, and with "Can you have dinner a month from Thursday?" becoming all too common a query. Sharing or taking turns with social responsibilities is often a sound idea.

Couples will also have to decide whether they're going to spend their joint social time only with other couples, or whether they'll include single friends as well. Many newlyweds I spoke with said that, without meaning to, they began to make plans almost exclusively with other couples after their marriage. But they also said they regretted having neglected their single buddies and wished they had made more of an effort to include them in their lives.

If you and your partner *are* going to spend time with single friends, it's crucial to make sure they don't end up feeling like "third wheels." Mushy displays of affection between you and your mate or rapturous commentaries on connubial life may well make your single pals feel awkward. Even worse, it may make them feel as if you're trying to rub their noses in the fact that they have yet to find Ms. or Mr. Right or, if they're divorced, that they have somehow failed. You should beware of emitting messages that seem to say "Ours is the only way of life that's right." Beware, too, of focusing all your energies on matchmaking. Chances are your single friends will have a better time in your company if you don't always insist on bringing along your just-divorced cousin Louie or your maiden aunt Louise.

A policy decision that you and your spouse will each have to make on your own is how much you are going to confide in your friends. Before marriage, you may each have had a special chum or two who served as confidants, lending an ear while you divulged your most intimate secrets and offering advice, sympathy, or encouragement as needed. Once wed, will you continue to tell such friends *everything* about your life, including every passing doubt about your marriage and its ability to withstand the test of time? If so, you may be doing yourself and your relationship a disservice.

On those days when your spouse can seem to do nothing right and when the question "Why did I marry this person, anyway?" becomes a nagging refrain inside your head, if you unload all your complaints and negative feelings on a well-meaning pal—or on your faithful hairdresser or trusty bartender—you may end up regretting it. By showing people only one side of your mixed emotions, you may give them a false picture of your marriage. Because they may not *realize* it's a false picture, they may be only too eager to agree that you've married a hopeless case. Once your positive feelings start to reemerge, you may feel guilty for having been disloyal to your spouse and somewhat silly for having run off at the mouth.

Every couple is entitled to have some secrets between

them, some areas of their life together that are marked "classified." The people in your life who really care about you will not think any less of you for refraining from spilling the beans. In fact, they will probably respect you all the more.

In-laws, stepchildren, ex-spouses, friends—they can be vexing and perplexing, annoying, aggravating, and sometimes infuriating. They can be hard to figure out, hard to factor in, and generally hard to live with. But the truth of the matter is that they are even harder to live without.

When the honeymoon phase of a marriage comes to an end and other people's presence begins to be felt again, there's no question that the marital boat may rock a bit as each partner tries to reconcile feelings toward others with feelings for his or her mate. But a greater threat to any marriage exists when both partners isolate themselves and shut out the rest of the world.

Today many couples live far away from their extended families. Some may never make the efforts required—the phone calls, the letters, the trips—to keep those bonds intact. Some new couples, too, are so preoccupied by their careers that their friendships, one by one, seem to fall apart. Such couples, by virtually making orphans of themselves, are handicapping their marriages by expecting marriage to meet all their needs all the time. Turning elsewhere now and again, for diversion, for conversation, for closeness, for companionship, and just for fun, is a much wiser course. Newlyweds who have too few others in their lives would do well to heed the advice of the immortal Ma Bell: "Reach out and touch someone."

10

The Proof of the Pudding

Love does not consist in gazing at each other, but in looking together in the same direction.

—*Antoine de Saint-Exupéry*

IT WOULD BE NICE if at the end of a couple's first year of marriage, after all the adjusting, all the attuning, and all the hard work, they could pop open a bottle of champagne and bid farewell to their problems as they raise their glasses to each other. It would be nice, but, alas, like so many things that would be nice—world peace, for example, or eternally perfect weather—it is most unlikely to occur.

Just as there are certain periods in the life of an infant when, as psychiatrist Daniel Stern puts it, "quantum leaps" of development take place, there are periods in the life of a marriage that are also epochs of speedy and significant growth and change. The first year, a time when clauses of the unspoken marital contract are almost continually renegotiated and when each member of a couple "hatches" (to use Margaret Mahler's delightful metaphor) from their joint symbiotic membrane, is no doubt one of them. Provided you make it through that year, other such times will follow.

These new epochs, sometimes heralded by major life events such as the birth of a child, the death of a parent, or a child's leaving home, sometimes ushered in by a psychic change in one of the partners—a "mid-life crisis" or a "seven-year itch"—will bring with them new dilemmas and, therefore, new work.

Couples who have, in the first year, laid a firm base on which to build their relationship will have a far better chance of withstanding later strains. They will have learned that, when it comes to having a durable marriage, the proof of the pudding is not in how well their wedding plans came off, not in how much fun their honeymoon was, not in how much bridal booty they raked in, but in how much each of them is willing to make an effort, *each and every day,* to show their love and respect for each other and to create a viable "third person" who will not crumble at a whiff of restlessness or discontent.

No marriage is perennially happy. I know no veterans of even the most successful unions who skip down the street each morning singing their mates' praises. When I spoke with couples whose marriages had endured for fifteen years or more, I did not ask them to tell me the secrets of a "happy" marriage. Rather, I asked them to share their thoughts on what it takes to make a "happy enough" marriage, one in which the amount of contentment significantly outweighs the degree of unhappiness, in which the good times outnumber the bad ones, and in which minor difficulties and even the occasional major crisis are not likely to rock the marital boat so badly that its inhabitants are tempted to abandon ship.

Their responses, together with a look at the research on the subject of long-term marriage, make it clear that the tasks of marriage's first year do not end with the pop of a cork and the exchange of a kiss on the first anniversary. Having weathered a year of continual surprises and inevitable disappointments, married couples are in a better position than ever to fine-tune the attitudes and strategies that got them this far and to hone in on the areas (be they financial, sexual, career-related, or family-related) that make up their marriages' particular vulnerabilities. They're better able to do such work because they tend to be not only a little bit wiser but a little bit calmer as well.

Don't be surprised if the following discussion of what constitutes a happy-enough marriage, in addition to raising some new things, also elaborates on what has gone before in this book. Moving beyond your first year of marriage does not mean you should promptly forget everything you've learned; it means you must remember it, use it whenever you can, and expand upon it. Each stage of marriage, after all, is a preparation for the next.

Passion, Intimacy, and Commitment Revisited

Passion, intimacy, and commitment are the cornerstones of a loving relationship. But if one is going to have a lasting "happy enough" marriage, one must accept the fact that the more time and habituation enter into it, the more passion will take a back seat. That's not to say it will disappear, but it *is* to say that it will lose some of its drama.

The continual, intrusive feelings of longing that you may well have had toward your mate at the outset of your relationship will seem increasingly like distant memories. You'll no longer feel as though you're walking on air merely because your love is reciprocated. The sense of invincibility that your beloved's attentions instilled in you, and which probably began to dissipate in your first married year, will doubtless continue to wane. This return to reality, however, is not a sign that you love any less or are any less loved. It's merely an indication that your brain and your body have stabilized.

According to Dr. Bernie Siegel, author of *Love, Medicine, and Miracles,* research done at the Menninger Foundation shows that people who are *in* love have an actual physiological response to their emotions that does indeed make them "stronger" in certain ways. Lowered lactic acid levels in their bloodstream make them less tired, and increased endorphin production by their brains creates chemically based feelings of euphoria along with a lessened sensitivity to pain. As this abnormal state gradually recedes, and as the natural cooling down of hot passion occurs, those who once felt superhuman begin to feel, little by little, as if they're all *too* human.

Now, all this may lead one to believe that marriage is a real party-pooper, the ultimate wet blanket. But fear not. Long-married couples who consider their relationships good almost universally say that they experience intermittent periods that do recapture, albeit to a far less hysterical degree, some of the exhilarating emotions they once felt toward each other.

The noted Italian sociologist Francesco Alberoni has written, "How do we know when we are in love? Because we repeatedly fall in love with the same person." According to those who are married "happily enough," Alberoni couldn't be more right. In spite of, or one might more accurately say *because* of, the inevitable periods of distancing that go on between any two partners, temporary periods of rekindled passion can be especially gratifying, providing not all but much of the sense of magic and delight that reigned early on.

Such interludes, tempered by Father Time, are far less likely to cause feelings of utter ecstasy than they are to create feelings of contentment and a certain lightheartedness, and they will probably not hamper, as they well might have at the very start, your ability to work or to relate to people other than your mate. But when you stop to think about it, that's all to the good. One can't expect to accomplish much else in life if one succumbs, again and again, to *total* concentration on affairs of the heart.

The noted psychologist Theodore Reik wrote insightfully about the quality of relationships: "Love can outlast passion. It need not die. It can survive, but only if it changes its character, or rather, if it gains real character." In marriage, that character takes the forms of intimacy and commitment, for without these other two elements, as psychologist Robert Sternberg notes, passion boils down to mere infatuation.

Dr. Phyllis Meadow, writing in the *Journal of Modern Psychoanalysis*, compares the intimacy of marriage favorably to a child's relationship to its mother. "It might be argued that marriage offers superior opportunities for intimacy to the mother-child kind [of relationship], in that new skills learned in maturity can be used to avoid the pitfalls an infant's relationship is subject to when conflicting emotions are experienced." But such superintimacy, not to mention the skills required for achieving it, does not develop in a hurry. In fact, the *more* time passes in a marriage, the greater its chances of coming into being.

Curiously, as Sternberg and others have pointed out, over the years marital intimacy may *seem* to be fading even as it grows stronger and stronger, and often one must consider a relationship quite carefully in order to determine the direction in which things are going.

If you and your spouse spend less time talking to each

other after you are married for five years that you did when you were married for five months, it may mean trouble; but then again, it may mean the opposite. You may have grown much more attuned to each other's nonverbal and paraverbal language. You may be spending less time disagreeing with each other or criticizing each other. And you may have substituted other forms of intimacy for talk, such as doing old familiar things together or sampling new experiences. Couples do run into problems, however, when one of the partners is afraid of intimacy in any of its manifestations.

There can be something downright spooky about someone knowing you as well as—or perhaps better than—you know yourself. In an effort to maintain a semblance of control over one's own existence and to keep from feeling "swallowed up," some people construct elaborate psychological barriers between themselves and their spouses.

Anyone can have a fear of intimacy—women as well as men. Though it's true that, in our culture, men are generally trained to play their emotions somewhat closer to the vest than women, it's not fair to assume, as many are wont to do, that husbands make up a special species of emotional oafs who would rather be strung up by their thumbs than acknowledge their own or their wives' feelings.

The problem with simplistically equating femaleness with a longing for intimacy, and maleness with a longing for autonomy, is that this perspective, carried to extremes, would inevitably lead one to share Benjamin Disraeli's opinion that "every woman should marry, and no man." But it doesn't take a Phi Beta Kappa to figure out that every time a woman gets married, a man gets married too. What's more, 75 percent of all divorced and widowed men *remarry*. If all men were as terrified by the prospect of intimacy as popular belief would have it, marriage would long since have gone the way of the dinosaurs.

Perhaps it would be easier to stop thinking about fear of intimacy as an exclusively gender-related trait if we could all remember that each of us embraces both masculine and feminine characteristics within our personality. Even Freud, who, despite his many awe-inspiring breakthroughs, was hardly the most enlightened being when it came to the subject of sex-related psychological characteristics, conceded, ''No individual is limited to the modes of reaction of a single sex, but always finds room for the opposite one.''

Social scientists who study gender differences have begun to ''discover'' that men, underneath it all, desire intimacy as much as women do. Why all this should come as a revelation is something of a mystery. Deep down, men and women have the same needs. They want to be understood and appreciated, talked to and listened to. They want, at the right times, to be cradled and comforted, encouraged and challenged, wooed and fussed over. They also want, at least every once in a while, to be left alone. When the desire to be left alone continually blots out all other desires, it's usually an indication that someone is frightened of being too close, too vulnerable, too exposed.

A long-term marriage thrives, to a certain degree, on both partners respecting each other's special areas of privacy. But when one partner, be it husband *or* wife, becomes unduly leery of being intimate, the other must act as the temporary guardian of the relationship's intimacy factor, helping the wary spouse to overcome those fears.

Long-married partners I talked with said repeatedly that when they felt their mates had backed off too far for too long, they tried to find some way of ''breaking the ice.'' Sometimes they did so by campaigning for a weekend together, climbing mountains or lolling at the beach, sometimes by using jokes and affectionate gestures to coax a silent spouse to say what was on his or her mind, sometimes by finding ways of reassuring their partners that they were loved and accepted. Though their methods varied, their goal was the same: to keep the bonds of intimacy from growing too slack.

It's important, too, for spouses who may be more skilled when it comes to achieving intimacy to praise and reward their partners when they do make an effort to open up. As family therapist W. Robert Beavers writes, "Most people enjoy doing what they do well, and relating to a spouse is no exception." To convey the idea that your spouse is getting high marks in intimacy is practically to assure more intimacy.

Commitment, the final element of the marital troika, represents not only the wish but the determination to make the marriage last. We already know that getting married represents a big commitment. Staying married, especially once the bloom is off the rose, represents a far greater one.

In Jeannette and Robert Lauer's survey of long-married couples, which they reported in *Psychology Today,* a gentleman married for over twenty years commented, "Commitment means a willingness to be unhappy for a while." That sounds sobering, but, then again, the truth so often does. In those inevitable moments when hot, passionate feelings for one's partner are on a back burner, and when it seems as though it would be easier to have a warm, intimate exchange with a three-headed Martian than with one's spouse, it is commitment that sees one through.

Staying married during marriage's "up" times is a cinch; during its "down" times, however, remaining committed can seem like a herculean chore. During a down time in marriage, partners don't feel as if they're *in* love at all. They may feel nagged or neglected, angry or anxious, fed up, frustrated, mistreated, misunderstood, or all of the above. They may also feel just plain bored and begin to imagine that anything, but *anything*, new would be better than *this*.

At times like these, if they're not truly committed they may begin by constructing fantasy-based contingency plans, like "If things don't change soon I'm going to hop on a freight train/board a jet plane/move in with my cousin Mo/buy my spouse a one-way ticket to the Yukon/become a monk," and end by taking more realistic measures aimed at dissolving their union, like asking their friends if they happen to know the name of the meanest, most merciless divorce lawyer who ever passed the bar.

If they are really committed, they'll either grin and bear—or, perhaps more likely, grit their teeth and bear—what to others might seem unbearable. Those who want their marriages to hold fast learn to tough out the tough times, secure in their belief that relationships often move in cycles, that circumstances and even people *do* change, that the dynamic part of life *can* be created within the context of a secure relationship, that no one who really pays attention to his or her marriage can be bored for very long, and, finally, that a promise (as in "forsaking all others" and "so long as we both shall live") is a promise. They'll keep on assuming that they're going to be married forever because that's what they agreed to.

Beyond Feelings

While feelings of commitment, intimacy, and passion are key in any long-term marriage, it's also important to note that *having* such feelings is not enough. One must *express* those feelings as well. As Robert Sternberg writes in his article "Explorations of Love," relationships are doomed to fail unless people are willing to "translate the three components of love into actions." In *The Art of Loving,* Eric Fromm writes, "If love were only a feeling, there would be no basis for the promise to love each other forever."

Expressing passion, obviously enough, can be done through making love, by flirting with your spouse, by creating opportunities for you and your mate to spend time alone together where romance can flourish. It can also be done through kissing, hugging, tickling, stroking, and so on. Equally important, however, passion can be fostered by sharing positive feelings with your partner and by complimenting him or her whenever you can.

Interestingly, despite the fact that couples with successful marriages generally say they are satisfied with their sex lives, many also say that they would, at least hypothetically, be willing to forgo sex altogether if they found all the other elements in their marriages to be fulfilling. What they would be less willing to give up are nonerotic gestures of affection—the ways in which their partners let them know, through words and through friendly or playful kinds of touch, that they are still the apples of their eyes.

Intimacy, we know, can be expressed by discussing things with each other, but it can also be expressed by fighting and by making up. A happy-enough marriage is *not* a marriage that is conflict free, and a good fight now and again can serve to clear the air. All the long-married couples I spoke with said they invariably locked horns now and again, though many said their quarrels did not escalate as quickly as they did in their early years together, partly because they had learned to exercise more restraint, and partly because they came to realize that certain things were not worth arguing about. As one woman, married for twenty-two years, explained, "There were things my husband and I used to argue about that always ended in deadlocks, things like where to spend our summer vacations, for example. My husband likes the country, I like the beach. Now we alternate between the two. It just dawned on us both at about the same time that if we kept fighting, we'd never go anywhere." As for making up, that seems to be one of the most crucial things couples who stay together do. As one veteran of a nineteen-year marriage put it, "Marriage is *about* letting bygones be bygones. If you can't do that, you might as well pack it in."

Intimacy is expressed, too, by being supportive, by giving each other pep talks, by being understanding when it comes to the demands of each other's work, and by giving each other enough psychic room to pursue individual goals. A lasting marriage is one in which both parties are enhanced and neither is diminished and where spouses keep under wraps the feelings of envy they have toward each other. When asked what he learned during his first year of marriage that most helped him in the following years, Dave Brown responded, "To stop being resentful of Megan's glamorous career, or at least to stop picking on her *because* of my resentment. It turns out I had a lot of ambivalence about what I was doing for a living. I felt I should push myself harder and now I am, by going to night school for another degree. I took the energy I used to expend being angry and put it toward positive ends." As for his wife, Dave says she's thrilled for him, even though his new aspirations mean he's out of the house two or three evenings a week.

In order for intimacy to flourish, partners need to display trust in each other—by *not* questioning each other's intentions, by *not* spying on each other (e.g., steaming open the mail, listening in on the extension phone), by *not* being unreasonably jealous. Couples who feel their marriages are successful have in common the fact that they really believe in each other's integrity and good judgment. What's more, many of them have learned the lesson that the more they trust their spouses, the more their mates tend to be trustworthy. Goethe put it well: "If you treat [an individual] as if he were what he could be, he will become what he could be."

Without sharing power and without cultivating interdependency, true intimacy would be impossible. As Phyllis Ross wrote in *Parallel Lives,* "Marriages go bad not when love fades—love can modulate into affection without driving two people apart—but when [the] understanding about the balance of power breaks down." Long-married couples say they do tend to consult each other about *most* decisions and don't see either one of them as being "the boss." As for interdependency, most long-married partners say they don't expect to be taken care of all the time or to be the constant care-giver in the relationship. Rather, they say they rely on each other for certain things and allow themselves to be relied on for other things. They like feeling needed, and they like having some of their needs routinely met by someone else. But, while they feel they function better as part of a pair, they don't believe they would be utterly helpless without their partners or vice versa.

Indeed, partners in most successful, reasonably non-neurotic marriages have a firm sense of who they are and what they can do, and that is one of the secrets of intimacy as well. People grow closer not by sacrificing their own identities but by being true to them. When asked what she thought the most important thing she had learned from marriage thus far was, Robin Turner answered, "The fact that you don't have to imitate your parents, that you do have choices." Robin is justifiably pleased with herself for having overcome her tendency to take on her mother's somewhat excessive preoccupation with neatness and cleanliness. What she may not be aware of *yet* is that people become especially prone to parent-identifications not only in the first year of marriage but also when they become parents themselves or when their own parents die. As a marriage progresses, husbands and wives must be particularly on their guard during these pivotal times, lest their partners suddenly feel that they are living not with the person they married but with some weird variation.

Perhaps one of the best ways that married couples can express intimacy is to laugh, play, and share good times. A couples therapist I know says the first question she asks couples who come to see her is, "What do you do for fun?" If they are hard pressed to come up with an answer, she knows they're in trouble. Happy-enough couples whose marriages have endured say they enjoy each other's company and have mutual interests that bring them both pleasure. They also say that they enjoy each other's sense of humor and like each other as people. In fact, they often use the term "best friend" when referring to their spouses.

As we can see, though intimacy may sound like a somewhat amorphous term, there are many concrete ways of putting it into practice. And that's true for commitment as well.

Commitment can be expressed symbolically, by wearing a wedding ring, for example, but sporting a band of gold means little unless it's backed up by fidelity, by concern for a mate's welfare, by respect for a partner's relationships with his or her parents, siblings, friends, and children (and this holds true whether or not the couple ends up having children of their own), by the ability to be flexible, and by tolerance for the ways in which one's spouse will change and *not* change throughout the years. To fend off or force change, on the other hand, is the very opposite of commitment. It's ludicrous to expect your spouse to stay exactly the same as the day you married (that really *would* be boring!), and equally unrealistic to expect your mate to conform to your every ideal just by virtue of being in your company year in, year out.

Many long-married partners I spoke with freely admitted that there are things their spouses do they wished they *didn't* do, from procrastinating to back-seat driving to leaving the cap off the toothpaste. But by stressing the commitment factor over the annoyance factor, they have learned to stop complaining and to overlook these irksome habits. As psychologist Daniel Goleman writes in *Vital Lies, Simple Truths,* "To some extent . . . the bonds of a relationship are strengthened by tacit blind spots."

Happy-enough married couples know that the best solution to certain marital problems is to refrain from seeking a solution. There's an old joke in which a man walks into a doctor's office, stands on his head, and stretches his legs forward and his arms backward until he resembles a giant pretzel. "Doc," he says, "it hurts when I do this." The physician looks at him incredulously and says, "Well, don't *do* that." As the punchline suggests, it's simply not pragmatic to re-create a painful situation for which there is no "cure."

Commitment in marriage is antithetical to the expectation of perfection. It means being able to live with compromise and sometimes not getting what you want exactly when you want it so that your spouse can get what he or she wants instead. As the young heroine says in *Romeo and Juliet,* "The more I give, the more I have, for both are infinite." But don't make the mistake of thinking that happy-enough spouses are nice only to each other; they are generally also pretty nice to themselves. Instead of letting their emotions get the best of them, they choose to focus on their best emotions, at least most of the time.

And when they do occasionally capitulate to pettiness, grumpiness, or gloominess, they grant themselves absolution and then move forward. As important as it is to accept a spouse for the good and bad he or she embodies, it's also important to accept the good and bad in oneself.

Finally, commitment involves setting goals within a marriage and working together toward those goals. A lot of people view getting married as one of their big goals. Once they've said their vows, they feel they've achieved an end rather than a beginning and promptly begin treating their spouses like impediments to the future rather than fellow travelers through life. With a comrade in arms at one's side, however, chasing one's dreams is a far more satisfying endeavor.

Getting Help

Almost all couples in their first year of marriage will do a little stumbling and bumbling as they pave the way for the years ahead. Though loving relationships tend to move from a sense of illusory harmony, through a stage of disappointment, to a phase of bargaining and adjustment, to a state of acceptance and a sense of constancy, there can be any number of blips along the bell curve. Not all couples will reach, at precisely the same moment, the point where they have mastered their initial marital tasks well enough to expand their efforts and work toward more long-range objectives in their relationships. As Eric Fromm wrote, "Anyone who imagines that all fruits ripen at the same time as strawberries knows nothing about grapes."

Now, maybe your marriage is a strawberry, maybe it's a grape, maybe it's even a papaya or a kumquat. But if, in your first year as husband and wife, it doesn't seem to be satisfactorily ripening of its own accord, you may find that you need a little help.

Sadly, for century upon century, newlyweds had no available forum in which to discuss the difficulties that may have beset them. Madame Bovary, during her first wedded year, was plagued by disillusionment and despair that marriage would not transform her humdrum existence, but she had no one to turn to. As Flaubert writes, "She might have liked to confide all these things to someone . . . [but] she had neither the courage nor the opportunity to speak."

Today, though, newlyweds *do* have an opportunity to speak—to marriage and family counselors, psychotherapists, psychologists, psychoanalysts, psychiatrists, or social workers who have been trained to work with couples who have problems they feel they cannot muddle through on their own. It does take a certain amount of courage to overcome the natural apprehensiveness that may accompany opening up to a stranger, even a qualified and compassionate one, but "being in therapy" no longer conjures up the negative associations it once did. Where people who sought help with their problems might have been stigmatized in the past, they're now more often applauded for their willingness to tackle the things that keep them stuck.

As a newlywed, how do you know when it's time to seek professional help with your marriage? How do you know when the problems you're having go beyond the routine stresses and strains of adjustment?

Couples therapist Joan Ormont says it's time to get help "when the couple begins to have lots of thoughts and fantasies about leaving each other." Few married people could say with a straight face that they have never, ever (not once!) harbored at least a fleeting impulse to bid their spouses adieu. But those who are obsessively preoccupied with such notions should consider them a warning sign.

Psychoanalyst James Morrell says it's time for couples to seek treatment "when there's a breakdown in communication." Poor communication is, in fact, the leading reason couples give for entering therapy. When one or both spouses refuses to talk or to listen, when conflicting signals proliferate, when one or both partners is dishonest much of the time or *too* honest too much of the time, the choices, ultimately, will boil down to calling it quits or calling for assistance.

Psychoanalyst Hyman Spotnitz advises that couples enlist the aid of a qualified professional "when they are unable to behave the way they want to and when they want to improve the marriage but can't figure out how to do so." If a couple is unable to keep conflicts about money, work, sex, in-laws, or stepchildren from being the continual focus of their relationship, if they're unable to keep transference issues from distorting their view of each other, or if they can't help themselves from reenacting the pathological scenarios that their parents and perhaps their parents' parents before them played out, they may, with the right kind of guidance, be able to purge their relationship of its destructive elements.

If one partner in a marriage thinks the relationship has no significant problems, but the other thinks there are tremendous ones, it's still a good idea for both to undertake some counseling or therapy together, at least until it's determined whether the source of the unhappy spouse's discontentment really springs from the relationship. Telling unhappy partners that their grievances are all imagined and sending them off to get help alone will only serve to reinforce their feelings of being uncared for. And even if both spouses already have their own therapists (not at all an uncommon situation) they may well benefit from working on marital issues as a team, either by visiting each other's therapists together or by finding a third person to help who has no previous history with either.

There are all kinds of schools of couples therapy. A therapist with a psychoanalytic orientation will try to help partners understand how conflicts from their pasts may be causing them to resist working cooperatively with each other and how their unconscious wishes may be undermining their conscious ones. A behaviorist will focus on correcting a couple's maladaptive ways of relating by training them to reinforce their own and each other's good behavior with various kinds of rewards. A family systems therapist will examine how the actions of each family member, including in-laws and children (who may well be encouraged to attend some of the couple's sessions), affect the actions of all the other family members. Some therapists work with couples in group settings, where it's hoped they will gain a clearer understanding of their own dynamics by observing and interacting with others. Some employ role-switching techniques, having husbands and wives "practice" empathy by play-acting each other's part.

Each of these approaches has something substantial to offer, and the nice thing about having a number of options to choose from is that if A doesn't suit you, B, C, or D just might. And keep in mind that there are many marital therapists who favor an eclectic approach, incorporating bits and pieces of many theories and techniques.

If you and your mate are in need of a couples therapist, don't hesitate to shop around until you find someone you both feel comfortable with, whose skills you have confidence in, and whose personality you find pleasing. In the long run, a marital therapist's philosophy is far less important than his or her perspicacity, dedication, and ability to facilitate the kind of hindsight, foresight, and insight that bring about concrete results on an emotional—rather than merely an intellectual—level.

If a therapist is helping you and your partner to talk without wounding each other's ego, to be able to glimpse the world and the relationship from each other's point of view, to abandon repetitive behavior that continually leads to misunderstandings, to recognize which of your premarital expectations were realistic and which were not, to make tradeoffs you both can live with, and to feel better about yourselves both as individuals and as a couple, then you are in the right place. If, on the other hand, you and your spouse are not getting equal time and attention from the therapist, are being delivered a "sermon on the mount" each time you go in for a consultation, or are being labeled, diagnosed, and picked apart in ways that serve to hurt rather than help you, you are in the wrong place. And if your therapist insists that the only cure for marital woes is to hit each other over the head with foam rubber bats, indulge in primal screaming, chant "om" together, or live apart except for the months of the year when both your moons are in Aquarius, remember that it's perfectly all right to giggle as you make a beeline for the door.

Even the best therapist, however, will be unable to have a positive effect on your marriage unless you do your part. If you want to be a successful patient, you must *be* patient. Don't expect instant improvements or you'll just be disappointed. Don't expect to be spoon-fed solutions to your problems, for the goal of any credible therapist will be to offer you and your mate ways of arriving at solutions on your own. No matter how much you're tempted, don't try to regale the therapist with your wisdom or "normality," or try to get him or her to join you in placing the blame for all your troubles on your partner, for marital therapy should not be treated as some sort of sanity contest.

There's another old joke: "How many shrinks does it take to change a light bulb?" The answer: "One, but only if the light bulb really wants to change." Too many husbands and wives embark upon marital therapy with the idea that all will be well once their mates are overhauled. As far as they're concerned, they're just along for the ride, and have no role in the treatment other than to gripe about the same old things over and over again. With an attitude like that, they only assure that their money and time will be wasted. Couples in treatment begin doing better only when both partners are willing to take an honest look at themselves and admit that, as clever as they may be, they may yet have a few things to learn.

Some Last Words

When people graduate from high school and college, they attend not a "termination" ceremony but a *commencement* ceremony, a rite of passage aptly named to remind them that the knowledge they acquired as students was designed to serve them well as they make their way in the world. The knowledge you acquire in your first year of marriage—about yourself, about your spouse, and about the way you function together—should likewise serve you well as you commence making your way through the years ahead. If you apply that knowledge, you and your spouse will stand a good chance of growing old together. If you don't, you may never have the pleasure of falling asleep beside someone who loves you, nurtures you, enriches you, and enjoys you even though your teeth are in a jar on your bedside table.

WHY DID I MARRY YOU, ANYWAY?

Eric Fromm has written that "concentration is a necessary condition for the mastery of an art." Marriage is an art, and that's why it's necessary to spend the first year concentrating on making it work, as opposed to concentrating on the reasons why you don't think it *will* work or "comparison shopping" for that elusive perfect spouse who—it's all too easy to imagine—is out there waiting for you the next time around.

As we all know only too well, not every marriage will last forever. Indeed, not all of them should. But in our "disposable" society, where everything from diapers to dining utensils is designed to be tossed after use and where everything from cars to toaster-ovens contains a built-in obsolescence factor, divorce is all too often looked on as the first rather than a last resort. And that's just lazy.

In computer lingo, there is a popular phrase: garbage in, garbage out. It means, simply enough, that the quality of what a computer produces can be no better than the quality of the data it's fed. If it's fed nonsense, it creates more nonsense. If it's fed good stuff, it produces even more good stuff. Marriage is like that as well. What you put into it, it tends to give you back—in spades. The more positive energy you devote to it, the more you'll get in return.

It would be unrealistic to hope that readers of this book will never experience moments of doubt, confusion, or trepidation in their first year of marriage. It would also be unwise. Marriage means growing up, and growing up involves having some of those feelings some of the time *without letting them control you.*

It is my hope, however, that those who have read these pages will, in contemplating their partially ever-changing, partially never-changing, part "good," part "bad," altogether fascinating and complicated spouses, know by now some of the answers to the ever-popular question "Why did I marry you, anyway?"

Why? Because I know who you are and love you—usually because of it, and sometimes in spite of it. Because, together, we can discover how to talk to each other and listen to each other, and forgive each other when we forget to do so. Because, though marriage will bring us closer to each other in important ways, we are secure enough and caring enough to value the ways in which each of us will remain our own person. Because I accept you, I accept myself, and I trust that you accept me too.

Quiz

Is Your Marriage Getting Off on the Right Foot?

The following quiz is designed to help you reflect on both your marital attitudes and your marital actions. These actions and attitudes will undergo significant changes as your first year of marriage moves along.

Although you can take this quiz at any time in your first year, don't concern yourself too much with scoring interpretations if you've been married much less than a full year. Rather, make a note of your score and retake the quiz as your first anniversary approaches. You may well notice a vast difference in the results.

Try to be as honest with yourself as possible when selecting your answers. Choosing an answer because you sense it's "correct" is self-defeating. The ultimate goal here, after all, is to learn more about yourself and your relationship—not to ace an exam.

Another way you can use this quiz is to have your partner take it, too. If your scores differ by more than 10 points, you may want to compare answers to see where your perceptions dovetail and where they diverge.

1. Before I wed my spouse I believed this marriage:
   A. Would bring a permanent end to feelings of loneliness and unhappiness.
   B. Would be an eternally romantic situation.
   C. Would prove to my family and friends that I was a lovable, worthwhile person.
   D. Would present certain difficulties that I felt optimistic about being able to handle.
   E. Would present certain difficulties that I felt doubtful about being able to handle.

2. My *main* reason for marrying my spouse was:
   A. Our mutual attraction and our terrific sex life.
   B. Our sense of camaraderie and ability to talk to each other.
   C. Our mutual desire to form a stable relationship and/or to start a family.

3. Before I wed, I thought my spouse-to-be:
   A. Was exactly like me.
   B. Was exactly the opposite of me.
   C. Was similar to me in certain ways and dissimilar in others.

4. I believed that after marriage:
   A. I would be able to cure my spouse of all his/her flaws.
   B. My spouse would stay exactly the same as he/she was before marriage.
   C. My spouse would change and mature.

D. My spouse would change in certain ways and stay the same in others.

5. In the weeks leading up to my wedding, I:
   A. Felt a little scared, but also happy and excited.
   B. Felt totally elated.
   C. Experienced occasional bouts of panic alternating with feelings of euphoria.
   D. Gave serious, repeated thought to calling the whole thing off.
   E. Was too busy with wedding plans to consider how I felt.

6. My spouse and I quarreled over wedding plans:
   A. Frequently, with difficulty making up.
   B. Frequently, with little difficulty making up.
   C. Occasionally, with difficulty making up.
   D. Occasionally, with little difficulty making up.
   E. Never.

7. My partner and I had premarital counseling:
   A. Because we were required to.
   B. Because we were not getting along too well and were concerned about it.
   C. To learn more about each other and what we were getting into.
   D. So we could be sure we would have no problems after marriage.
   E. We had no premarital counseling.

8. After marriage, when I first became annoyed with or disappointed in my spouse, I:
   A. Felt betrayed and was resentful for quite a while.
   B. Was reasonably philosophical about it, realizing it came with the territory.

C. Wondered, briefly, if I'd made a mistake, and then calmed down.

D. Felt like an idiot for having been so blind in the first place.

E. I've never been annoyed with or disappointed in my spouse.

9. When my spouse first began to do certain things on his/her own, I:
   A. Became depressed and sullen.
   B. Became angry.
   C. Felt a little relieved to have some time for my own interests.
   D. Felt thrilled that I would no longer have to entertain or "babysit" him/her all the time.

10. When my spouse first expressed opinions or preferences that were different from my own, I:
    A. Tried to change his/her mind through reasonable persuasion.
    B. Tried to change his/her mind by crying, yelling, or threatening divorce.
    C. Let my spouse have his/her way because I was afraid of being abandoned if I didn't.
    D. Kept an open mind and was persuaded he/she was right.
    E. Worked toward compromise.

11. I notice myself mimicking one of my parent's less attractive traits:
    A. Often.
    B. Occasionally.
    C. Rarely.
    D. Never.

12. I have conflicts with my spouse that are reminiscent of conflicts I had with one or both my parents:
    A. Often.
    B. Occasionally.
    C. Rarely.
    D. Never.

13. I tell my spouse what I am thinking:
    A. 100 percent of the time, no matter what.
    B. Never. He/she should know my thoughts without being told.
    C. Hardly ever.
    D. Sometimes.
    E. Sometimes—usually when I think he/she is ready to hear it.

14. I compliment my spouse:
    A. Often.
    B. Occasionally.
    C. Rarely.
    D. Never.

15. Check off the phrases that apply. My spouse and I:
    — Call each other by nicknames.
    — Tell each other jokes and/or do impressions.
    — Make funny faces at each other.
    — Tease each other affectionately.
    — Perform funny physical antics for each other.
    — Buy or make each other silly, inexpensive gifts for no special reason.
    — Write each other funny notes.
    — Wink at each other.
    — Goose or tickle each other.
    — Laugh at the same things.
    I checked:

   A. Six or more.
   B. Three to five.
   C. Fewer than three.

16. My partner and I fight:
   A. Often.
   B. Occasionally.
   C. Rarely.
   D. Never.

17. Check off the phrases that apply. When my spouse and
   I fight, we:
   — Trade tit-for-tat accusations.
   — Bring up past conflicts and problems.
   — Criticize each other's parents, siblings, or children
     when the argument is not primarily about them.
   — Shout simultaneously.
   — Threaten to leave the marriage.
   — Call each other insulting names.
   — Swear.
   — Storm out of the house in the middle of a quarrel.
   — Fight in public and/or in front of the kids.
   — Fight about the same things over and over again.
   I checked:
   A. Six or more.
   B. Three to six.
   C. Fewer than three.

18. After a quarrel, my spouse and I usually make up:
   A. Within a day or so.
   B. Before bedtime.
   C. After several days of silent sulking or cursory con-
     versation.
   D. We don't really make up. We just take rests be-
     tween arguments.

19. My attitude toward money is best described by the following:
    A. Money means love. When someone spends money on you it means he/she loves you.
    B. Money means power. The person in a relationship who makes more money should have more say-so than the one who makes less.
    C. Money is sexy. People who have lots of money have an attractive aura about them that excites me.
    D. Money is money. It comes and goes. It's nice to be financially comfortable, but money itself is not the most important thing in my life.

20. My spouse and I have financial arrangements that I feel:
    A. Are fair to both of us.
    B. Are much better for my partner than for me.
    C. Are much better for me than for my partner.
    D. Are sometimes slightly better for my partner than for me and sometimes the other way around. We take turns helping each other out when necessary.

21. When my spouse and I discuss budgets and financial planning we:
    A. Always end up in a bad fight.
    B. Become confused and anxious.
    C. Generally are able to remain calm and objective.
    D. Do it with the help of a professional.
    E. We never discuss this sort of thing. We just play our financial life by ear.

22. When it comes to domestic chores:
    A. We share the responsibility.
    B. I do the majority of the work.
    C. My spouse does the majority of the work.

D. We've decided to let some things go and/or to rely on outside help.

23. When my spouse talks about his/her work, I:
    A. Listen, ask questions, encourage, and offer advice if asked.
    B. Think he/she doesn't love me anymore.
    C. Tune out.
    D. Try to change the subject to my work instead.

24. My spouse and I go on vacation alone:
    A. Often.
    B. Occasionally.
    C. Rarely.
    D. Never.

25. My partner and I try new activities together:
    A. Often.
    B. Occasionally.
    C. Rarely.
    D. Never.

26. My attitude toward sex is best described by the following:
    A. Sex generally gets better the more you get to know and care about someone.
    B. You can only have really great sex with someone you don't know too well.
    C. The quality of lovemaking is more important than how often you do it.
    D. If I don't have a lot of sex all the time, I'm discontent.

27. When it comes to lovemaking:
    A. My partner and I have about the same level of sex drive.
    B. I want sex more than my spouse does.
    C. My spouse wants sex more than I do.

28. I talk to my spouse about my sexual likes and dislikes:
    A. With some difficulty.
    B. With relative ease.
    C. Never.

29. My spouse and I engage in kissing, hugging, flirting, "necking," or "petting" that does *not* lead to sex:
    A. Often.
    B. Occasionally.
    C. Rarely.
    D. Never.

30. I make it a point to look attractive and well groomed around the house:
    A. All the time.
    B. More often than not.
    C. Once in a while.
    D. I never pay attention to the way I look unless I'm going out in public.

31. When my spouse eyes a member of the opposite sex appreciatively, I feel:
    A. Furiously jealous.
    B. Frightened and insecure.
    C. Glad that he/she is obviously alive and well.
    D. Somewhat uncomfortable, but I try not to let him/her know.

    E. As though I want to retaliate by doing the same thing.

32. I would describe my relationship to my spouse's family as:
    A. Generally good.
    B. Pretty bad. I resent them and feel they resent me.
    C. We all adore each other and my spouse is delighted.
    D. We all adore each other, though I sense my spouse sometimes feels left out.
    E. What relationship?

33. When my spouse goes out to spend time with a friend I don't like, I:
    A. Sit home, watch the clock, and feel sorry for myself.
    B. Imagine his/her friend is saying all sorts of terrible things about me.
    C. Am glad not to have to be involved.
    D. Spend that time with a friend of my own or find something else interesting to do.

34. My spouse and I socialize with friends:
    A. Fairly often (with couples and singles).
    B. Fairly often (just with couples).
    C. Once in a while (with couples and singles).
    D. Once in a while (just with couples).
    E. Rarely.

35. My spouse and I want the same things out of life.
    A. Very true.
    B. Somewhat true.
    C. Not at all true.

36. As time goes by in my marriage, my spouse and I reach compromises:
    A. More easily than at the start.
    B. Less easily than at the start.
    C. We never compromise. I'm the boss.
    D. We never compromise. My spouse is the boss.

37. As my relationship moves long, I find I trust my spouse:
    A. Less and less.
    B. More and more.
    C. I never trusted my spouse and still don't.

38. As time passes, I find I am:
    A. More and more tolerant of my partner's shortcomings.
    B. Less and less tolerant of my partner's shortcomings.
    C. What shortcomings?

39. The longer I am married:
    A. The more certain I am that my spouse and I will be married forever.
    B. The less certain I am that my spouse and I will be married forever.

40. The longer I am married:
    A. The more pleased I am with my ability to be a good spouse.
    B. The more I feel like a failure.

Scoring and Explanations

1. Marriage is not a cure-all or a mere extension of courtship. Nor should it be entered into to prove anything to anyone. Those who realize marriage will be problematical at times tend to have easier adjustments, and the more optimistic they are that loving feelings and good sense will see them through, the better. Score 1 point for E, 2 for D.

2. Passion is one of life's great pleasures, but when it's the *principal* reason for marriage, real problems can set in. Those who are committed to the institution of marriage tend to weather its storms better than others, but people who think of their spouses-to-be as intimate friends tend to do best of all. Score 1 point for C, 2 for B.

3. People who think they're marrying a clone can be bitterly disappointed when inevitable differences surface. Those who search for their exact opposite secretly dislike themselves and tend to either overidealize their mates or engage in lots of projection. Score 2 points for C.

4. Those who envision themselves performing miracle makeovers on their spouses are inevitably let down hard. So are those who never expect their partners to surprise them. Marriage should indeed cause people to grow and grow up, but some habits and aspects of character resist revision. Score 1 point for C, 2 for D.

5. Mixed emotions before a wedding are utterly normal, even if they occur in a seesaw sequence, but the more

integrated those emotions, the better the prognosis that later marital ambivalence can be resolved with relative ease. Experiencing undiluted premarital elation or terror without acknowledging the other side of the coin can be a sign that one is out of touch with part of the emotional spectrum, while ignoring one's emotional life completely never bodes well. Score 1 point for C, 2 for A.

6. A certain amount of fighting over wedding plans is perfectly natural, though too much may suggest that other important issues are being glossed over. Not fighting at all during such a pressured time is a little suspect. It may mean that too many negative emotions are being stored up for later. As with all kinds of fights, making up is the most important part. Score 1 point for B, 2 for D.

7. Some premarital counseling is advisable, and even if it's involuntary, parts of it often sink in. Those who seek it to help ease prewedding discord or to give themselves an opportunity to reflect on their relationships display an admirable willingness to confront reality. On the other hand, those who look upon it as a magical process are deluding themselves. Score 1 point for A, 2 for B or C.

8. It's not unusual to have a few fleeting second thoughts when the honeymoon ends, but the more one can take a little bit of letdown in stride, the better. Clinging to negative feelings—whether one turns them on one's spouse or on oneself—is destructive, but never allowing oneself to acknowledge them at all is just as dangerous. Score 1 point for C, 2 for B.

9. A little distancing after the intense closeness of the honeymoon phase is a fine thing, and acting mournful or resentful may make a spouse feel guilty for no good reason. But while craving a little time and space to oneself at this stage is natural, feelings of jubilation at having one's spouse out of the way indicate that the relationship is a bit stifling. Score 2 points for C.

10. Capitulating out of fear and tyrannizing through histrionics are counterproductive strategies. Reasonable dialogue is always a productive strategy, whether it ends in one party's being swayed by the other's sound arguments or by partners meeting somewhere in the middle. Score 2 points for A, D, or E.

11. Overidentification with a parent's negative traits is bound to cause marital problems. On the other hand, virtually everyone is bound to succumb once in a while. Those who answered "Never" may be unwilling to take a hard enough look at themselves and, therefore, powerless to put a halt to identification-based behavior when it crops up. Score 1 point for B, 2 for C.

12. If these conflicts happen often, a destructive transference is being acted out in the marriage. Of course, some elements of parental transference tend to persist in most intimate relationships. Again, those who answered "Never" may be unwilling to examine the underlying dynamics of their marriages and, therefore, unable to alter them for the better. Score 1 point for B, 2 for C.

13. In a marriage, sharing all one's thoughts is just as dangerous as being too unforthcoming. And expecting one's spouse to be telepathic is silly. While it's sometimes quite constructive to let a spouse know exactly what's on one's mind, it's best to offer certain kinds of communications when the emotional climate is such that they can be clearly heard and understood. Score 1 point for D, 2 for E.

14. Praise is one of the greatest love potions that exists. Score 1 point for B, 2 for A.

15. Couples who don't laugh and play together are missing out on one of marriage's greatest pleasures and probably don't feel as intimate with each other as they should. Score 1 for B, 2 for A.

16. Couples who fight too much of the time haven't learned the art of compromise, but those who shun fighting altogether inhabit a precarious "paradise." Score 2 points for B or C.

17. Fighting fair and exercising some self-control is crucial, especially when one's blood is boiling. Score 2 for C.

18. It can't be said too often or too emphatically: couples who don't make up are in danger of break-up. To nurse postfight blues for days on end is to accentuate the negative, and people who can never bring themselves to apologize should remember the old adage that pride comes before a fall. Score 2 points for A or B.

19. Confusing money with love or power gets a lot of couples into trouble. People who find money an aph-

rodisiac are in danger of turning off to a spouse in a financial slump or having their heads turned by anyone more prosperous than their own partners. A rational, relatively de-emotionalized approach to money makes marriage infinitely easier. Score 2 points for D.

20. Resentment can build when either spouse feels constantly overburdened on the financial front, but there's nothing unfair about taking on a little more than one's rightful share of expenses from time to time if circumstances warrant it. Score 2 points for A or D.

21. Whether couples do it on their own or with help, it's necessary to have practical discussions about money in a marriage, lest partners wind up working against rather than with each other. Score 2 points for C or D.

22. If one spouse is the designated "Cinderella," sooner or later something's got to give. If neither spouse has the time or inclination to do housework, farming out chores or letting a few of them slip is fine, providing both agree that help is affordable or that a little mess is acceptable. Score 2 points for A or D.

23. Husbands and wives who show interest in each other's work show respect for what their spouses do and an understanding of who they are. Score 2 points for A.

24. All couples need time alone to refuel their relationships and get reacquainted. Score 1 point for B, 2 for A.

25. Learning about new things together is a way of continuing to learn about each other and to increase intimacy. Score 1 point for B, 2 for A.

26. Those who equate sexual satisfaction solely with frequency or with the thrill of the unknown are prone to indifference to marital sex—and perhaps even prone to infidelity. Score 2 points for A or C.

27. Whether partners' sex drives are high, low, or somewhere in between is far less important than whether or not they generally agree on how much sex they want. Score 2 points for A.

28. A lot of people are slightly uncomfortable discussing sex, but even doing it with some hesitation or awkwardness is better than not doing it at all. Score 1 point for A, 2 for B.

29. A little smooching, nuzzling, and ogling goes a long way when it comes to making a spouse feel admired and appreciated. Score 1 point for B, 2 for A.

30. Looking good in private gives one's spouse the message that he or she isn't taken for granted. On the other hand, being obsessed with one's appearance at all times may indicate an unwillingness to relax and let down one's guard. Score 1 point for C, 2 for B.

31. It's only human for men to admire women and vice versa. Providing a spouse is "just looking," it's a waste of emotional energy to be angry, scared, or vindictive. Still, if such feelings persist and one can control them without acting on them, that's a sign of maturity. Score 2 points for C or D.

32. Obviously enough, a good relationship with a partner's family is better than a bad one. An idealized relationship may lead to some later disillusionment, but, providing one's spouse does not feel excluded, it's better than no relationship at all. Score 1 point for C, 2 for A.

33. Moping is never any fun, and neither is paranoia. What's more, giving in to such feelings probably will result in a none-too-friendly greeting when one's spouse returns home. Better to count oneself lucky at having missed what might have been a difficult encounter, and better yet to amuse oneself in a way that will bolster, rather than dampen, one's mood. Score 1 point for C, 2 for D.

34. As Bette Midler says, "You've got to have friends," and the more varied a couple's friendships, the more their relationship will be enhanced. Score 1 point for B or C, 2 for A.

35. Shared goals and values help keep couples together. It's easier for partners to be future-oriented when they both agree they want to end up in more or less the same place. Score 1 point for B, 2 for A.

36. Never to compromise is never to create that all-important "third person." Couples who find it more difficult to compromise as time passes are moving backward instead of forward. And relationships where one spouse rules unequivocally are always at risk of mutiny. Score 5 points for A, and *subtract 5 points from your score for any other answer.*

37. Trust is the backbone of a successful marriage. If trust isn't growing, it's a sure sign that something is wrong. Score 5 points for B, and *subtract 5 points from your score for any other answer.*

38. As a marriage progresses, partners should become increasingly able to accept each other's flaws and/or look the other way when they surface. Becoming more critical instead of less so is another way of moving backward, while keeping a spouse on a pedestal indicates that rose-colored glasses are being worn too long. The latter is a good way to stay stuck in "together-together land." Score 5 points for A, and *subtract 5 points from your score for any other answer.*

39. Believing things doesn't always make them so, but it sure helps. Score 5 points for A, and *subtract 5 points if you chose B.*

40. As with all new undertakings, one should gain confidence as one goes along. Self-punishment, even if one makes mistakes, never does any good. It's impossible to truly love another without loving and, when necessary, forgiving oneself. Score 5 points for A, and *subtract 5 points if you chose B* (then forgive yourself).

What Your Score Means

95—A perfect score. But as we all know, no one is perfect and neither is any relationship. Subtract 5 points from your score for fudging.

81-94—Things look good, and there is reason to believe they will stay that way. Congratulations on being a good sport and a good spouse.

65-80—Your marriage still has some rough spots, and some initial work on the first year's tasks still needs to be tackled. If you and your partner remain optimistic and pay special attention to problem areas, you should do fine.

Below 65—Maybe you're just in a bad mood. Wait a few days and then take the quiz again. If you still score below 65, you and your mate need to do some talking. Perhaps you could use a little assistance from a professional. Don't despair, but do take care.

Selected Bibliography

This selection includes all sources referred to in the text as well as books and articles that, although not cited explicitly, were particularly useful to my research.

Alberoni, Francesco. *Falling in Love.* Translated by Lawrence Venuti. New York: Random House, 1983.

Beavers, W. Robert. *Successful Marriage: A Family Systems Approach to Couples Therapy.* New York: W. W. Norton & Co., 1985.

Betcher, William. *Intimate Play: Creating Romance in Everyday Life.* New York: Viking Penguin, 1987.

———. "Intimate Play and Marital Adaptation." *Psychiatry* 44 (February 1981): 13–33.

Blumstein, Philip, and Pepper Schwartz. *American Couples.* New York: William Morrow & Co., 1983.

Bok, Sissela. *Lying: Moral Choice in Public and Private Life.* New York: Pantheon, 1978.

Botwin, Carol. *Is There Sex After Marriage?* Boston: Little, Brown & Co., 1985.

Briffault, Robert. *Marriage: Past and Present.* Boston: Porter Sargent Publisher, 1956.

Cherlin, Andrew. *Marriage, Divorce, Remarriage.* Cambridge, Mass.: Harvard University Press, 1981.

Deutsch, Claudia H. "Prenuptial Decrees Up; Prenuptial Trust Down." *The New York Times,* November 19, 1986, p. C1.

Dicks, Henry V. *Marital Tensions.* London: Routledge & Kegan Paul, 1967.

Dinnerstein, Dorothy. *The Mermaid and the Minotaur:*

Sexual Arrangements and Human Malaise. New York: Harper & Row, 1977 (paperback).

Ekstein, Rudolph. "Normality and Pathology in Marriage." *Modern Psychoanalysis* 2, no. 1 (1977): 35–42.

Eliot, George. *Middlemarch.* London: Penguin English Library, 1965 (paperback). (Originally published in 1871.)

Ephron, Delia. *Funny Sauce.* New York: Viking Penguin, 1986.

Ephron, Nora. *Heartburn.* New York: Alfred A. Knopf, 1983.

Erikson, Erik H. *Identity and the Life Cycle.* New York: W. W. Norton & Co., 1980 (paperback).

Flaubert, Gustave. *Madame Bovary.* New York: Bantam, 1959 (paperback). (Originally published in 1857.)

Freud, Sigmund. "An Outline of Psychoanalysis." In *The Standard Edition,* vol. 23. Edited by James Strachey. London: The Hogarth Press, 1964. (Originally published in 1940 [1938].)

———. "Group Psychology and the Analysis of the Ego." In *The Standard Edition,* vol. 18. Edited by James Strachey. London: The Hogarth Press, 1964. (Originally published in 1921.)

———. "On Narcissism: An Introduction." In *The Standard Edition,* vol. 14. Edited by James Strachey. London: The Hogarth Press, 1964. (Originally published in 1914.)

Friedan, Betty. *The Feminine Mystique.* New York: W. W. Norton & Co., 1963.

Fromm, Eric. *The Art of Loving.* New York: Harper & Row, 1956.

Goleman, Daniel. "Patterns of Love Charted in Studies." *The New York Times,* September 10, 1985, p. C1.

———. "Who Are You Kidding?" *Psychology Today* 21, no. 3 (March 1987): 24–30.

———. *Vital Lies, Simple Truths*. New York: Simon & Schuster, 1985.

Hatfield, Elaine, David Greenberger, Jane Traupmann, and Philip Lambert. "Equity and Sexual Satisfaction in Recently Married Couples." *Journal of Sex Research* 18, no. 1 (February 1982): 18–32.

Kaplan, Helen Singer. *Disorders of Sexual Desire*. New York: Brunner/Mazel, 1979.

Kaplan, Louise. *Oneness and Separateness: From Infant to Individual*. New York: Simon & Schuster, 1978.

Kaufman, William. "Some Emotional Uses of Money." In *The Psychoanalysis of Money*. Edited by Ernest Borneman. New York: Urizen Books, 1976.

Kernberg, Otto. "Boundaries and Structure in Love Relations." *Journal of the American Psychoanalytic Association* 25, no. 1 (1977): 81–113.

Klagsbrun, Francine. *Married People: Staying Together in the Age of Divorce*. New York: Bantam, 1985.

Klein, Melanie, and Joan Riviere. *Love, Hate, and Reparation*. New York: W. W. Norton & Co., 1964.

Larsen, David. *Who Gets It When You Go?* New York: Random House, 1982.

Lauer, Jeannette, and Robert Lauer. "Marriages Made to Last." *Psychology Today* 19, no. 6 (June 1985): 22–26.

Lederer, William J., and Don D. Jackson. *The Mirages of Marriage*. New York: W. W. Norton & Co., 1968.

Lorenz, Konrad. *On Aggression*. New York: Harcourt, Brace & World, 1966.

Mahler, Margaret S., Fred Pine, and Anni Bergmann. *The Psychological Birth of the Human Infant*. New York: Basis Books, 1975.

Martin, Judith. *Miss Manners' Guide to Excruciatingly Correct Behavior.* New York: Atheneum, 1982.

Mason, A. A. "Paranoid and Depressive Positions in Marital Relations." *Modern Psychoanalysis* 2, no. 1 (1977): 43–55.

May, Rollo. *Love and Will.* New York: W. W. Norton & Co., 1969.

Meadow, Phyllis. "The Treatment of Marital Problems." *Modern Psychoanalysis* 2, no. 1 (1977): 15–23.

Minuchin, Salvador. *Families and Family Therapy.* Cambridge, Mass.: Harvard University Press, 1974.

Morris, Desmond. *The Naked Ape.* New York: Dell, 1984 (paperback).

Peck, M. Scott. *The Road Less Traveled.* New York: Simon & Schuster, 1978.

Reik, Theodor. *Of Love and Lust.* New York: Farrar, Straus, Giroux, 1957 (paperback).

Rice, David. *Dual Career Marriage.* New York: The Free Press, 1979.

Rose, Phyllis. *Parallel Lives: Five Victorian Marriages.* New York: Alfred A. Knopf, 1983.

Rosenbaum, Jean, and Veryl Rosenbaum. *Stepparenting.* Corte Madera, Calif.: Chandler & Sharp, 1977.

Sager, Clifford J. *Marriage Contracts and Couples Therapy.* New York: Brunner/Mazel, 1976.

Schopenhauer, Arthur. *Parerga and Paralipomena,* vol. 2. Translated by E. F. J. Payne. Oxford: Clarendon Press, 1974.

Scott, George Ryley. *Curious Customs of Sex and Marriage.* London: Torchstream Books, 1953.

Siegel, Bernie S. *Love, Medicine, and Miracles.* New York: Harper & Row, 1986.

Spitz, René A. In collaboration with W. Godfrey Cobliner. *The First Year of Life.* New York: International Universities Press, 1965.

Spotnitz, Hyman. "Problems of the Marriage Partnership." *Modern Psychoanalysis* 2, no. 1 (1977): 4–14.

Stannard, Una. *Married Women v. Husbands' Names.* San Francisco: Germainbooks, 1973.

Stern, Daniel N. *The Interpersonal World of the Infant: A View from Psychoanalysis and Developmental Psychology.* New York: Basic Books, 1985.

Sternberg, Robert J. "Explorations of Love." In *Perspectives in Interpersonal Behavior and Relationships.* Edited by D. Perlman and W. Jones. Greenwich, Conn.: JAL Press, 1987.

Sternberg, Robert J., and Michael L. Barnes. "Real and Ideal Others in Romantic Relationships: Is Four a Crowd?" *Journal of Personality and Social Psychology* 49, no. 6 (1985): 1586–1608.

Sternberg, Robert J., and Susan Grajek. "The Nature of Love." *Journal of Personality* 47, no. 2 (1984): 312–19.

Tavris, Carol. *Anger: The Misunderstood Emotion.* New York: Simon & Schuster, 1982.

Tennov, Dorothy. *Love and Limerence.* New York: Stein & Day, 1979.

Tolstoy, Leo. *Anna Karenina.* Translated by David Magarshack. New York: American Library Signet Classics, 1961. (Originally published in 1877.)

Updike, John. *Marry Me.* New York: Alfred A. Knopf, 1971.

Westermarck, Edward. *A Short History of Marriage.* New York: Humanities Press, 1968.

Winnicott, D. W. *Through Pediatrics to Psychoanalysis.* New York: Basic Books, 1975.